KINGSHIP AND LAW

D1493410

STUDIES IN MEDIAEVAL HISTORY

It is hoped that this Series, intended in the first place for students in the Universities, may help to bridge the gap between the text-books and the learned monographs in which English and continental scholars of the present day are re-writing the story of the Middle Ages. Its object is less to furnish an outline of facts, than to introduce the student to major problems of interpretation.

KINGSHIP
AND LAW
in the MIDDLE AGES

I. The DIVINE RIGHT OF KINGS and the RIGHT OF RESIST-
ANCE in the early MIDDLE AGES

II. LAW and CONSTITUTION in the MIDDLE AGES

Studies by

FRITZ KERN
Professor in the University of Bonn

Translated with an Introduction

by S. B. CHRIMES
*Professor of History in the University
of South Wales and Monmouthshire,
Cardiff*

BASIL BLACKWELL · OXFORD

1968

First Printed 1939
Fourth Impression 1968
631 00330 4

PRINTED IN GREAT BRITAIN
BY COMPTON PRINTING LTD., LONDON AND AYLESBURY
AND BOUND BY
THE KEMP HALL BINDERY, OXFORD

PREFACE

By the TRANSLATOR

THE DATE at which Professor Kern's monograph GOTTESGNADENTUM UND WIDERSTANDSRECHT IM FRÜHEREN MITTELALTER, was published—his preface was dated 1st August, 1914—was such as to prevent his work from becoming known to English scholars until some years later, and even to-day it is not so widely known to English-speaking mediaevalists as it deserves to be. When, therefore, Professor Kern, with great liberality, conveyed to me the right to produce a revised English edition of his book, I intended to arrange for a translation of the entire work, text, footnotes, and appendices complete. Only in this way could the full measure of Professor Kern's profound scholarship be made available to English readers. But in face of practical difficulties, this counsel of perfection had to be abandoned. The footnotes and the appendices to the work, containing a large mass of references to and quotations from original and secondary sources, are very extensive; the 515 footnotes occupy something like half of the 295 pages of text, which is followed by thirty-eight appendices spread over another 150 pages. The labour of translating the whole of this material would have been extremely heavy, and the cost of publishing it prohibitive. Moreover, the task would have been in part superfluous. For, although it is true that a great deal of matter is contained in these notes and appendices which scholars and specialists cannot afford to ignore, a large part of them naturally consists of references to older authorities which Professor Kern's book has in effect superseded. There is consequently little object in reproducing these notes and appendices in full. The principle of omission having been accepted, it was obvious that the English edition could not be a substitute for the original German edition for the exacting purposes of detailed scholarship, as was at first intended. Instead, I resolved to curtail still further the amount of annotation, and to devote the accruing space to making more of the author's general conclusions available

v

to the English-speaking student. With that end in view, the vhole text of the GOTTESGNADENTUM, incorporating a number of revisions generously supplied by the author himself, together with only about one eighth of the footnotes, is here edited and translated. The seventy-odd footnotes which have been selected are confined almost entirely to quotations from original authorities which seem to be especially illuminating, or to remarks by the author of special interest to English readers. The appendices have been omitted entirely, but a list of their titles is provided as a guide to those who may wish to refer to them in the original edition.

The space thus available has been devoted to a translation, with some of the footnotes, of very nearly the whole of another of the author's works, his article entitled RECHT UND VERFASSUNG IM MITTELALTER, which appeared in the *Historische Zeitschrift* in 1919. The translation of these two fundamentally important studies side by side has seemed to be a more fruitful undertaking than the reproduction of every note and reference in the larger of the two works.

I can only hope that the rendering here given reflects accurately Professor Kern's meaning. The task of making a translation of this kind can never be simple nor devoid of hazardous pitfalls, and would be hopeless to those as inexpert as myself, but for the generous encouragement and help of others. If errors of translation and of style have been avoided in the version that follows, the credit is mainly due to my wife, to my friend Herr cand. jur. K. J. Blanck, of the Universities of Frankfürt a. Main and Edinburgh, who in their several ways gave much time to improving my text at its different stages; and above all, to my friend Mr. Geoffrey Barraclough, whose task as General Editor has been no sinecure, and whose patient and able co-operation has been indistinguishable from collaboration. For the errors that remain I must take responsibility, and I shall welcome any suggestions for amendment that may occur to readers.

S. B. CHRIMES

University of Glasgow.

1st August, 1939.

CONTENTS

THE FIRST PART

THE DIVINE RIGHT OF KINGS *and* THE
RIGHT OF RESISTANCE *in the* EARLY
MIDDLE AGES

vii

THE SECOND PART

LAW AND CONSTITUTION IN THE MIDDLE AGES

INTRODUCTION

By THE TRANSLATOR

MANY scholars to-day would agree that the way in which Constitutional History, especially on its mediaeval side, has been, and is commonly presented in this country is no longer altogether satisfactory. For one thing, it is usually treated with excessive insularity, with very slight reference to the cognate constitutional experiences of other countries; for another thing, its subject-matter is often expanded too far in some respects and curtailed too far in others. On the one hand, we are encouraged to believe that the origins and foundations of our Constitution were as peculiar to England as its later developments, which is not in fact the case. On the other hand, disagreement and confusion as to what is the proper subject-matter of Constitutional History as distinct from other aspects of History often prevent us from obtaining in full measure the fruits of specialised cultivation and treatment. Consequently, even at this comparatively advanced hour in the History of History, a certain lack of focus hinders a realistic and general understanding of the most characteristic and lasting contribution of the British people to the common heritage of mankind.

The reasons for the prevailing insularity with which English Constitutional History is treated, are not, of course, far to seek. They are to be found mainly in the nationalistic lines along which history in general is still almost universally approached, and there is no need to pursue the matter here. The evils of nationalism, in historical studies as elsewhere, and the narrow-mindedness thereby begotten, are doubtless sufficiently familiar and repellent to most of those who are likely to read these remarks.

But the point which perhaps is not always realized by constitutional historians (to say nothing of others) is that for their purposes, " International History " as commonly understood, is no adequate substitute for National History

The study of several national constitutional histories alongside each other is no doubt a valuable corrective to national
prejudices and narrow outlook, but it is not enough in itself.
What is needed for the satisfaction of essential scientific
purposes is a genuine study of constitutional history on
comparative lines: a study which, instead of merely making
an addition-sum, as it were, of national histories, shall seek
the common factors underlying constitutional experience in
a number of different but closely cognate countries, more
especially those of Western Europe, and shall bring out as
never before their common characteristics as well as their
divergences.   Only by the serious application of the comparative method to this field will the national constitutional
histories themselves come to be rightly understood, and also a
proper perspective for European history be obtained.
English scholarship so far has almost totally neglected this
great task, and it is much to be hoped that Professor Kern's
masterly studies, here introduced, will encourage fruitful
work in this field.   No doubt in any event, far more stress
ought to be laid upon the reading of modern languages as a
part of the essential training of historical scholars than is at
present usual, but no greater incentive to that end can be
offered to students than the prospect that their labours,
rightly directed, may result in a deeper understanding and a
greater illumination of the common bases of European
civilisation, and may even contribute something indispensable to the very preservation of that civilization.   It is
time, and more than time, that English constitutional historians, as well as others, should abandon their splendid but
often delusive isolation, and take stock of the common
factors in European constitutional history, for the sake not
only of broadening the scope and content of historical
studies, but also for the sake of gaining a better and fuller
understanding of English history itself.

Moreover, sooner or later, we cannot evade the question of
what is the proper subject-matter of Constitutional History,
nor ignore the need for more precision and definition in
making up our minds as to what we mean by that aspect of
History.   We need to do so not for the sake of any pleasure

we may feel in drawing nice distinctions, but for the sake of the clarification of issues and the better advancement of knowledge. Unfortunately, reluctance to make definitions is deeply ingrained in English historical studies, with the result that the utmost confusion prevails both as to the theory and the practice of historiography, confusion of a kind that would not be tolerated in any other branch of learning.[1] This reluctance to define one's terms is no doubt due in part to the well-known national distrust of what is called " too much logic," " inelastic rigidity," " artificial distinctions," and so forth. That attitude is doubtless necessary and proper in practical life, but it is the very reverse in scientific endeavour of any kind. Science—and History, of course, in so far as it is an endeavour to find and state the truth about something, is no more and no less a science than all other such attempts—cannot advance by compromising logic with life. On the contrary, the whole method of scientific study consists essentially in the application of logic to life, and is therefore in a sense an " artificial process," though in another and better sense it is a natural one, being itself a manifestation of life.

Now we all know that the Universe is one, and that the garment of Clio is a seamless web. All history is one stem without any branches—history in the sense of the Past. But that is no reason why we should not make for our own purposes branches of History in the sense of the study of the Past.[2] For of course History in the sense of the study of the Past, being only an intellectually differentiated piece of the study of the Universe, is itself an artificial and arbitrary branch of study or science. Yet most of us would admit that History in general is quite a legitimate and even necessary sphere for investigation; even those who most dislike, dis-

---

[1] The contradictory and even self-contradictory assertions of many eminent historians on this matter are notorious. They may be briefly studied in an excellent pamphlet by L. S. Wood entitled *Selected Epigraphs* (Historical Association, 1932).

[2] Many discussions of historiography have been vitiated by failure to distinguish between these two senses of the same word. It is unfortunate that the same word does duty for both the study and the thing studied. In what follows I write " History " for the former, and " history " for the latter.

trust, or unconsciously ignore the " artificial " departmentalization of History into political, economic, constitutional, and so on, seldom feel themselves obliged to treat the whole Universe as the indivisible entity that it is in " real life."

But if, then, there need be no compunction about the differentiation of History into various branches for the purposes of study, there can be no objection to the rationalization of that differentiation. True, of course, we can no more understand fully a branch of History without taking into account general History, than we can understand general History without taking the Universe into account. But the limitations of the human intellect being what they are, we have to take some things for granted, and can advance knowledge only by way of specialized approach. Or, putting the essential point more precisely, it is very necessary for historical scholars (as they do) to divide up Clio's otherwise seamless web, and at the same time (as they are often reluctant to do) to admit frankly that the portion fallen to their lot is but one piece of the garment, and is not some other piece or pieces. In short, Constitutional History is not, and should no longer be written as though it were, an indeterminate hybrid of biographical, political, economic, social, administrative, and other sorts of history. Naturally all these go to make up History, but it is the business not of the constitutional historian as such, but of the general historian, to make the ultimate synthesis, and only he can do it with anything better than a vague and illusory plausibility. A Constitutional History should be the History of the Constitution, and it may safely omit odds and ends of other things by way of (usually tendentious) " background."

But the menaces to genuine advance in Constitutional History do not come only from inconsistency in distinguishing its field from other fields (i.e., from the very human desire to have one's cake and eat it). The perils come perhaps even more from an excessive, though more or less unconscious reaction away from that kind of inconsistency. Nowadays it is quite the fashion to treat constitutional history as though it were merely the history of institutions, as though to string together (no matter how disjointedly) the history of a few government departments and administrative devices were all that need be done. Constitutional History undoubtedly includes, or at least is in part based upon institutional History, and may include something of administrative History in so far as administrative methods may modify the Constitution itself, but it is a great deal more than that. Institutions and administrative devices are only means to the ends of the Constitution, whatever these may be at any time. Institutions and administration exist only in virtue of their being the means, effective or ineffective, for realizing in practice the rights and duties in government which together make up the Constitution. Hence it is to these rights and duties themselves that we must look, as well as to the institutions which embody some of them, if we would comprehend a Constitution as it really is at any time. It is these rights and duties alone that give life and meaning to an otherwise unintelligible agglomeration of machinery and devices.

But governmental rights and duties themselves exist only in virtue of their recognition by law or by what in effect has the force of law.[3] Most of us would agree that a Constitution at any time is not made up of any rights or duties other than those which pass as legal rights or duties, or at least as quasi-legal rights or duties, howsoever they may be distributed. Yet there is often reluctance to face the obvious inference that if Constitutional History is to be what it pretends to be, and is to have any content of its own genuinely distinct from that of other branches of History, it needs to be treated primarily as itself a branch of legal history. If constitutional history is not primarily (I do not say exclusively) the history of constitutional law (law in theory and practice and law in the broadest sense including convention), it is exceedingly hard to say what it is, but it has the appearance of being a myth.

For, when all is said and done, in referring to the present-

---

[3] It is hardly necessary to enter here into a discussion of the nature of constitutional conventions. But I take it for granted that a convention is only a convention because it is regarded as in effect as binding upon the parties concerned as is the law proper, whether it could be enforced in the law-courts or not.

day Constitution (as it actually is, not as we may think it ought to be or will become), most of us have no hesitation in pointing to a well-defined body of law and custom; we do not point to all kinds of political, social, and economic facts and fancies, or to lists of departments. If we want information about our Constitution as it is, we consult the lawyers rather than the sociologists, economists, political theorists, and politicians. Presumably, then, in seeking the Constitution of the past, we do well to look primarily for past law and custom and their changes, not political incidents and social phenomena. No doubt in both past and present we may wish to know more than the law and custom of the matter, and may wish to relate these to other considerations, political, economic, social, and so on. But if we do, we shall be engaging in synthesis of some kind which neither the constitutional lawyer nor the constitutional historian can make within, so to speak, his own terms of reference. It is the business of the general historian, or should be, to co-ordinate the work of specialists in every field, and to discover (if he can) how politics, economics, and so on, have reacted upon constitutional development, and vice versa. This ultimate analysis, these supreme tasks of historical science ought not to be attempted in facile and incidental fashion, nor by way of avowedly specialized approach. The work of synthesis, indeed, is itself a specialized task (or should be), requiring (but not often obtaining) very special gifts and discipline of its own. It is, any rate, high time we were spared the further multiplication of self-styled Constitutional Histories of England which are in fact neither Histories of England nor of its Constitution, but which are something of both mixed together in varying proportions according to each author's taste and private recipe.[4]

We should no doubt all agree that Constitutional History is more than simply the history of Constitutional Law,

---

[4] It would be invidious to refer here to particular writers, but it is only fair to say that, in my opinion, our latest (1937) survey of *The Constitutional History of Mediaeval England* shows in general a marked advance upon previous works of the kind in this question of the selection of material. Certainly the irrelevant is excluded from this work, even though sometimes the relevant is also.

because in at least one respect, we need, as constitutional historians, to go further than the purely legal historian. We need to enquire how far the governmental rights in question were empty rights, and how far the duties were unfulfilled. But we sometimes forget that at all events Constitutional History is certainly nothing less than the History of Constitutional Law. And the painful but plain truth is that the history of English Constitutional Law still remains to be written. It will not and cannot be written until constitutional historians admit to themselves that their study is a branch of legal rather than of political history. For the constitutional historian is, or should be, *ex hypothesi* primarily interested in the effects of political (and other) forces *upon* a branch of law and custom, *not* in the history of those forces themselves. He is concerned with changes in the Constitution, that is, in governmental law and custom, not in something else. In making this admission, we may meet with a good deal of prejudice and disapproval, because of the modern divorce between historical and legal studies, which has left their offspring, Legal History, in the custody of the lawyers. But the historian who will regard Constitutional History primarily as Legal History, has an important function to perform in reconciling those once so devoted parents, a reconciliation which is likely to have far-reaching and beneficial effects not only upon the ultimate advancement of knowledge, but also more immediately upon the training received by historical students. For, on the one hand, past civilizations cannot be properly understood apart from the law and legal ideas without which they could not have existed as they did; and on the other hand, the legal way of thought is a very necessary element in any kind of intellectual training.

To treat Constitutional History as a branch of Legal History, is, maybe, to narrow its scope in the sense of concentrating its light as in focal point, but it is at the same time to intensify its illuminative power, also as in a focus. For Legal History of any kind cannot be written without taking into account concepts and ideas as well as rules and institutions. " Past actualities," as Professor Kern would say, cannot be rightly understood apart from their conceptual environment. This fact, very much neglected in English historiography, which alas! scarcely knows any *Geistesgeschichte*, needs no demonstration to those who are familiar with Professor Kern's work. Professor Kern does not concern himself primarily with "actualities"; indeed, he hardly mentions them, and yet his work undoubtedly puts a very different complexion upon much of what habitually pass as the realities of our constitutional history.

His two works, here translated under the titles of THE DIVINE RIGHT OF KINGS AND THE RIGHT OF RESISTANCE, and LAW AND CONSTITUTION, both in the Middle Ages, are exceptionally valuable to English students on account both of their method and their conclusions. Together they form an important corrective to the common presentation of English Constitutional History.

Professor Kern's avowed purpose is to study certain common factors in the constitutional history of Western Europe in the early Middle Ages, roughly from the fifth to the twelfth and early fourteenth centuries. He is enabled to do so because he seeks the common ideas underlying the various national manifestations of the same things, such as monarchy, law, and constitution in general. In the first of these studies, he devotes himself, as he says, not to the history of any one monarchy, but to the history of the idea of Western monarchy in general, and the same may be said of his treatment of the ideas of law and constitution in the second study. He is able to do this with great effect because he refrains from limiting his attention to merely institutional history, and seeks rather the ideas fundamental to the very existence of governmental institutions. He produces his results by working in the border-lands between what the Germans call *Geistesgeschichte* or the History of *Weltanschauung*—for which as yet there is no exact equivalent in English—and Legal (Constitutional) History. He is thus enabled to throw a powerful light upon the ideas and concepts which the early Middle Ages tried to realize in their institutions, and in so studying the basic forces of all Western constitutional history, he illumines in a remarkable way its whole field. Moreover, by studying political ideas in close relation to actualities and as understood by practical men and the people at large, he avoids the unfortunate abstraction and academic character which pervades almost all Histories of mediaeval Political Thought.[5] Here we find the assumptions and ideas not of philosophers and scholastics, but of the men who governed and were governed—notions of far greater importance to all students except historians of Philosophy than learned systems of political doctrine.[6] Professor Kern's method is one almost unexampled in the work of English historians, but it is amply justified both for its own sake and for the sake of its striking results.

A detailed analysis of these results is the less necessary here because the author himself provides a full and skilful summary of the first study, and his second and less intricate essay is itself sufficiently succinct. It may, however, be useful to some readers if an attempt is here made to co-ordinate the two essays, and to bring out the principal ways in which they together tend to modify our views of English history as generally conceived. Many of Professor Kern's conclusions, of course, have long been familiar to English-speaking scholars, but it can hardly be said that their general effect has yet been worked into the common presentation of Constitutional History, and it therefore may not be superfluous to review them with that end in mind.

Broadly speaking, the general effects of Professor Kern's work, as they seem to the Translator, are, on the one hand, to put back to a remote date the essential ideas fundamental to the emergence of the modern constitutional State; and, on the other hand, to reduce very considerably the place that is to be assigned to feudalism in the evolution and inter-action of those essential ideas. He shows that the basic ideas and concepts were not so much non-feudal as pre-feudal in origin. This very important conclusion is particularly manifest in his demonstration that the notion of (feudal)

---

[5] Not even the most recent and admirable works of this kind, as, for example, C. H. McIlwain, *The Growth of Political Thought in the West* (1932), or A. P. D'Entrèves, *The Mediaeval Contribution to Political Thought* (1939), can escape criticism from this point of view.

[6] Cf. what Prof. Kern himself has to say, *infra* p. 142.

contract was not the primary nor the principal source of the right of resistance, nor even an original source at all. On the contrary, the contractual idea was a great deal later in date than the right of resistance, which derives not from the feudal right of *diffidatio*, but from the ancient Germanic customary right to resist the monarch's breach of the law.

This conclusion, however, is explicable only in the light of early mediaeval notions of kingship and of law. Professor Kern begins his first study by pointing out that the fully developed theory of the Divine Right of kings in the seventeenth century combined in one doctrine elements which in fact had had entirely different origins. The notion of the exclusive rightness of the monarchical form of government mingled with belief in a single monarch's indefeasible right to the throne, and these came to be inextricably bound up with hereditary right (legitimism), sacral consecration of the king, and eventually with irresponsibility and unlimited absolutism.

The origins of these various ideas, no matter how closely associated with each other and seemingly inter-dependent in the seventeenth century and later, were quite independent of each other, and are to be found in early Germanic custom, in the political doctrines of the early Church, in the revived study of Roman law in the twelfth century, and in the influence of all these upon each other.

The monarchical principle itself was inherent in Germanic ideas and practice, and was accepted by the Church from the earliest times, and it penetrated every early mediaeval form of government, even those forms which nominally were not monarchies. The popular basis of Germanic kingship, symbolized in the election or at least the acclamation of the new king, never entirely disappeared from the monarchy of Western Europe, whilst the transcendental element in the authority to rule, present even in pagan times, came to be enormously strengthened and emphasized by the Church's participation in and blessing upon the king's inauguration.

The early Germanic kings, however, did not come to the throne through a simple personal right of succession. At best they possessed only a " privileged throne-worthiness," in virtue of their descent; election or at least acceptance by the people alone gave them a legal right to the throne (a *ius in re* as distinct from a mere *ius ad rem*).   Kin-right, not hereditary right, was the Germanic custom, but it was kin-right transmuted by other ideas that was the source of later divine hereditary right.   This transmutation was brought about largely by the effect of certain ecclesiastical (non-Germanic) concepts and practices.   For one thing, the Church adopted a strongly theocratic view of the royal position, viewing it as an office carrying duties, imposing upon its holder the duty of acting as the Vicar of God. The Church's theocratic view of monarchy had little in common with the Germanic notion of monarchy based upon popular election and blood-right, but in time the Church bridged the gulf between the two by its practice of blessing an individual man's right to rule.

The participation of the Church in the establishment of kingship had immense consequences upon the nature of monarchy itself.   Notwithstanding the great strengthening of the conception of the kingship as an office carrying duties, and therefore accountable to God and His servants—the pope and the bishops—in the long run the effect of the ecclesiastical consecration of the monarch was the exaltation of the State more than of the Church, and to provide an apparent legitimation for the prevailing Erastianism of the period.

But the consequences of these changes could not be pushed to their logical extremes in the early Middle Ages, because the fundamental conceptions of the State and of the Law prevented it.   No full-blown doctrine of monarchical irresponsibility could be evolved whilst the Law was regarded as supreme, and no distinction was drawn between ideal and positive law.   The Law was regarded as sovereign, so far as any sovereign existed at all, throughout the early mediaeval period.   The State existed for the realization of the Law, and therefore the Law was primary, the State only secondary. The monarch's function was to realize the Law in practice, and he was therefore bound to the Law.   Both Church and people agreed on that, but the two entertained different notions as to what the Law was. The deeply-rooted Germanic idea of law was that of the good, old law, unenacted and unwritten, residing in the common sense of justice, the sum total of all the subjective rights of individuals; the king's right to rule was but his private right, a mere parcel of the law itself. The Church, on the other hand, regarded divine or natural law as the universally obligatory law, and insisted that it was the king's duty to realize this law in practice, even if it conflicted with the good old customary law. This view sometimes had the highly important effect of releasing the king from the fetters of existent law, but in either sense the king was definitely bound to and limited by a law outside his own will. A legally absolute king, therefore, could not exist, even though some early mediaeval kings at times acted, or seem to have acted absolutely in practice. But in fact a king acted absolutely only if he encroached upon the rights of others (i.e., violated the law) without at the same time acting in accordance with the legal conscience of the community. There were no hard and fast rules as to how the king was to seek that accord. We must not, therefore, be deceived by the seemingly absolutist forms of royal " declarations " of law. For the king might declare the law by means of any of three degrees of consent. He might declare it with merely tacit consent, i.e., in absolutist *form*; or with the advice and assent of some counsellors (the *meliores et maiores*), vaguely representative of the community; or he might declare it by way of formal judicial verdict, i.e., with the advice and assent of the wise in the law. These different methods of securing harmony with the legal feeling of the community were all equally valid; the king's promulgations of law (which in fact though never in theory might be modifications of the existing law), since the king acted as always on behalf of the people, were all equally valid, no matter which of the three methods he adopted. But no such declaration, promulgated by whatever degree of consent, would be valid if in the long run it were rejected by the common conviction of justice.

For there was not, in the early Middle Ages, any distinction between ideal law and positive law. There was only one kind of law: the Law. This fundamental idea, is, as Professor Kern points out, vital for constitutional historians to bear in mind. As there was no difference between ideal or moral law and positive law, nor between objective and subjective law, since king and people were subject to one and the same law, everyone was authorized, and, indeed, obliged to protect and safeguard the existent law. Ideal and positive law being the same thing, there was only one Law, timeless in quality: the good old law residing in common conscience and tradition, innovation in which, theoretically, could take the form only of restoration; new law could never be recognized as such.

But since it was the right and the duty of everyone to protect the existing law, in particular to protect one's own personal rights, it was manifestly a right and a duty to resist the king himself if he were to violate that law or those rights. This right to resist, Professor Kern shows, was not based upon a contractual idea. True, the elements of a mutual compact were visible in, and were claimed as being seen in, the king's promises at his coronation to uphold the law, but the legal bond between king and subjects did not rest upon a contract. The king and the people did not simply co-exist as partners in a private-law contract. On the contrary, both were bound together in and to the objective legal order; both had duties to perform to God and the Law. The right of resistance, therefore, was not primarily the right of a party whose contract has been violated, nor was it even exclusively the subjective right of a citizen against an unjust ruler; principally it was a duty of resistance which the citizen owed to the objective legal order which has been disturbed by the ruler, and which is now to be restored. The contractual idea (which when asserted in the eleventh century was alien to Germanic political theory) does not suffice as a basis for either obedience or resistance, for the breaking of a contract essentially only frees the other party from his obligations. No doubt, as Professor Kern points out, later feudal theory of contract and diffidation emphasized a contractual element in the relations between king and subject, and lent a certain juristic sharpening and formality to the right of resistance, which otherwise always remained formless and clumsy. But the essential point, apt to be overlooked, is that the right of resistance against the king who violated the law was inherent in the ancient and pre-feudal Germanic ideas, and was itself a universally recognized and well-established part of early mediaeval constitutional law.

The full realisation of the implications of these facts should seriously modify the whole conception of our early mediaeval constitutional history. For example, Professor Kern is able to bring out with considerable effect an aspect of *Magna Carta* which is not always given its due emphasis and recognition by constitutional historians. Veneration for that famous document has been so great that, from Coke to Stubbs, there was a tendency to overlook the fact that many of its provisions are concerned largely with private law and have little bearing upon constitutional matters. But for a generation and more it has been realized that most of the provisions of Magna Carta are concerned with questions which have little or no bearing on public law. Certain sections of it, however—notably, among others, the famous " security-clause "—have been singled out as important constitutional innovations. Yet even the " security-clause " is not very remarkable when considered in relation to its European background, as Professor Kern considers it; for the king had in theory always been below the law and liable to lawful resistance if he infringed the law. The genuine novelty about § 61 of Magna Carta, as Professor Kern shows, is that it took the pre-existing right of resistance, which would still have been an effective check upon the king with or without Magna Carta, and gave it a place in the written public law of the realm. The popular (non-feudal) right of resistance institutionalized itself into a committee of five-and-twenty barons.[7] True, this striking attempt at

[7] It is obvious that comments such as McKechnie's on this section (*Magna Carta*, 474), to the effect that " Rebellion, even where morally justified, is necessarily illegal," are quite beside the mark. As Kern in effect shows, such a statement as this would, in the early mediaeval view, have been a self-contradiction; moreover *Magna Carta* itself manifestly legalizes coercion of the king in the form set out in the section in point.

giving an institutional embodiment to the right of resistance may have been crude, and no more than a temporary expedient, which the barons who devised it, never applied; prevention may have expressed itself only in the constitutional establishment of repression, in the constitutional organization of self-help. But this was none the less a remarkable instance of the setting-up of an institution to keep the king to the law or at any rate a part of it; and the committee of resistance, even if short-lived, has its place in the beginnings of what is rightly called constitutional monarchy.

Professor Kern elsewhere shows how, long before this date, the Germanic right of resistance had in times and in places been affected by the ecclesiastical notion of the right to resist the *tyrannus*, a notion which was originally based upon the right of the Christian minority to resist, at least passively, the actions of an unchristian or heretical authority. The limits of obedience to the State were clearly set for the Christian, and the doctrine had been evolved that a monarch who violated his lawful duty ceased *ipso facto* to be king, and *ipso facto* became *tyrannus*. The ecclesiastical view of these matters assisted the development of a regular judicial process against such a king, in contrast to the characteristic formlessness of the popular right of resistance; for the king as a Christian, was, like everyone else, subject to the disciplinary powers of the Church; moreover, the bishops, having participated in the king's inauguration, were presumed to possess some kind of admonitory, even coercive power over him. But human judgment over the king, no matter whether ecclesiastical or secular, always remained purely declaratory, not constitutive in character. It was the king who deposed himself in the very act of his wrong-doing.

The subjection of the king to spiritual penalty could not be seriously denied even in the heat of the Investiture Contest. But the question whether spiritual correction should have political and legal consequences was far more debatable. On this question, opinion was sharply divided in the eleventh and twelfth centuries. On the one hand, the ancient doctrine of the Church itself, inculcating passive obedience to the powers that be, came to the rescue of monarchy threatened by clerical aggression, and this doctrine, strengthened by others, was to triumph in the long run at the expense of all rights of resistance, ecclesiastical and secular. But for the time being, the notion of the responsibility of all to build the *Civitas Dei* held the field, and militated against any unconditional respect for authority. The alliance of the clerical right of resistance with the secular was a combination stronger than Germanic monarchy could withstand, and because of that alliance, Gregory VII was able to dare the extremes against the German Emperor.

But almost immediately the excesses of the Church militant reacted in favour of the monarchy.[8] To meet the boundless claims of the Church, royalism broke away from its customary mediaeval moderation, and preached the doctrines of the passive obedience of the subject, and of the irresponsibility of the monarch. The fully-fledged theory of the Divine Right of Kings began to take shape, but this theory was never completed in the mediaeval world; for theoretically the king could not be absolute, being below the law. Nevertheless, if the king were responsible to no earthly court, he was in practice, though limited in certain respects by the law, uncontrolled—and that was substantially the position of the monarch in England as elsewhere at the end of the Middle Ages.

It was, then, the struggle between the *sacerdotium* and the *regnum*, and the interaction of secular and ecclesiastical ideas that made possible the intellectual conditions necessary for the emergence of the modern sovereign State, and therefore, in the long run, of modern constitutionalism. For the excessive claims of the *sacerdotium* provoked an exaltation of the monarch, which was in some measure also encouraged by the revived study of Roman law, and all this in turn elicited the doctrine of popular sovereignty. Manegold of Lautenbach turned the tables on the royalists who argued that the authority of the people had been transferred to the monarch, by admitting the transfer but denying that it was

---

[8] Cf. A. Brackmann in this Series, vol. III, pp. 286 *sqq.*

irrevocable.   The king, he insisted, was dismissible like any
other servant, if he were unfaithful to his trust.

This revolutionary theory of popular sovereignty, however, never caught on in the mediaeval world.   The struggle
remained a struggle between monarchical principle and the
right of resistance; from the eleventh century, between passive obedience and the doctrine of *tyrannus*.   The prevailing
lack of public law encouraged both restraint of the king on the
one hand, and practical absolutism on the other.   It was
necessary for new institutions to be evolved before these
extremes could be reconciled, and they appeared only in the
thirteenth and fourteenth centuries.   Efforts at converting
repression into prevention, such as the setting-up of an earl
palatine, a court, or a *judex medius*, as in some way superior
to the king, proved to be abortive, except perhaps as regards
the electoral princes of Germany in relation to the Emperor.
The problem was eventually solved only by the gradual
formation of Estates of the realm in one shape or another;
by organizations which could exert some restraint upon the
king without dissolving into mere committees of resistance.
Only with this development was definite form given to the
consensus fidelium.   On the one hand, by this means better
definition was given to the king's limitations; and on the
other, his government was freed from its old rigid subjection
to customary law.

When eventually the history of the English parliament
comes to be put into its proper perspective, no doubt it will
constitute the best illustration of this extremely important
technical improvement in the practical realization of mediae-
cal constitutional aims.   But this improvement was essentially mediaeval in spirit, and the modern State cannot be
directly attributed to it.   At best, it amounted only to the
creation of a standing preventative device in place of the
older casual repressive one.   The right of resistance was not
thereby abandoned; the essential aims were still the preservation of individual rights, and the limitation of the power
of the State.   But the Estates achieved important improvements in technique; a clearer definition of the organs of
government; the adoption of the fiction of majority consent.

Two closely connected developments, coming from outside these spheres, were needed before the modern sovereign constitutional State was possible. For one thing, the monarch had to acquire sovereignty by shattering the old mediaeval idea of the ruler being bound to the existent law, which was accomplished by the doctrines of *raison d'Etat* and necessity of State; for another thing (inseparable from the previous one), the conception of law itself had to be fundamentally modified by the drawing of sharp distinctions between ideal and positive law. The monarch or the State could then become above positive law, whilst remaining below natural law and natural rights.

Yet, notwithstanding these changes, the fundamental aims of the modern constitutional State are still essentially the aims of the mediaeval constitution. The binding of the government to law of some sort; the participation in some way of the people or their representatives in government; the responsibility of the government to the people in some sense; all these aims were inherent in the common stock of the political ideas of the earliest Middle Ages, of the pre-feudal era in Western Europe. Only the enormous technical improvements, unimaginable then, and to that blunt age inconceivably circumambulatory, distinguish the modern constitution from the early mediaeval one. The difference is essentially only one of form, not of substance. This difference of form may be so stupendous as to seem substantial, but to realize the fundamental identity and continuity of purpose, is to put constitutional history into true perspective, and to recognize the truth, often hidden, that at bottom the problem of human government is at all times and in all places the same.

Most of us will agree that we do well to bear in mind the " eternal Middle Ages " in reading our constitutional History, and that Professor Kern's work is indispensable for a right understanding of much that otherwise remains mysterious and even incomprehensible in our early history. We cannot afford to neglect either his method or his conclusions in building up our account of that history in its darkest period. And before our Constitutional History can be written as fully and as lucidly as it may be, we shall need to carry his method into every period, mediaeval and modern. Then, and only then, will the story become real, for institutions are largely meaningless when abstracted from the rights and duties which they embody and which give them life and purpose.

I have said " into every period " advisedly, because Professor Kern concerns himself mostly with the early Middle Ages, not even with the mediaeval period as a whole. He wished to limit himself to the period running roughly from the fall of the Roman Empire in the West up to the threshold of what he calls the *Ständestaat*, to the beginnings of the organization of *consensus* upon a basis of representative Estates. As he points out, this period has a well-marked character of its own, which divides it off from the later Middle Ages, from the thirteenth, fourteenth, and fifteenth centuries ; and although naturally many of the ideas current in the earlier period survived into the later, it would be a serious mistake to assume that what is true of the one period is also true of the other. We must not generalize for the whole mediaeval period on the basis of the materials which Professor Kern here provides for us. His particular conclusions must not be torn out of their early mediaeval context and applied without due modification to the later period. This reservation is especially necessary, for example, in respect of the conception of law and legislation. As Professor Kern rightly shows, although legislation in the sense of law-making inevitably occurred in practice in the early period, the general conception of law as being the good old law prevented such legislation from being recognized for what in fact it was. But in the later period undoubtedly the changes in the conception of law (including the partial differentiation between positive and ideal law) had made that recognition both possible and actual. This profound modification naturally was bound up with the emergence of the *Ständestaat*. The State organized upon the basis of representative Estates soon lost the character of being, as Professor Kern would say, a *Rechts- und Ordnungs- Staat*.

The theory that whatever the king enacted or declared with
the *consensus* of the Estates was necessarily in accord with
the common conviction of justice and right, preserved the
old notion in the sense that the resulting promulgation was
lawful (so long as not contrary to natural law), but it
abandoned the old idea in the sense that legality now no
longer meant harmony with pre-existent custom. True,
there was a short period of rivalry and struggle between
new statute-law and old customary or common law; a
period of uncertainty as to whether a statute had force
enough to break ancient custom when in direct conflict with
it.   But the triumph of statutory law over common law
was achieved long before the mediaeval period was passed,
unless we choose to reject such a statement as this as being
a contradiction in terms, as perhaps we ought, since we can
scarcely speak of a mediaeval period *minus* its essential
conception of law.   However, if we prefer to adhere to the
conventional temporal division into periods, we need to bear
in mind that the *Weltanschauung* of the early Middle Ages
was far from being in all respects identical with that of the
later, and we must avoid the supposition that the " mediaeval
mind " was fossilized for a millennium.   Ideas, of course, are
vastly more sensitive to change than institutions, and they
need to be studied on their own account as well as in relation
to their contemporary institutions.   Only thus can the historians' besetting sin of anachronism (which is equally
vicious whether in the form of prochronism or parachronism)
be avoided.

There would be no object in attempting to provide here an
elaborate bibliographical apparatus.   Full references to
original and other sources are given in the footnotes and
appendices in the German edition of the GOTTESGNADENTUM,
which also supplies a twenty-one page Bibliography of
secondary and other sources available at the date of its
publication.   Professor Kern's work, within its bounds, had
the effect of superseding the older books, and the reproduction of the titles here would be superfluous.   Nor is there
much to add to the list since 1914, for Professor Kern's

book, being a classical exposition in its kind, has needed neither emendation nor expansion. But it may be useful for students if some allusion be made here to work since that date which may be regarded as in some measure supplementary to or cognate with his, and which is also reasonably accessible to English readers.

The place of the right of resistance in later political thought has been thoroughly treated by Kurt Wolzendorff in his book *Staatsrecht und Naturrecht in der Lehre vom Widerstandsrecht des Volkes gegen rechtswidrige Ausübung der Staatsgewalt.*[9] In this work the subject is treated from the point of view of legal history as well as from that of abstract theory, with special reference to both public and positive law, and the book forms an important contribution to modern constitutional history. The later history of the right of resistance has been sketched also by Hans Fehr in his article *Das Widerstandsrecht.*[10] Building on the foundations laid by Professors Kern and Wolzendorff, Dr Fehr summarizes the mediaeval history of the right, and estimates the influence of Calvin, of Luther (whom Professor Kern himself has studied in this connection[11]), of Althusius and Rousseau upon its subsequent history, in a short but illuminating article. Those who may wish to consider further the religious and theological bearings of the doctrine of divine grace and the spiritual character of the king, may profitably refer to two articles by Franz Kampers entitled *Vom Gottesgnadentum,*[12] and *Rex et Sacerdos,*[13] whilst Professor Kern has also written a short note on the pictorial representation of the king-priest in early mediaeval art.[14] The most striking addition

---

[9] Gierkes Untersuchungen zur deutschen Staats- und Rechtsgeschichte CXXVI (1916).

[10] Mitteilungen des Instituts für österr. Geschichtsforschung, XXXVIII, (1918), 1–38.

[11] *Luther und Widerstandsrecht,* Zeitschrift der Savigny-Stiftung für Rechtsgeschichte, XXXVII (1916), Kanon. Abt, VI, 331–340.

[12] Mitteilungen der Schlesischen Gesellschaft für Volkskunde, XXVI, Breslau, (1925), 25–59.

[13] Historisches Jahrbuch, XLV, (1925), 495–515.

[14] *Der Rex et Sacerdos in bildlicher Darstellung,* Forschungen und Versuche zur Geschichte des Mittelalters und der Neuzeit (Festschrift D. Schäfer dargebracht), Jena (1915), 1–5.

to. our knowledge of this aspect of the question, however, has been provided by a recent study of the mediaeval treatises on the princely vocation, the *Fürstenspiegel*. Analysing these writings in historical sequence, Dr Berges has been able to lay bare the metamorphosis in the theory of kingship which occurred between the date of John of Salisbury's *Policraticus* and the end of the mediaeval period. In this illuminating and stimulating work a new method of approach has been successfully opened up.[15]

Closely connected with the sacral character of kingship is the question of the thaumaturgical powers of the king, and this whole subject has been exhaustively treated by Professor Marc Bloch in his admirable book, *Les Rois Thaumaturges*.[16] This is a book that should be consulted by all interested in the history of royalism, showing as it does that thaumaturgical powers were first claimed in England by Henry I, who seems to have deliberately imitated the Capetians in that respect.

The coronation ceremonies offer material of first-rate importance for constitutional history, reflecting as they do the mingling of popular, ecclesiastical, and legitimist ideas of royal inauguration; and the coronation oath contains, as Professor Kern reminds us, the germ of constitutional monarchy. The history of the English coronation has been surveyed, with emphasis upon its constitutional bearings, by Professor Percy Schramm,[17] who, moreover, in a series of invaluable articles, has firmly laid the foundations for the comparative study of coronation ceremonies in Western Europe.[18] Taken together, Professor Schramm's works comprise the principal authority for this whole subject, and in many ways they supplement what Professor Kern has to say upon it. In addition, the coronation oath of Edward II

---

[15] W. Berges, *Die Fürstenspiegel des hohen und späten Mittelalters*, Schriften des Reichsinstituts für ältere deutsche Geschichtskunde, II (1938).

[16] Strasbourg (1924).

[17] *A History of the English Coronation*, trans. by L. G. Wickham Legg, Oxford (1937).

[18] For a full list of these articles, which deal in turn with the coronations in the mediaeval Empire, in the kingdoms of the West Franks, the Anglo-Saxons, France, England, and Aragon, v. Schramm, *op. cit.*, 239–240.

of England has been specially studied by Professor B. Wilkinson.[19]

Professor Kern has some occasion for referring to the depositions of Edward II and of Richard II of England, without going into any details. Indispensable information upon these events and their significance is to be found in Dr Gaillard Lapsley's articles on *The Parliamentary Title of Henry IV*.[20] The same subject has been in part treated in my book, *English Constitutional Ideas in the Fifteenth Century*,[21] which, if I may be permitted the observation, may be regarded as in some measure a first attempt to do for merely one century of English history what Professor Kern has done in masterly fashion for eight centuries of European history

S.B.C.

[19] *Historical Essays in honour of James Tait*, ed. J. G. Edwards and E. F. Jacob (1933), 405–416.
[20] *English Historical Review*, XLIX (1934), 423–449, 577–606. Cf. also H. G. Richardson, *Richard II's Last Parliament*, ibid., LII (1937), 37–47, and Dr Lapsley's reply, *ibid.*, LIII, (1938), 53–78.
[21] Cambridge (1936).

ABBREVIATIONS

EHR. = English Historical Review.
MGH. = Monumenta Germaniae Historica.
 PL. = Patrologia Latina.
RBS. = Rerum Britannicarum medii Aevi Scriptores
         (Rolls Series).

THE FIRST PART

THE DIVINE RIGHT OF KINGS
AND
THE RIGHT OF RESISTANCE
IN THE
EARLY MIDDLE AGES

Whose rights are to predominate in the State, the rights of the ruler or those of the people, the rights of the governed or those of government? It is this vexed question which produces tension in the structure of constitutional monarchy—a tension which may only make itself felt on exceptional occasions, but then shakes the whole edifice to the point of collapse. Divine Right and the Right of Resistance, their struggles for dominance in the State from the seventeenth to the nineteenth centuries, still live in the consciousness of the present.

In order to find the origins of these doctrines, it is necessary to go back to a time when the slogans of Divine Right and Popular Sovereignty, Resistance and Non-resistance were not yet coined, though the ideas underlying them already formed the battle-cries of parties. Our path leads into a double and at first divided world of ideas, into the doctrines of the ancient and mediaeval Church, and into the early history of the Germanic States. We shall see how these two sets of influences, interacting in conflict and alliance during the ninth, eleventh, and thirteenth centuries, by their mutual repulsion and stimulation prepared the ground for a new outlook in the relations between the ruler and the ruled, and laid the foundations both of absolutist and of constitutional theory.

I

THE DIVINE RIGHT OF KINGS

WE turn first to the right of the monarch, or, to be more precise, to the origin of that complex of rights which is comprised under the name of " Divine Right."

Within this concept the fully developed theory of the seventeenth century combined many elements which, although wholly diverse, had gradually been assimilated in the course of historical development: (i) the notion of the exclusive rightness of the monarchical form of government (the monarchical principle); (ii) the belief in an individual monarch's particular right to govern, a right inalienable and independent of human agency, which derived from (*a*) hereditary right (the principle of legitimism), and from (*b*) divine consecration (the sacral character of the king); finally, (iii) the assertion of the irresponsibility of the king, together with the corollary, usually closely connected, that he is unlimited (absolutism).[1]

To its later adherents, the union of all these elements in Divine Right seemed natural and indissoluble, but in fact they have entirely different historical origins.

§1. THE MONARCHICAL PRINCIPLE

In the early Middle Ages, no controversy arose as to the desirability of the monarchical form of government. Germanic political ideas and the *Weltanschauung* of the Church both combined to give expression to the divinely-willed *a priori* necessity of monarchy.

Before the thirteenth century, that is to say, before the formulation of a genuine theory of the State, there could

---

[1] Cf. for example, the Address of the University of Cambridge to Charles II (1681): We still believe and maintain, that our kings derive not their title from the people, but from God; that to him only are they accountable; that it belongs not to subjects, either to create or censure, but to honour and obey their sovereign, who comes to be so by fundamental, hereditary right of succession, which no religion, no law, no fault or forfeiture can alter or diminish. Figgis, *The Divine Right of Kings*, 6.

not be in any strict sense a conscious monarchical principle; but in practice monarchy dominated Western political life. Even if some of the Germanic peoples entered into history without kingship, and even though it is said that at the time of the folk migrations, as a result of some strange impulse, they temporarily abolished an existing monarchy, possibilities of this kind were soon forgotten in the Middle Ages proper, just as the fundamental doctrines of antiquity about the sovereignty of the people and the popular will passed into oblivion.   As yet the towns were too unimportant and politically too undeveloped to suggest in matters of constitutional law a comparison of republican ideas with the only recognized type of monarchical government.   Indeed, even in towns such as Venice, where something of the independent spirit and brilliance of an ancient republic re-appeared at an early date, two circumstances hindered the emergence of any profound antipathy to monarchy.

On the one hand, political societies that were organized not on a monarchical but on a communal basis consisted only of such communities as were not in the ultimate sense independent, but were rather in some way subordinate to a monarch, even if only to the supreme world-monarch, the Emperor.   In the Empire, Christendom found once for all its monarchical centre;   in this both late. classical and mediaeval Germanic beliefs unreservedly agreed.

On the other hand—and this in our context is still more important—the idea of monarchy permeated even the communal societies which, in contrast to the monarchies, were based upon the principle of equality;   even the aristocracies and the democracies of the early Middle Ages always contained a monarchical element in their constitution.   To the mediaeval mind, the freely elected head of a communal society was similar, as regards both rights and duties, to the ruler of a kingdom, who, as we shall see, was also elected; and this similarity was far more decisive than the differences that divided them.   Moreover, even the communal head was in certain respects a monarch;   and the mediaeval monarch, in a certain sense, was merely a communal head.   The concrete rights of the two differed in some measure, but both were so very much alike in their fundamental relations with the communities which they respectively governed, that the subtle modern distinction between the wielder of sovereignty, the monarch, and the republican magistrate or president, must have seemed utterly insignificant in the early Middle Ages. For even in the communal society of the Middle Ages the head was not by any means merely an officer of the community; he administered a mandate " from on high," a mandate which may perhaps best be described as a guardianship over the community.

The Church Fathers' definition of government as the extension of a benevolent *patria potestas* influenced notions of magistracy of every kind, in the narrowest as well as the widest human spheres. Christian magistracy in all its grades, up to and including that of the Emperor, " the guardian of the world," was something more than merely a mandatory power conferred by the community. It did not, indeed, as we shall see later, lack popular support; but side by side with and superior to this popular basis, it was endowed with a theocratic sanction which was not derived from the will of the community at all. This " guardianship " over the community was an office to which God rather than the community appointed, and to God the ruler remained responsible for the performance of his office. All government was conceived of as the image in miniature of the divine government of the world. Just as the macrocosm of the world was eternally ruled by God, and the microcosm of the body was directed by the soul, so the intermediate body politic, the political commonwealth, was thought to be guided by the magistracy, which presided as a head over the members, and was not derived from them. There was an element in the idea of monarchy which could not be derived from the will of the subjects. The official duty of the man entrusted with power to rule was regarded as a perpetual right independent of the will of the community. And if this was plainly the case with all authority, in the home, in industry, in the municipality, and in the State; and if all power was derived from God, there is no doubt that the magistracy's independence of the subjects, the general theocratic and monarchical element inherent in every kind of authority, was particularly manifest in the case of the head of a political community and the possessor of full powers of government.[2]

The conviction that an element not derived from the " folk " lay in all magisterial authority was strengthened by the characteristics of spiritual authority. Whilst in modern times Catholic political doctrine has emphasized the difference between the divinely-ordained quality of the spiritual power and the purely empirical origin of the secular power, which it has regarded as emanating from the will of the people, the Middle Ages emphasized above all the affinity of the two authorities; both are simply imposed on the subject-peoples, and both contain a transcendental element. And this divine aspect of government was deemed to be most satisfactorily manifested when one single person ruled as " God's vicar."

In the Christian world, as in China, monotheism and monarchy supported each other. At first this profited monotheism: Athenagoras, for example, inferred from the fitness of human monarchy for its purpose that the divine government of the harmonious cosmos similarly could not be split up polytheistically. But in the Middle Ages such analogies were advantageous to monarchy. With the re-discovery of Aristotelian political theory in the thirteenth century, discussion first began, in the light of experience, of the relative worth of different forms of constitution, monarchy, democracy, and so on. But precisely because monarchy was thus compelled to justify itself scientifically, it revealed

[2] That is, in the case of a ruler of a *regnum*, which was the political unit of government, and included even duchies and countships, as contrasted with communal or free associations. The importance which life-long and personal fealty gained in the early Middle Ages as a fundamental idea of public law, rested upon the monarchical character of magistracy, and it, in its turn, strengthened the monarchical order. As early as about 1300, it was observed that the feudal constitution did not suit republics, but that bureaucratic administration was more appropriate to them. Like-wise, the monarchical principle went better with the sacral consecration of the ruler; only a life-long ruler could be " the Lord's anointed," just as in the ancient world monarchy and the deification of the ruler went to-gether; no temporary elected magistrate could be the " son of God."

its strength more than ever before; its assumptions developed into a monarchical principle in the theoretical discussions of the late mediaeval philosophers and jurists. Its essentials proved themselves to be as deeply rooted in mediaeval thought as in the practical constitutional needs of the time.

In this connection, indeed, we must never forget that the Middle Ages were concerned only with the universal validity of monarchy as such. They emphasized its exalted character, and its independence of the people, but there was no desire to claim universal validity for any particular type of constitution, such, for example, as hereditary monarchy. The monarchical principle of the mediaeval thinker is, therefore, something much more general, flexible, and abstract than that of the modern political theorist. The difference between the head of any community and the monarch was deemed to be no profound contrast, but merely a difference of degree, and there was, as we shall shortly see, no ruler entirely a " law unto himself." Moreover, the comparison of magistracy with the divine government of the world, and its derivation from God, did not necessitate government by a single person. The Byzantine soldiers justified collective rule with the singular orthodoxy that " we believe in the Trinity; we crown three Emperors," when in the year 669 they took it into their heads to elect two new Emperors in addition to the existing one. If to all this we add the statement, to be discussed more fully in the following sections, that even the monarch who was the sole ruler of an independent State owed his power both in fact and in law to a decision of the people, to the election or acclamation of the community, then we shall entertain no doubts at all that the monarchical principle of the early Middle Ages did not possess the strength attributed to it by the advocates of Divine Right in modern times; namely, the monarch's independence of popular will in respect of his whole legal position. On the contrary, monarchy possessed, as we have seen, a sanction independent of the people, and, as we shall see later, a sanction dependent upon the people, and these two sanctions co-existed and were even mutually dependent. The theocratical and monarchical element in all forms of government did not, therefore, make the king "sovereign" in the modern sense; the dependence of the monarch upon God and His commands—a dependence that sprang from the ruler's divine mandate—was broadly enough conceived to allow the monarch to be dependent also upon the will of the community in so far as monarchy itself was based upon a popular as well as a divine mandate.

Certainly, the monarchical principle even in this form precluded any idea of popular sovereignty; the people in the Middle Ages were no more regarded as "sovereign" than was the monarch. If we wish to use this inappropriate expression at all for the Middle Ages, we may only say: God is sovereign, and the Law, which binds both the monarch and the community, is equally sovereign, so long as it does not run counter to God. The monarch on the one hand, and the community on the other, are joined together in the theocratic order in such a way that both are subordinate to God and to the Law. This fundamental conception will be fully discussed later; the point here is that in the Middle Ages the monarchical principle (or the monarch's divine mandate) had not yet freed the monarch from dependence upon popular will as the later theory of Divine Right freed him. The monarchical principle was, indeed, strong enough to hinder the emergence of a democratic principle at a time when even the head of a local community was conceded some measure of self-sufficiency in the exercise of his functions, when he was entrusted with a mandate for which he was responsible only to God, with a "guardianship." But the monarchical principle was an ideal concept rather than one of positive law. It did not relieve the individual possessor of power from the particular legal obligations which he assumed towards the community at the time of his admission to office or afterwards. There was a transcendental element in government as such, but the individual holder of power, whether in a small community or in a monarchy, could not base his personal and subjective claim to rule upon this entirely general principle; a particular legal title was essential, and such a title could, in the early Middle Ages, be obtained only from the people.

Let us glance again at the fully-developed theory of Divine Right as maintained in later centuries. In those centuries the absolutism of the modern period was leading to a separation of the personal, subjective right of the individual king from the popular will, and was attributing to the individual prince the same independence which had for so long undisputedly belonged to the monarchy as such, though not to any individual ruler. Two things furthered this development: legitimism and sacral consecration. The history of the origins of both these principles leads back into the early Middle Ages. It is true that legitimist principles in the later sense were then still quite unknown; the monarch, though God's vicar, had his sanction not only from God, but from the people as well. Nevertheless, even in this period, the way was being prepared for the rôle which legitimism was to play in world history.

In the fully developed theory of Divine Right in modern times there is no doubt that the monarch differs from the republican magistrate in as much as the personal royal rights of the individual king—not only the inalienable prerogatives of monarchy itself—derive from God, and originate without any act of human will. The concrete expression of this notion is the hereditary right of the ruler. The accident of birth, an act of nature, wherein the will of God must be venerated, indicates the person who is to be king, and the king owes exclusively to God not only the essential content of his power but also his subjective and personal claim to the throne. Since the community has not given this to him, it can neither question nor withdraw it. The prince's inalienable birthright thus raises the throne above popular sanction.

This principle of " legitimism," the divine right of the hereditary monarch in such a form as this, is a comparatively modern product. Neither Germanic nor ecclesiastical law contained originally any theory of hereditary rule. One of the concepts that established for the individual occupant of a throne a *ius in re* in the government was the *ius ad rem* acquired by birth. But an act of the people as well as hereditary right was an essential factor in obtaining

the power to govern.   The early mediaeval monarch customarily owed his position to an act of the community or its
representatives; thus in principle he was never established
solely by divine grace but always also by the people.

But we must now examine in more detail the significance
of the ruler's hereditary *ius ad rem*, and must indicate its
fortunes prior to the rise of modern legitimist principles.

§2. GERMANIC KIN-RIGHT

The early mediaeval king did not come to the throne
through a simple personal right of inheritance.   He did, it is
true, as a rule possess a certain hereditary reversionary
right, or at least a privileged " throne-worthiness " in virtue
of his royal descent.   But it was the people who summoned
him to the throne with the full force of law, in as much as
they chose from among the members of the ruling dynasty
either the next in title or the fittest.[3]   The part played by
the people or their representatives in the elevation of the
monarch fluctuated between genuine election and mere
recognition (or acceptance) of a king already designated.

[3] As a rule the sons of the king had a right of succession to the throne
similar to a private right of inheritance, but usually only if they were
suitable for the position of ruler.   A requisite for suitability, especially
when danger from enemies threatened, but also normally in the Germanic
States, was capacity to be a leader in the field.   As a result of this, a
preference for the first-born king's son to succeed to the throne as against
younger brothers came into existence.   Nevertheless, even the brother of
a deceased king could be preferred to the king's son on precisely these
grounds.   Thus three possible ways of succession arose: (i) primogeniture,
(ii) " seniorat " (or " tanistry "), i.e., the succession of the oldest relative,
(iii) " majorat," i.e., the succession of the oldest relative of the same
grade as the next in blood-relationship.
    The question of practical importance was the decision taken between the
rights of the king's son and those of either the oldest or the best qualified
agnate.   It was the logical corollary of the elective principle that this
decision should be taken by a verdict of the electors.   Hence, even if in
general the king's sons, and in particular, where individual succession
existed, the oldest son, possessed a presumptive right, his claim was still
subject to the proviso that the electors recognized his suitability.
    The preference for the hereditary right of the oldest collateral rather
than for that of the children of a deceased king (" seniorat " or " tanistry ")
had its principal root in the need for having an experienced and respected
leader.   The hereditary right of the children had often exposed the community to the dangers of anarchy.   " Tanistry," therefore, is found in the
most diverse parts of the earth, and at very different periods.   Ireland,
Poland, Hungary, Serbia, Kiev, the Vandal kingdom, and Anglo-Saxon
England from 858 to 900 and in 946, may be mentioned as examples from
mediaeval Europe.

But at least the community gave legal assent to the prince's accession to the throne, and solemnly installed the new king in power.[4]

Thus, the difference between the mediaeval king and the head of a smaller community, like that between the *rex* and the *princeps* of Tacitus, was one of degree rather than of kind, even in the method of attaining the throne. We have seen above that the principles of monarchy held good for both the king and the magistrate, so far as the content of their power was concerned; it is now obvious that both, in virtue of their election by the community, are akin also in the way in which they attained their power. What distinguished the king from a freely elected official was his hereditary right to the throne; but this was an hereditary right not of any individual ruler, but of a ruling family.

This claim of the family, this " kin-right " or " blood-right," apart altogether from his election by the people, conferred upon the individual ruler an independent, subjective *ius ad rem*. The whole dynasty, not merely the individual, was called to the throne, and when in exceptional circumstances a man from another family had to be raised to the throne, a new royal dynasty came into existence. A king from a new family ruled as the founder of a new dynasty. The word " king " itself expressed " kin-right," for etymologically it signified " son of the king " or " scion of the ruling family." All members of the ruling family are royal.[5]

The origin of this mingling of hereditary right with elective right is lost in the darkness of primitive times. It seems to derive from old religious beliefs no less than from sound political insight. For a special virtue, a mysterious " manna " was inherent in the lord of a primitive people, a

---

[4] Both features, the power of the " folk " to elect or acclaim their king, and the restriction of their choice to members of the royal line already appear in the terse brevity of Tacitus's sentence, *Germ.* 7 : " reges ex nobilitate (duces ex virtute) sumunt." The phrase " ex nobilitate " does not mean " from among the nobles," but " in virtue of nobility," i.e., out of the noblest stock.

[5] Cf. *Grammaticus de differentiis* (Brunner, *Zeitschr. f. Rechtsgesch., Germ. Abt.* xviii (1884), 228 sq.): " inter regem et regalem hoc interest, quod regius puer est regalis, rex qui regit regnum."

magic which brought him close to God, as a priest, a hero, or even as a divine being.   But the Germanic peoples normally attached this inviolable sanctity not to a single lord but to his whole kindred; it was an inheritable commodity.   The kin might trace its genealogical tree back to the gods, or might be qualified only by ancestral merit and divine grace to reign on a plane partly human and partly superhuman; but the special claim to lordship possessed by the noblest kin among the folk always rested upon some distinctive inner virtue—a virtue which could be seen in the beaming eye of a prince of royal blood.   It was the virtues of their blood that lifted the sons of Woden, [6] the Astings, the Amals, and so on, out of the ranks of the folk, though without bestowing upon any individual prince a right to the throne independent of popular will.   The family's possession of the throne was as inviolable as the right of any individual prince to succeed to it was insecure.

There is no need to deny that in most cases kin-right was supported by the overwhelmingly superior power and wealth of the royal house, and also by considerations of political expediency, which at all times have militated against a purely elective monarchy.   Nevertheless, here where our principal purpose is to understand the fundamental convictions of the period, it must be emphasized that mere expediency is entirely insufficient to explain the tenacity with which folk-belief held fast to the notion of royal magic, to the special right of the *sanguis regis* or of the *genus purpuratum*.   Thus, as Procopius relates, about the year 545, the uncivilized Herules, after they had killed their king near Belgrade, sent envoys to remote Thule to see if they could find among the Herules there a royal descendant of the ruling house.   The envoys encountered many such descendants in Thule, and from their number they chose the ablest.   He died on the way; the envoys returned once more, and selected another.   During the long interval, however, the Herules who were settled on the Danube began to think

---

[6] The kings of the Anglo-Saxons especially passed as such. " Voden, de cuius stirpe multarum provinciarum regium genus originem duxit." Bede, *Eccles. Hist.* I, 15 (ed. Holder, 24).

that they might do better to set one of themselves on the throne instead of making a legitimist experiment. Nevertheless, despite their superficial Christianity, they did not venture to accomplish this breach with ancient folk-belief on their own responsibility, but—no doubt from political motives as well—they turned to the Emperor, just as later, in 751, the Franks in a similar position turned to the Pope. Justinian selected a king for them from their own ranks, not a member of the old dynasty, but a man of political ability and familiar with their affairs; they did homage to him and were content with him. Then the envoys arrived back with the stranger-prince. The new king prepared to resist him by force of arms; the Herules supported his resolve to fight, but when only a day's journey separated them from the true royal scion, they threw all discretion to the winds, and during the night went over *en bloc* to the stranger. Thus they broke with the Emperor, and before long they fell under the sword of the superior forces of Byzantium.

Another example admirably shows how the belief in kingship crystallized into a strong sense of the exalted character of the ruling line. When wicked relatives handed scissors and sword to one of the Merovingian queens so that, in the words of Gregory of Tours, she might choose whether her grandsons should be shorn " like the rest of the people " —whether, that is to say, they should be deprived of the long locks which were the distinctive symbol of Merovingian royalty—or whether they should be executed, she instinctively, in the agony of her dilemma, chose death for her loved ones, as being the more tolerable alternative.

Nothing throws more light upon the magical character of primitive Germanic kin-right than the physical insignia of royal descent that have just been mentioned. The king must receive his sceptre or sword of state from some one else, but the *reges criniti* wore their ornamental hair not as the sign of an office conferred upon them by the people, but as proof of hereditary personal dignity and virtue. Nor was it an empty symbol; like Samson, the family sometimes found that its strength reposed in its locks; for the hair-symbol passed current as a true and lawful sign of eligibility for the throne. To shave a Merovingian meant excluding him from the throne. If, on the other hand, the restoration of a shaven Merovingian was proposed, it was necessary to wait until his hair had again grown long. With his new head of hair he received a new name, a new legal personality, and the dignity fitting him for his new position.

The Franks, as late as the eighth century, were willing to tolerate kings from the Merovingian house, even after they possessed little or nothing more than their flowing locks. The superstitious aversion of the people from parting with this phantom-like dynasty; the expedient—well-nigh unexampled in world history—of the rule of Mayors of the Palace, which was the expression of that aversion;[7] the unsuccessful attempt, veiled by the fiction of adoption, which Grimoald, one of the Mayors, made to supplant the legitimate Merovingian ; finally Pipin's extraordinary caution and anxiety in setting aside the last of the puppet-kings; all these facts show with special clarity how closely the right of the king even at this date was bound up with the primitive beliefs and legal sentiments of the Germanic peoples. Such feelings were largely transmitted by popular tradition to later centuries, especially when the twofold blessing of age and success hallowed a *stirps regia*.

Even at the height of the Middle Ages, when the people, or at any rate the magnates, exercised with comparative freedom their right of election, kin-right was still a decisive force. In Germany, for example, no royal election occurred before Gregory VII's time in which the blood-relationship of the candidate to preceding kings was not a major consideration. Even at the election of the anti-king Rudolf of Rheinfelden in 1077, an important part was perhaps played by the fact that at any rate his wife was a king's daughter. To many of the people, it still seemed intolerable to be ruled

[7] Einhard, *Vita Karoli*, 1 (*MGH., Schulausgabe*[6], 2*sq.*) : " Gens Meroingorum . . . nullius vigoris erat, nec quicquam in se clarum praeter inane regis vocabulum praeferebat . . . Neque regi aliud relinquebatur, quam ut, regio tantum nomine contentus, crine profuso, barba summissa, solio resideret ac speciem dominantis effingeret, legatos undecumque venientes audiret eisque abeuntibus responsa, quae erat edoctus vel etiam iussus, ex sua velut potestate redderet; cum praeter inutile regis nomen et precarium vitae stipendium . . . nihil aliud proprii possideret, quam unam . . . villam. .. At regni administrationem . . . praefectus aulae procurabat."

by a prince from an ordinary family. A candidate for the throne who was not related to the royal line, left himself open to the taunt: " Don't you know your cart lacks its fourth wheel? "[8] On the other hand, it is true that a ruler had to reckon with the possibility that in exceptional circumstances the choice of the people might at some time be withheld from his own line before it became extinct.[9]

The older a family, the more worthy of the throne it seemed. Hence the Carolingian claim to rule remained imprescriptible throughout the Middle Ages. It was not the privilege that Pope Stephen II was held to have conferred upon the Carolingian dynasty that brought this about, but the immortality which popular sentiment accorded to the oldest and most distinguished stock. In Germany, the genealogical tree of Henry I came to be traced back to Charlemagne. In France, the Capetian house had reigned undisputed for two hundred years, and had long been revered, when Philip Augustus brought home a wife from the family of a German count; she was slighted on account of her inferior descent; but when it became known that a drop of Carolingian blood flowed in her veins, that was enough for both people and court to celebrate the " *reditus regni Francorum ad stirpem Caroli,*" and for all the older Capetians to be openly designated as usurpers. The belief was widespread among the people that the Capetians must die out after seven generations, and that before the world came to its end, the government must revert once more to the unforgettable line of Charles the Great. The principal object of French policy, the " recovery " of Lorraine and the Rhine frontier, rested in the long run upon the kin-right of the

---

[8] " ' Num,' inquid, ' currui tuo quartam deesse non sentis rotam? ' "— This was the reply received by Ekkehard of Meissen from a count who was asked to explain his opposition to Ekkehard's candidature during the electoral proceedings in 1002 after the death of Otto III. Cf. Thietmar, *Chron.* IV, 52.

[9] Thus Otto I in his charter of 936 for Quedlinburg (*MGH., Diplomata,* I, 90), where, after supposing that royal power will be in the hands of " aliquis generationis nostrae," he goes on to consider the position " si . . . alter e populo eligatur rex," in spite of the fact that his line has not died out (" nostrae namque cognationis qui potentissimus sit "). But this was exceptional, and Otto I himself would hardly have repeated it at a date more remote from his own election.

Carolingians, in which was included the claim to the empire of Charlemagne.

On the other hand, some people in the ninth and tenth centuries felt it necessary to justify the transference of the German, French, Burgundian, and Italian crowns to persons not of the Carolingian line, by asserting that the Carolingian house had died out.

Since in all Western opinion, capacity to rule was bound up with kin and blood, a series of legal rules or claims was built up, based upon the special sanctity of the royal blood. The most important of these legal innovations was the introduction of equality of birth among all princes ; the most peculiar, perhaps, were the special rights claimed by those born in the purple.

More than once in the early Middle Ages, princes " born in the purple " claimed a better title to the throne than their elder brothers born before their father's accession.[10]   In other words, the father as king begets a lineage of higher rank than he does as duke; only the younger son is a " king's son."   This claim, particularly frequent in the tenth century, never became a regular part of public law, for even before the formulation of a strict right of primogeniture, the right of the elder brother prevailed for obvious reasons in most cases.

[10]In Germany, when the question of a successor to Henry I was being discussed in 936, one party wanted Otto I as king, " quia aetate esset maior et consilio providentior," but many preferred Otto's younger brother, Henry, " quia natus esset in aula regali." Cf. *MGH., Script.* IV, 289. England in the tenth century offered an exact parallel to the German throne-contest of 936.   When after Edgar's death (975), a contest between his two minor sons or their supporters broke out, it was argued against the elder Edward, " quia matrem eius, licet legaliter nuptam, in regnum tamen non magis quam patrem eius, dum eum genuit, sacratam fuisse sciebant" (Eadmer, *Vita Dunst.* 35).

A curious inversion of the preference for princes " born in the purple " is found in the argument with which the anti-king Louis of France supported his claim to the English throne against John Lackland.   The incapacity of John to succeed to the throne was deduced from his condemnation in the French royal court (1203) : " tunc . . . nobis tanquam vero haeredi cessit ius regni Angliae, maxime cum adhuc de carne sua heredem non haberet." Rymer, *Foedera*, I, 140.   Therefore the whole of John's posterity born after the condemnation were to be disinherited.   But the English did not accept this deduction.   Cf., however, Matthew Paris (1216), *Chron.* II, 660: " Consuetudo est in regno Franciae, quod ex quo aliquis est damnatus ad mortem, quod proles suscepta post sententiam damnationis succedere non debet; geniti tamen ante sententiam succedere debent."

On the other hand, the principle of equality of princely birth gradually won its way in spite of opposition from the law of the land, unrestricted marriage-customs, and dynastic traditions. For although, as we shall see later, the older Germanic law regulating the private position of princes did not exclude the offspring born of misalliance, nor even the bastard, from eligibility for the throne, yet the matrimonial politics of the Middle Ages seem from an early date to be based upon the principle of upholding the sanctity of the family and of enhancing its lustre by marriages among the equal-born. Even if it was not an inviolable rule, it was certainly considered fitting and desirable that noble house should unite with noble house, royal house with royal house, and even imperial house with imperial house, in order to avoid lowering the worthiness of the stock. The existence of two Empires, contrary as it was to the strict ideas of the age, became as a result more tolerable, and it was of considerable practical value, especially to the less distinguished Western Empire, to be able to enhance the prestige of one Imperial house by inter-marriage with the other. The illustrious Eastern Empire, however, lacking as it did any established principles of kin-right, attached less importance to these matrimonial possibilities, and seldom emerged from its traditional sullen jealousy.

Thus kin-right gave rise in the first place to a definite marriage-policy; but in the course of centuries, it also resulted in a special law of equality of birth among ruling families, since the principle that like united with like become ever more rigid and increasingly narrow in application. This exclusiveness, so far as it concerned the legal position, at first affected not so much the ruling families as the high nobility. The equality of the offspring from all marriages between free people, it is true, is proclaimed by the *Sachsenspiegel* in Germany as late as the thirteenth century; but recent research has proved the existence, from at least the ninth century, of a status of nobility by birth. In the late Carolingian period, the marriage of a candidate for the throne with a count's daughter did not as yet prejudice his right to the throne, but his union with a knight's daughter was considered to be a misalliance by which kin-right suffered. A long time elapsed before a special status by birth for the ruling families grew out of the status of nobility by birth. The tendency in practice for rulers' children to marry only rulers' children appeared much earlier than the assertion of a definite legal preference for such marriages. But a dynastic caste of equals by birth was ultimately created in Europe, though not until modern times; a ruling cast which at least according to the strict rules of family law, can on principle propagate itself only through itself, and which loses the attribute of eligibility for the throne as a result of the slightest admixture of common blood. Before such a situation arose, however, other factors had to play their part. Had it not been for such factors, the royal houses of Europe, because of their limited numbers, could never have entirely avoided marriages with commoners, or at least could never have avoided considering the " peers " as equals in birth. But in Germany, where political consolidation was achieved not by the monarch but by the princes, several hundred sovereign princes came into existence, all possessing to the same extent the precious virtue of " blue-blood." These German princes in the course of time supplied nearly all the dynasties of Christendom with their privileged blood, and so constituted what has been called the " princely stud " of Europe.

These developments, though not achieved until long after the period which we are describing, amounted in essence only to a fuller expression and strengthening of the early mediaeval ideas confining eligibility for the throne to a definite kin. During the thirteenth century in Western Europe, at all events, it was considered more distinguished to be the blood-relation of an hereditary king than to be the recipient of a crown by election; this was the explanation offered for a French prince's refusal of the elective crown of Germany. [11]

" Kin-right," the right of the blood, was the most import-

[11] " Credimus enim dominum nostrum regem Galliae, quem linea regii sanguinis provexit ad sceptra Francorum regenda, excellentiorem esse aliquo imperatore, quem sola provehit electio voluntaria; sufficit domino comiti Roberto, fratrem esse tanti regis." Matth. Paris, op. cit., III, 626 sq.

ant contribution of Germanic traditions to the development of the theory of Divine Right. It had not, at first, anything in common with the Christian and theocratic principles of Divine Right. On the other hand, the Germanic and the Christian elements in monarchical right could ultimately be fused, and in the modern theory of Divine Right, legitimism derived from Germanic kin-right has entirely blended with the theocratic formulae of monarchical doctrine. But, even so, an essential difference between the two persists. Christain principles of monarchy evolved from the idea of the duties inherent in office, the fulfilment of which makes the ruler the vicar of God on earth. Germanic kin-right, on the other hand, contained no idea of office at all, but only a claim for the family, and the original foundations of this right were not so much a duty enjoined upon the family, as an unusual power, a fortunate virtue, a special divine vocation, with which legend at all times loves to enwrap the figures of the founders of dynasties.

But what especially differentiates the kin-right of the early Middle Ages from later legitimist principles is the lack, already mentioned, of a strict claim to the throne for any individual member of the ruling line. The possession of the throne by the whole family, and the kin's eligibility for it were universally recognized; but the succession of any particular prince of the blood depended as a rule upon many fluctuating circumstances, and particularly upon the will of the people.

There were, indeed, two ways of transmuting the incontestable claims of the family as a whole into a definite right of an individual prince to succeed to the throne, of converting kin-right into hereditary right, and of excluding the participation of the people in the acts by which the throne was filled, or of reducing popular intervention to an empty form.

1. The older way was to declare all members of the ruling house not only equally eligible for the throne, but also equally entitled to it. Something of this sort is said to have been a principle of public law under the Merovingians. But in fact hereditary ideas never reached such extremes. There did exist, however, at least a direct right to the throne for all male lineal descendants of a king; for the practice

under the Merovingian kings of partitioning the State as a private legacy among the heirs of the blood amounted to something like the realization of this principle. The political unity of the Frankish kingdom was not entirely destroyed by these partitions, but they involved the destruction of the popular basis of the Germanic monarchies, since the people, at any rate in the sixth century, had no voice in the purely private or dynastic affair of inheritance and partitioning of the State. The principle of equal or similar hereditary right for all blood-relations, however, was never fully carried out. The self-interest of individual kings combined with political motives to prevent the dismemberment of the State beyond a certain limit; hence collateral lines were excluded, whilst the innumerable offspring of the kings were decimated in wars of mutual extermination.

Moreover, the magnates, especially after the seventh century, contested with some measure of success the encroachment of private hereditary rights upon the power of the State. Nevertheless, succession to the throne involving the partition of the realm still prevailed in a mild form in the Carolingian period, and the weakening of authority and other political evils resulting from this, as well as the selfish hostility of royal relatives to one another, were hardly less conspicuous in the ninth century than in the Merovingian period. Even after the principle of impartibility and individual succession had been secured in the States of the post-Carolingian period, the hereditary right of all the heirs was once again revived during the later Middle Ages, as a result of the custom of granting apanages, and even in this much weakened form it proved—in France, for example— to be a serious menace. The grant of apanages had already caused Otto I some moments of grave anxiety; for even if the development of the electoral principle had, after the death of Louis the Child, done away with the partitioning of the inheritance, it still had not obviated claims to the throne and strong ambition for power on the part of the agnates.

2. Nevertheless, after the downfall of the Carolingians, the idea of individual succession prevailed over these tendencies to such an extent that from that time onwards there was no

longer any question of an hereditary right for all the sons of a king. Henceforth there remained only the less ancient way of transforming kin-right into hereditary right: by concentrating in a single person the whole family's eligibility for the throne. Family custom and the law of the land built up strict rules on this matter, and the presumptive right to the throne, which was always given to age, male sex, and close relationship to the last king, gradually grew into an exclusive claim to the throne for one certain member of the ruling dynasty. In this way, the different forms of hereditary succession—the right of the " majorat," the right of the " seniorat," and the right of the first-born[12]—originated, and the last of these three forms, the right of primogeniture, attained by far the greatest importance, and by degrees so hardened that the kin-right of the dynasty merged into the right of the first-born.

At the time of its highest development, the blood-right of the whole kin had extended not only to the innumerable adult male members of the family, but also as a rule had included women and minors, although in certain cases their unsuitability for military and political leadership had excluded them from the succession. Again, in principle, the right to succeed also belonged to bastards in the early Middle Ages; many of the greatest rulers of the period—Theodoric the Great, Charles Martel, William the Conqueror, Manfred, and others—were born out of wedlock, and this indifference to the ordinary law of marriage and of inheritance was, after all, only logical, since the claim to rule rested on the fact that the claimant actually possessed a ruler's blood in his veins.

Not until the ninth century, as we shall see, was the right of royal bastards to succeed checked by the Church, and eventually set aside. Further restrictions of kin-right were brought about by the exclusion of women from the succession, and by the passing-over of collateral heirs. But the final settlement of the right of the first-born to succeed was still a long way off, and for centuries more, until modern times, direct succession from father to son remained precluded. In France, which was actually the most definitely

[12] Cf. n. 3, *supra* p. 12.

hereditary monarchy of the West, a special act of the community was needed for every recognition of the son's right to succeed, until the very end of the *ancien régime*, and primogeniture was not established as a principle until 1791. But already during the Middle Ages, where conditions were favourable, and especially where for centuries there was unbroken succession from father to son within a single dynasty, primogeniture existed in practice.

No sudden change occurred, but a gradual transition from kin-right to hereditary right set in; the father's designation of the son as successor to the throne, or the crowning of the next heir as co-ruler during the life-time of the father, permitted the almost imperceptible growth of the custom of primogeniture in France, as early as the thirteenth century.[13]

Only after this transformation of kin-right into hereditary right, at first in practice and finally in principle, did the successor to the throne receive his powers immediately of God, or at the hand of Nature. The election to the kingship dwindled to a mere ceremony, and the elimination of election and the steady li.nitation of kin-right, led to the emergence of the divine right of birth, the so-called principle of legitimism. Kin-right, the right of the line to beget any number of *principes* or potential rulers, is implicit in the idea of " prince "; the individual's reversionary right, on the other hand, his hereditary and independent right to succeed to the crown, is implicit in the idea of " crown-prince." The principle of private law, that " only God can make an heir," is expressed most strongly in the law of succession to the throne, which, being divine law, overrides even the sanctity of oaths.[14] Struggles for the throne henceforth arise not

---

[13] The usual method, which formally preserved the electoral right of the community, but which increasingly deprived it of its importance by making it into a mere ceremony, consisted in the election and crowning of the son during the father's life-time. This way had its inconveniences, as the frequent revolts of such pre-crowned kings against their fathers, especially in Germany, showed. But mediaeval kingship could not do without this method, if it wished to obtain a genuine hereditary character.

[14] When, for the first time in England, strict hereditary legitimism came to be treated as divine natural law, during the revolt of the Duke of York, the Duke's reply to Henry VI's objection that he had sworn him an oath of allegiance, was that: Oaths are invalid in conflict with divine and natural law (i.e., his claim to inherit the crown). Cf. Figgis, *op. cit.*, 82; Chrimes, *English Constitutional Ideas in the XVth cent.*, 30.

from disputed elections and the like, but from the rules of hereditary descent; the period of the wars of succession sets in during the fourteenth century, after the old Germanic elective idea had sunk into insignificance as compared with the hereditary principle.

Only at this stage could the legitimist principle be blended with both the monarchical principle and the theocratic notions of office. The same God who universally established authority over the people, and who imparted to the ruler a mandate from on high, also raised each individual heir to the kingship, without human intervention or co-operation. For the first time a gulf opens out between the right of the ruler and the will of the people, and henceforth only the inscrutable fate that rules over life and death determines succession to the throne. With the possible exception of a curtailed and formal election-ceremony at his coronation, there was no longer anything to remind the absolute king of the sixteenth, seventeenth, and eighteenth centuries of the earthly source of his power; the principle of legitimism was for him a sufficient warrant for his position as God's viceroy, and he had every reason to regard legitimist Divine Right as the basis of the whole of public law. The hereditary succession of the first-born, along with the doctrine of the equal birth of princes, created that legitimist mysticism which already in the later Middle Ages prepared the ground for Absolutism. In the fifteenth century, the English judges, when invited to give an opinion on the duke of York's claim to the throne, stated that the matter was too high for their learning; it was outside the scope of the law, and therefore they could not dare to discuss anything so exalted.

The early Middle Ages, on the contrary, until the thirteenth century, maintained the essentials of kin-right, without taking the final step towards individual hereditary right. The whole period, despite its emphasis on the divine origins of government, never forgot the earthly basis of the ruler's powers. However exalted authority was over the subjects, the power to rule was always considered to be made by human hands. The ruler, as the heir of the family, received his mandate from God; and, as an elected prince, he also received it from the community. He was ruler in virtue of divine grace and through an act of human will. Throughout the period, this idea was expressed in a variety of ways, and even mature scholastic theory maintained that God, the *causa remota* of government, permitted rather than precluded the actual establishment of the ruler's power by an act of the people.

But though blood-right and election supplemented each other, and though a mystical throne-right in which the people had no share did not exist, these two factors, blood-right and election, were not the only forces which contributed towards establishing an individual ruler's personal right to govern. Yet another factor was the voice of the Church, whether affirmative or negative. The Church in the early Middle Ages also claimed to share in the setting-up of a king.

We have seen that, according to the monarchical principles of the Middle Ages, everybody in authority was expected to be the vicar of God, and in return was endowed with transcendental powers. We also saw, on the other hand, that the individual's concrete right to rule came into existence through the union of kin-right with popular election—a union in which there was no question of theocratic duty. It was the Church which provided the connecting-link between the abstract theocratic principle of monarchy and the subjective claim of the individual ruler. The Church applied the idea of office and of the duties of office to each individual monarch, in the form of concrete demands and the exaction of promises; but in return it conceded to him a divinely attested title to the throne, transcendental and subjective, distinct from kin-right and popular election.

This result came about because the Church, by means of consecration, gave its sanction to an individual prince's right to govern and thereby marked him out as God's vicar on earth. But to this confirmation of the ruler's powers, the Church attached certain conditions arising from the insistence in Christian views of magistracy upon the ideas of office and duty. The inevitable corollary of the endorsement of a ruler's rights by ecclesiastical consecration was a reminder of the ruler's duty. Thus, the participation of the

Church, both by introducing divine warranty for the ruler and by strengthening the idea of royal duty, put the foundations of Germanic kingship upon a fresh basis.   From the beginning, ecclesiastical notions were woven into the fabric of mediaeval Divine Right.   We now turn to these elements in the law of monarchy.

§3. CONSECRATION OF THE MONARCH

A. The Theocratic Conception of Office

The most ancient traditional lore of the Church laid down that every power possessing authority in the State ought to be recognized as a divinely ordained magistracy.   From the time of Paul to that of the Emperor Constantine, this rule took the purely negative form of indifference to the State, and was the expression of the Christian renunciation of active politics.   Nothing was more remote from the Church's ambition in the pagan State than to attempt to assess by either earthly or heavenly standards the lawful title of rival Emperors.

But in a State that had become Christian, the question inevitably arose whether Christianity would continue to accept without scrutiny the established powers, or whether the Church would seek to apply an ethical test to the ruler as to every other Christian—a test which, under certain circumstances, could be enforced by the disciplinary authority of the Church.

We shall deal here with only one of the many points arising from this question; namely, that in a Christian commonwealth a definite ethical duty must be assigned to the head of the State in person.   As a consequence criteria were established which determined whom the faithful should in doubtful cases recognize as possessing authority, and whom not.   But the inevitable result of such a recognition or denunciation by the ecclesiastical authorities was to stamp an existing political authority either as divinely ordained or as godless.   Thus a new criterion of monarchy came into being, in addition to those set up by rights of blood or by election: the sanction of the Church, which followed only rules of its own.[15]

Magistracy, according to the doctrines of the Church Fathers, did not derive its lawful sanction merely from itself, but from something higher than the State, from the law of nature or from divine law.   The *Leitmotif* of all ecclesiastical political theory is the dictum: What is right, ought to be law.   The State, in this view, exists for the purpose of transforming ethical rightness into binding positive law. This civilizing function of the State also determines the choice of ruler.   The true ruler can be recognized only by his fitness to fulfil the divine mission of the State.   Consequently the Church, in approving a ruler, was much less concerned with his legitimism than with his suitability.   As Clement of Alexandria said: " He is king who rules according to law."   Nothing less, but also nothing more, was inherent in the clerical concept of the true ruler.

The ruler, therefore, according to ecclesiastical standards must possess two things: the goodwill and the power to put God's law into practice.   Let us first consider power, the narrower but indispensable attribute of the ruler.

When the Church had to choose between a powerful and righteous but illegitimate ruler, and a prince favoured by blood-right and by election but lacking in power, it unhesitatingly decided for the former—not, indeed, in all cases, but certainly in those in which it most obviously followed its own principles.   Thus the Church allied itself with force, and sanctioned force by this very alliance.   Germanic principles of legitimism, like every other sanction of the right to govern based upon secular standards, remained at heart alien and indifferent to the aims of the Church.   The Church would, of course, support a legitimate ruler where a strengthening of his authority seemed to serve the maintenance of order and of Christian government.   But when the furtherance of those objects required a different course, the Church often

---

[15] The principal Biblical texts for the theocratic idea of office (of the ruler as *minister omnium*) are as follows: Mark x, 42; Mark ix, 35; Matthew xx, 26*sq*; Luke xxii, 26.   The theocratic idea of office matured especially early in that Germanic State where the clergy and the clerical hierarchy received the central place in the administration; namely, among the Visigoths.

set powerful usurpers in the saddle.[16] Pope Zacharias, in his famous decree to the Franks (751) laid down the principle that suitability was more important than legitimism, and defeated it if the two conflicted. " It is better," he is reported to have said, " that he who possesses power be called king, than he who has none."[17]

The pronouncement here made by the Church in favour of the Carolingians against the Merovingions was, four generations later, unhesitatingly turned by the Frankish bishops against the Carolingians themselves, when power had slipped from their hands; they blessed the rising power of non-Carolingian usurpers, " so that order should be maintained." Never again were there Mayors of the Palace ; it was so much easier to replace an unsuitable dynasty with the co-operation of the Church.

Since, in clerical theory, capacity, not inherited right, makes the ruler, the Church combated the right of minors to the throne. With more success, it also attacked the eligibility of bastards, whose very existence made mockery of the sanctity of marriage.[18] Next to the baptismal vows,

[16] There is no doubt that not the Church but God was officially considered to be the power that could replace the principle of legitimism by the principle of " suitability." As Adhémar of Chabannes stated in connection with the revolution of 987: " Regnum pro eo accipere voluit patruus eius Carolus, sed nequivit, quia Deus iudicio suo meliorem elegit." (Recueil des Hist. des Gaules et de la France, X, 144, C.) Gregory VII, with complete lucidity, emphasized in 1081 that the setting aside of Childerich III had occurred not so much because of his lack of moral qualities as because a powerless ruler was politically useless: " Romanus pontifex Zacharias . . . regem Francorum non tam pro suis iniquitatibus quam pro eo, quod tantae potestati non erat utilis, a regno deposuit; et Pipinum Caroli Magni imperatoris patrem in eius loco substituit; omnesque Francigenas a iuramento fidelitatis, quod illi fecerant, absolvit." (Registrum, 8, 21.)

[17] " Zacharias papa mandavit Pippino, ut melius esset illum regem vocari, qui potestatem haberet, quam illum, qui sine regali potestate manebat." (Ann. Regni Franc., a. 748.)

[18] This attack began as early as the sixth century, and is illustrated by a characteristic episode in the life of St Columban (MGH. Script. Mer. IV, 87): " filios Theuderici, quos de adulterinis permixtionibus habebat, ad virum Dei adducit; quos cum vidisset, sciscitatur, quid sibi vellint. Cui Brunichildis ait: ' Regis sunt filii; tu eos tua benedictione robora.' At ille: ' Nequaquam,' inquid, ' istos regalia sceptra suscepturos scias, quia de lupanaribus emerserunt.' " Cf. also the English synod of 786 (MGH., Ep. IV, 23 sq.): " legitime reges a sacerdotibus et senioribus populi eligantur et non de adulterio vel incaestu procreati; quia sicut nostris temporibus ad sacerdotium secundum canones adulter pervenire non potest, sic nec Christus Domini esse valet et rex totius regni, et heres patriae, qui ex legitimo non fuerit connubio generatus."

which early in the Christian Roman Empire had become the first personal requirement in a ruler's eligibility for the throne, birth in wedlock became, from the tenth century, the second canonical qualification for the *"regale minister-ium."* In this respect, however, the clerical demand for " suitability " is opposed to the Germanic principle of " kin-right," not because the Church is supporting power against impotence, but because it is determined to exact definite religious or moral standards from the ruler of a Christian State.[19] These standards could be formal, like the requirement of legitimate birth; but it is noteworthy that the more formal criteria of " suitability " could be dispensed with, if broader issues were at stake. Thus the Church favoured Tancred of Lecce in 1189 and 1190, although he was a bastard, in order to prevent Southern Italy from falling into the hands of a *genus ˈpersecutorum.*

We shall not be able to understand fully the ways in which theocratic principles often defeated the secular right of the mediaeval ruler to the throne, until we have discussed the Right of Resistance. But before we come to that, we still have to consider the deadly blows which the Church, at the height of its influence, dealt to the principles of blood-right.

[19] Already the Council of Paris (829) emphasized the insignificance of rights of blood in order to enhance the importance of regarding kingship as *ministerium.* Government is office and duty, not proprietary right. This basic idea among others is to be found in cap. 5 : " Quod regnum non ab hominibus, sed a Deo . . . detur." (*MGH., Conc.*, II, 655, no. 50, § 59): " Nemo regum a progenitoribus regnum sibi administrari, sed a Deo vera-citer atque humiliter credere debet dari . . . Hi vero, qui a progenitoribus sibi succedere regnum terrenum et non potius a Deo dari putant, illis aptantur, quos Dominus . . . inprobat, dicens: Ipsi regnaverunt et non ex me; principes extiterunt, et non cognovi. Ignorare quippe Dei procul dubio reprobare est." But in order to reign *per Deum*, neither royal descent nor legal title is needed: " Qui pie et iuste et misericorditer regnant, sine dubio per Deum regnant."

The most authoritative statement of " suitability " is that made by Gregory VII (*Registrum*, 8, 26 (1081)) : " Preterea admonendi sunt omnes in partibus vestris Deum timentes . . . : ut non, aliqua gratia suadente aut ullo metu cogente, properent eam temere personam eligere, cuius mores et cetera, quae regi oportet inesse, a suscipienda christianae religionis defen-sione et cura discordent. Melius quippe fore arbitramur, ut aliqua mora secundum Deum ad honorem sanctae ecclesiae rex provideatur idoneus, quam nimium festinando in regem aliquis ordinetur indignus. . . . Nisi enim ita oboediens et sanctae ecclesiae humiliter devotus ac utilis, quemadmo-dum christianum regem oportet, . . . fuerit, . . . ei . . . ecclesia non favebit sed etiam contradicet . . . Qua de re quid promissionis iuramento . . . ecclesia ab illo requirat, in sequenti significamus."

In the twelfth and thirteenth centuries, when papal theocracy was at its zenith, it was alleged that a prince's descent
from a dynasty hostile to the Church, a *genus persecutorum*,
was sufficient in itself to destroy his eligibility for the throne.
But in the application of this threat, the Church did not
merely propose to visit the sins of the fathers upon the sons.
More generally still, direct descent from any ruler, no matter
whether good or bad, so far from establishing a claim to the
throne, was held rather to be proof of ineligibility. Innocent III wrote in 1202, with regard to the disputed election
in Germany, that if Philip of Swabia obtained the realm,
and if the crown remained, as hitherto, in the hands of the
Hohenstaufen, then the many equally noble and powerful
German princes of other houses would be prejudiced in their
prospects of attaining the throne.

The indifference of the Church towards dynastic principles
here amounted to unreserved hostility, and this repudiation
of the ruling dynasty's special rank and eminence was
coupled with a lively concern for the preservation—in reality,
the aggrandisement—of the elective principle. Hence it
finally came about in thirteenth-century Germany, which
was more exposed than other countries to the reiterated
attacks of clerical principles, that the duly qualified son of a
qualified king lost the reversion of the throne precisely
because of his descent, and the setting aside of the next-of-
kin was applauded as though the matter were merely one of
excluding nepotism at an episcopal election.

Only in Germany, however, did the ecclesiastical idea of
office, in alliance with the unscrupulousness of the electoral
princes, lead to so impudent a reversal of kin-right, and even
there it was only transitory. The beginning of its influence
dates from the election at Forchheim in 1077, when for the
first time a rival king was elected in place of the ruling house,
in the common interest of the Curia and of the German
princes. Already on this occasion the elected candidate,
Rudolf of Swabia, had to make a declaration, in defiance of
all Germanic sentiments and traditions, that he mounted the
throne as an individual prince, not as the founder of a
dynasty. But though the self-interest of the electoral

princes, supported by the ecclesiastical idea of "suitability," had by the thirteenth and fourteenth centuries resulted in a complete destruction of dynastic right, the transformation of Germany into an elective State, devoid of any *stirps regia*, was not permanent. Under the Luxemburg and Hapsburg houses, the proscribed kin-right again emerged, though only in a weakened form, after the fashion of other European States and the German principalities. The community's instinct for self-preservation culminated in resistance to the electoral confusion which prevailed in the century after the Interregnum. To be sure, praise for the official elective principle was as little lacking in Germany as in Byzantium, just as the hereditary monarchies of Western Europe, once they were well-established, found their theoretical defenders. Pure hereditary principle was in theory incompatible with the Empire until the year 1806, as it had already been in classical times.

The claim of the spiritual power to examine the "suitability" of the ruler sprang in the first place from the leading part played by the theocratic ideal in every sphere of life, and also from the inclusion of the State within the *Ecclesia*, as understood in mediaeval thought. Moreover, the Church had in addition a definite constitutional opportunity for proclaiming its judgment as to the fitness or unfitness of a ruler; namely, his consecration. The importance of this opportunity will be discussed in the following sections; here it need only be pointed out that the right of the popes to consecrate the Emperor explains the special interest which the Curia had in curtailing the hereditary principle in Germany. The Curia had, indeed, at times formulated in general terms the claim to exclude any unsuitable king from the throne; but, on the other hand, many popes, from the ninth century onwards, based their claim to confirm the election of German kings expressly upon their share in the Emperor's coronation.[20] The fundamental claim of the

[20] Cf. Pope John VIII to archbishop Anspert of Milan in 879 (*MGH.*, *Ep.*, VII, 133, no. 163): " Et quia Karolusmannus corporis, sicut audimus, incommoditate gravatus regnum retinere iam nequit, ut de novi regis . . . omnes pariter consideremus, vos predicto adesse tempore valde oportet. Et ideo antea nullum absque nostro consensu regem debetis recipere, nam ipse, qui a nobis est ordinandus in imperium, a nobis primum atque potissimum debet esse vocatus atque electus."

spiritual power to examine a candidate's eligibility for the throne was not derived from the papal right to consecrate the Emperor, but from the theocratic conception of the royal office.   Nevertheless, it was the papal right of consecration that gave the Curia a political excuse for exercising in Germany its right to scrutinize candidates, and for furthering the principles of " suitability," and of election, at the expense of the principles of dynastic legitimacy.   The Curia had to acquiesce in what it considered the " abuse " of blood-right by other kings, but it was able to resist dynastic claims in Germany, and was obliged to resist them, lest its power to dispose of the Imperial crown should vanish.

The value of the Church's recognition varied from ruler to ruler in the Middle Ages.   A king who mounted his father's throne might enjoy sufficient support in the dynastic conceptions of Germanic society to be able safely to dispense with ecclesiastical confirmation.   In that case, consecration by the Church came to be at most a declaratory or affirmative act devoid of constitutive importance in the establishment of his right to govern.   It was otherwise with rulers who had no hereditary claim to the throne—who, in contrast with the rulers possessing an hereditary right, might perhaps be raised on the shield.   Even though these rulers considered election by the people to be the true legal basis of their kingship, they normally desired not only such an election—which was independent of blood-right and sometimes hostile to it—but also the sanction of the Church. Government, which was deemed to be not simply a mandate from the people, but to possess independent rights of its own, ought, at its establishment, to receive an exalted sanction independent of popular will; this was what general feeling demanded.   The elected king, therefore, sought support and confirmation either in kin-right or in ecclesiastical consecration, or in both.

Thus ecclesiastical sanction became a constituent factor in all governments not supported at their establishment by dynastic rights.   This sanction could be expressed either by a simple declaration of ecclesiastical support or approbation, or by the participation of the episcopate in the election of a ruler. But in the early Middle Ages, consecration became the usual method of such approval. Ecclesiastical acts, in accordance with the faith of the time, were commonly associated with visible rites of a definitely ceremonial character. When, therefore, the Church sanctified a ruler's office by its confirmation, it was natural that it should express its blessing in a formal legal act which symbolized the divine legitimation and endorsement of the right to the throne. The development of this legal act, which was both ecclesiastical and political in character, was completed in the period between the sixth and ninth centuries.

B. Ecclesiastical Consecration of the Ruler as a Sacral Rite

The pagan monarchies of the East, down to the time of the Sassanids, offered many examples of royal consecration at the hands of priests. But we may ignore these proceedings, as well as the earliest mediaeval coronations, which took place in Byzantium, since these precedents, if they were known at all in the West, certainly exerted no influence there. It was rather the Old-Testament account of the anointing of Saul and David by Samuel that provided the West with an example of royal consecration.

Where royal unction appeared in the West, among the Britons in the sixth century, the Visigoths in the seventh century, and the Anglo-Saxons and the Franks in the eighth century, the precise occasion for its introduction remains almost entirely obscure. But it is clear enough, in the case of the Britons, Visigoths, and Franks, as well as in Byzantium, that its introduction was connected with the irregular and disturbed positions in which their monarchs found themselves. The monarchy itself, in those States where it had lost peaceful possession of its hereditary powers, made a place in public law for the new ecclesiastical usage. The foundation of the Carolingian monarchy is the most striking example of this connection of consecration with insecurity; for the Franks alone of all the Germanic peoples completed the introduction of consecration in the full light of history, and here, in the most important State of the West, all the

elements of early mediaeval monarchical right are fused
together as in a crucible.

When, in the year 751, the Franks resolved to do away at
last with the division of government between the legitimate
kings and the powerful Mayors of the Palace, and to set on
the throne the family of the Arnulfings, who had ruled for a
century and a half, the monstrosity and outrageousness of
this design in the eyes of contemporaries consisted not so
much in abandoning Childerich III, as in destroying the
dynastic rights of the Merovingians. Although the *reges
criniti* had never received a special consecration by the
Church, they none the less possessed a supernatural sanctification in the old, pagan, mythical roots of their rights, and
at that time such sanctification meant more, in the consciousness of the people, than the benediction of the Church. A
single Merovingian could be displaced, but no assembly of the
" folk " could lawfully deprive the race of Clovis of its claims
to the throne. If a few years earlier, it had been thought
necessary to place a Merovingian once again on the long
vacant throne, in order to maintain control of the dependent
provinces, no less confusion in the State was to be expected,
if the symbol of its unity, the royal dynasty, vanished, and a
race, no more noble than many ducal and comital families
in the provinces, took possession of the realm.

In these circumstances, the Franks turned to the Pope,
the oracle of divine law, who alone was capable of defeating
the Merovingian blood-right. The decision of Pope Zacharias is already known to us. The election of Pipin by the
Franks followed in November, 751; the last Merovingian,
designated a " false king " by the papal decree, was deprived
of the long hair which symbolized his blood-right. But the
great revolution was still not concluded by this double act.
The election by the people had doubtless transmuted the
de facto power of the Arnulfinger dynasty into a power *de
jure*; but Pipin went further and had himself anointed, probably at the hands of Boniface, the papal vicar and the most
eminent prince of the Church north of the Alps. This act
was altogether an innovation in the Frankish kingdom. It
gave the new dynasty a supernatural sanction, which in some

measure compensated for the loss of the sanctity that the *reges criniti* had possessed; an ancient pagan symbol gave way to a modern theocratic one.

From that day onwards, the ceremony of consecration, evoked by the political needs of the new dynasty, never disappeared from the usages of Western monarchy, and soon became one of the principal features of Divine Right.

1. The Ecclesiastical Significance of Royal Consecration.

From the start, consecration of the monarch signified more than a mere ecclesiastical intercession and invocation of divine benediction. Pope Gregory the Great typified it by stating that the consecration bestowed upon the secular authority was a " sacrament." Sacramental doctrine was still very fluid in the early Middle Ages. The Augustinian idea of sacrament allowed, and even insisted, that all rites and usages which revealed to the faithful a supernatural gift of grace, a *sacra res*, were to be conceived of as sacraments. When, from the twelfth century onwards, the sacramental doctrines of the Church was defined, and the number of sacraments was limited, monarchical consecration was, however, no longer included among them. But the three distinctive features which mediaeval doctrine attributed to all sacraments, still belonged in some measure to royal consecration; and since in the early Middle Ages, consecration had been regarded as a distinct sacrament, it continued to be regarded as at least a quasi-sacrament in the well-defined dogma of the later Middle Ages. Consecration, which according to the early mediaeval Church, was a vehicle of supernatural virtue, brought results, expressed in symbolical form, which were both psychological and religious on the one hand, and ecclesiastical and legal on the other. Its external symbols were seen in the ministrations of the priest who crowned and anointed; its inner efficacy was in the soul of the princely recipient; its outward efficacy was manifested in the " character " that it conferred upon the person of the crowned and anointed prince.

(*a*) The inner efficacy of consecration, by the mystical power of God, changed the anointed prince into a new man, conferred upon him the sevenfold gifts of the Holy Ghost. " The grace of God hath this day changed thee into another man, and by the holy rite of unction hath made thee partaker in its divinity," declared the archbishop of Mainz, in biblical phrase, to the German king. The king, like a priest, was anointed with the oil of the grace of the Holy Ghost, and the theological parlance of Carolingian court-circles once again exalted the anointed prince, as in Old-Testament times, to the rank of an adoptive son of God.[21]

(b) But with this inner mystical virtue, consecration also transmitted a legally significant outward character. As early as the middle of the ninth century, a Carolingian king himself inferred that he had received from the anointing " a quality that could not be taken away without the verdict of the Church." The general belief of the ninth century in the legal importance of the anointing is clearly shown by the fact that a Roman Council of 898 declared in one case that such an anointing was valid, but in another that it was void, because it was surreptitious. But it is more difficult to define the content of this special " character " transmitted by anointing, than to establish its existence.

From the beginning, there was above all a strong belief in the close affinity between monarchical and priestly consecration. Since the substance, the chrism, was the same in both cases, and since the inner efficacy, the bestowal of spiritual virtue, was in both considered to be very similar, or even identical, the " character " which royal " consecration " or " ordination " conferred was from an early date compared with the consecration of a priest. In both cases, the act

---

[21] For the mystical efficacy of royal consecration cf. especially the prayer *Prospice* in the coronation order of the ninth century (Eichmann, *Quellensammlung z. kirchl. Rechtsgesch.*, I, (1912), 58sq., no. 31) and the German formula of the tenth century (*ibid.*, 71sq.), where we read (p. 72): . . . " ut sicut manibus nostris indignis oleo materiali oblitus pinguescis exterius, ita eius invisibili unguine delibutus inpinguari merearis interius eiusque spirituali unctione perfectissime semper imbutus. . . ."

Smaragdus proclaims the spiritual adoption of the ruler by God : " Deus omipotens te, o clarissime rex, quando voluit et ubi voluit, de regali nobilique genere nobiliter procreavit . . .; caput tuum oleo sacri chrismatis linivit et dignanter in filium adoptavit. Constituit te regem populi terrae et proprii Filii sui in coelo fieri iussit heredem. His etenim sacris ditatus muneribus rite portas diademata regis." (*Via Regia Prol.*, ed. Migne, *P.L.*, 102, 933B.)

consecrated an office-holder graced with holy power, whose authority could not, or could not exclusively, depend upon human conferment.

Early mediaeval ideals of the City of God, moreover, in contrast to the outlook of the later Middle Ages, allowed considerable scope for the assimilation of the spiritual and secular authority; the priestly kingship of the Old Testament was a pattern not only for a Charles the Great, but for his theologians also. And if the Church exalted the ruler by this supernatural, mystical transmission of dominion, the king himself acknowledged that the affinity of his office to that of priests and bishops, was the holiest element in his own majesty; and this fact was no small gain for the clergy, who as yet scarcely ventured to protest against the theocratic and proprietary control exercised by the State over the Church.

This point of view reached its zenith in the tenth century. Royal consecration was more and more assimilated to priestly ordination. The words: " And here the lord pope makes the Emperor-elect into a clerk," now found a place in the formulae of the imperial coronation service. In the coronation-rite of the German kings which was composed in the same century, the archbishop of Mainz said to the king: " Receive the crown of the realm at the hands of the bishops . . . and through this thy crown know thyself partaker in our office." Moreover, the coronation liturgy led to close definition of the priestly character of the anointed king. The monarch, even if he was not exactly raised into the clerical estate, was nevertheless lifted out of the ranks of the laity ; he was to be mediator between clergy and people. The monarch, side by side with the bishops and allied with them by his office as God's vicar on earth, must take over only the external aspects of this dual spiritual and secular regiment, and must leave the care of souls to the bishops.[22]

[22] V. the imperial coronation order of the tenth century: " Finita oratione vadit electus ad chorum sancti Gregorii cum predicto cardinalium archipresbytero et archidiacano, quibus quasi magistris uti debet in toto officio unctionis, et induunt eum amictu et alba et cingulo, et sic deducunt eum ad dominum papam in secretarium, ibique facit eum clericum, et concedit ei tunicam, et dalmaticam . . . "(Eichmann, *op. cit.*, I, 82sq., no. 39). Cf. the German royal coronation formula of the tenth century, which was also

The assimilation of the anointed king with the clergy gave rise to peculiar customs; even in a much later period, for example, the Emperor on his coronation was admitted to a canonry in the chapter of St Peter's in the Vatican.

Such symbols remained important as an expression of the legal relationship between king and bishops. The Emperor Henry III invoked them even before the Investiture Controversy. When Bishop Wazo of Liège made a demand prefaced by the remark that the bishop was anointed with the holy oil, the Emperor insisted that he himself was similarly anointed, and used the argument to induce submission to his will. The Investiture Controversy led to even bolder deductions from the fact of royal consecration. The " Anonymous of York " built up a system of royal theocracy or " caesaro-papism " on this basis. His writings, which at the height of the Gregorian movement presumed to justify the prince's supremacy over the national church, derived their strength not only from Augustine, who at that time was made to serve the interests of both parties, but still more from contemporary views of the sacramental character of monarchical consecration. These views the " Anonymous " attempted to re-inforce by additional arguments, especially by an ingenious interpretation of the coronation ceremonies.

The inviolability which the virtue of being the " Lord's Anointed " bestowed upon its recipients benefited even those rulers who could claim this title only metaphorically, and had never been actually anointed.[23] But if the supporters of royal control in the national churches could appeal

---

used in France and England (*ibid.*, 75, no. 37): " Postea metropolitanus reverenter coronam capiti regis imponat, dicens: Accipe coronam regni, quae, licet ab indignis, episcoporum tamen manibus capiti tuo imponitur, eamque sanctitatis gloriam et honorem et opus fortitudinis expresse signare intelligas, et per hanc te participem ministerii nostri non ignores, ita ut, sicut nos in interioribus pastores rectoresque animarum intelligimur, tu quoque in exterioribus verus Dei cultor strenuusque contra omnes adversitates aecclesiae Christi defensor regnique tibi a Deo dati et per officium nostrae benedictionis vice apostolorum omniumque sanctorum tuo regimini commissi utilis exsecutor regnatorque proficuus semper appareas. . . .et quanto clerum sacris altaribus propinquiorem perspicis, tanto ei potiorem in locis congruis honorem impendere memineris, quatinus Mediator Dei et hominum te mediatorem cleri et plebis in hoc regni solio confirmet te. . . ."

[23] According to the text: " Nolite tangere christos meos."

during the Investiture Controversy specifically to the biblical qualities of the ruler, and placed the two *christi domini*, king and bishop, on an equal footing because of their consecration and anointing, it was mainly because the concrete and visible elements in the consecration of a king gave cogency to such arguments.[24]

(c) Accordingly, the external forms of royal consecration in all countries were modelled ever more closely upon the rites of episcopal consecration, and these externals endured until well beyond our period—in part, indeed, until the present day. Even an ecclesiastical reformer like Peter Damiani, in the middle of the eleventh century, counted royal consecration among the sacraments of the Church,[25] and traces of the view that the king became through his anointing more than a layman, survived into the canonical literature of the twelfth century.

2. The Political Significance of Royal Consecration.

Because of the sacerdotal character which consecration conferred upon the king, its mystical effects were reflected in the law of the Church, and in consequence of the close bonds between Church and State, church law could hardly have failed in any circumstances to influence constitutional law. In fact, however, it was precisely the constitutional importance of the anointing which, from the very beginning,

[24] Cf. Wido of Osnabrück: " Quamvis rex a numero laicorum merito in huiusmodi separetur, cum oleo consecrationis inunctus sacerdotalis ministerii particeps esse cognoscitur." (*MGH., Lib. de Lite*, I, 467, 8sq.). Similarly Guido of Ferrara (*ibid.*, I, 566, 34sq.) : " Cur videatur indignum, si per imperatores et reges fiant ordinationes ecclesiarum, cum maiorem unctionem et quodammodo digniorem ipsis eciam sacerdotibus habeant? Unde nec debent inter laicos computari, sed per unctionis meritum in sorte sunt Domini deputandi." The conclusion to be drawn, from the point of view of the relations between Church and State, is that a layman ought not to interfere in ecclesiastical affairs; but the king by his anointing receives a share in the priestly office; consequently he may confer investiture, since in this respect he no longer belongs to the ranks of the laity. Cf. also *Orth. Def. Imp.*, c. 6 (*MGH., Lib. de Lite*, II, 538): " reges et imperatores propter sacram unctionem christi nuncupantur et sic suorum ministerio vel officio sive prelatione sacramentis eclesiae sunt uniti, ut in nullo debeant separari."

[25] *V.* Peter Damiani: " Quintum est inunctio regis. Sublimis ista delibutio, quia sublimem efficit potestatem." (Sermo 69, Migne, *P.L.*, 144, 899 D, no. 374sq.). Cf. *Liber Gratissimus*, c. 10, *MGH., Lib. de Lite*, I, 31, 16sq.: " reges enim et sacerdotes ... dii ... et christi dici repperiuntur propter accepti ministerii sacramentum."

mattered most to the rulers themselves; to them, the constitutional results of consecration were at least as important as the sacramental conferment of transcendental virtue. Secular politics, as we have seen, were the effective reason for the introduction of anointing into the constitutional law of the Frankish State, and it seems as though Pipin, with consummate statesmanship, used consecration as an instrument of dynastic interests even after the year 751.

We have already noted the latent hostility between Germanic kin-right and the ecclesiastical principle of " suitability "—a hostility which at times culminated in open conflict. It is therefore a remarkable fact that when consecration was introduced into the Frankish empire, its purpose was to re-inforce and confirm the rights of kin and blood. When the Franks set Pipin on the throne in 751, there is no doubt that they wished to raise not only Pipin himself but also his whole house to royal status. The general belief in kin-right left no other alternative; moreover, the Arnulfingers already possessed a quasi-legitimate standing as a dynasty of Mayors of the Palace. The anointing of 751 was therefore adjusted to these considerations; in accordance with traditional dynastic principles—the authorities imply—not only Pipin but his family also were elevated to the throne.[26]

Hence, Pipin's wish to restrict eligibility for the throne to his own sons, by excluding collateral branches of the Arnulfinger dynasty, especially the offspring of his brother Carlmann, was not altogether fulfilled. On the one hand, the new royal kin-right of the Pipinids was not clearly distinct from the common right of the Arnulfinger family as a whole; on the other hand, the claims of Merovingian pretenders who might perhaps arise with renewed power, were not yet clearly enough invalidated to satisfy Frankish sentiment. Pope Zacharias had, after all, only defined the king as " he

---

[26] Cf. *MGH.*, *Script. Mer.*, II, 182: " Pippinus electione totius Francorum in sedem regni cum consecratione episcoporum et subiectione principum una cum regina Bertradane, ut antiquitus ordo deposcit, sublimatur in regno." As Brunner (*Rechtsgesch.*, II, 27) and others point out, the anointing and elevation of the queen implies the raising of the whole dynasty, and not only of Pipin himself.

who has the power." Be that as it may, Pope Stephen II, when in 754 he went to the Frankish kingdom to implore aid, and besought the king to fight the Lombards and to found the papal State, offered in return no equivalent worldly benefits for these heavy demands. All he promised was a repetition of the anointing of 751, but this time at his, the pope's own hands. This renewed anointing, which took place in 754, must have been of great value to Pipin; for it was granted not only to him personally, but also to his two sons. According to a text of doubtful credibility, the pope at the same time pronounced eternal anathema on all Franks who should at any time dare to choose a king from a stock other than that which sprang from the loins of Pipin. Stephen II thereby gave the sanction of the Church to a legitimist principle which was alien, if not directly hostile, to the ecclesiastical principle of " suitability."

Nevertheless, Stephen's action on this occasion was not afterwards used as a precedent in favour of the dynasty which it protected, to so great an extent as we should expect, and, as already remarked, doubts have been raised regarding the authenticity of the whole story. There need be no doubt that Stephen II showed favour towards the Frankish king, but it must remain questionable whether that favour could, in the opinion of the eighth century, go the length of a sanctification of the dynasty's legitimacy. At all events, by the end of the ninth century, the Church had begun to abandon the right of the declining Carolingians to the throne, in spite of Stephen's alleged anathema. On the other hand, there is no doubt that the popes of the eighth century regarded the race of Pipin and his sons as divinely summoned. The religious mission of the Frankish monarchy, including protectorship over the Roman Church, was emphasized by the anointing more clearly than ever before, and Pipin himself acknowledged by his deeds the binding force of his duties towards the Church of God, and especially towards the Church of the Princes of the Apostles, Peter and Paul.

One of Pipin's sons, anointed at the same time as his father in 754, was Charles the Great. Under him the designation " *Dei gratia* " first became a permanent part of the royal title. The almost simultaneous appearance of the anointing and of the formula : " by the grace of God," under the Frankish kings is no accident. The idea underlying all Christian theories, that government springs from God, received a concrete expression in the anointing, and the insertion of the pious formula in the ruler's title, like his consecration, emphasized his independence in his relations with the Frankish people. The later developments which were to make the words " *Dei gratia* " accompanying the royal name into the permanent device of absolute government, could, of course, not be anticipated in the eighth century. But the introduction into royal charters of the formula, which had been used by clerics from the early days of Christianity, not only proclaimed from the very beginning an increase in Christian humility, but also underlined the gulf between the authority established by " God's grace " or by " God's mercy," and " crowned by God," and the subject people answerable to the officers of God.

The concrete emanation of divine will which the ruler received through his anointing, must, as we saw, tempt princes whose throne was insecurely established, to seek in consecration a valid constitutional title. It was to the interest of the anointed ruler and also of the princes of the Church, who had the privilege of performing the ceremony, to enhance the legal value of the unction. Through this community of interests, a constitutional theory of anointing emerged as early as the middle of the ninth century, according to which the conferment of consecration settled a disputed claim to the throne, and eliminated all rival claims; it made a doubtful right watertight. Just as the weakness of rulers, or their lack of legal title had favoured the introduction of royal consecration, so, from the middle of the ninth century, the same factors encouraged the extension of clerical influence over the acts by which a ruler was set on the throne. In this respect, Charles the Bald was the man of destiny. He was crowned in purely secular fashion by his father in 838. But when at Orléans in 848 he became king of Aquitaine, and when at Metz in 869 he became king of Lotharingia, on both occasions he was depriving another

Carolingian of his rights.   On both occasions, therefore, not only did he have himself anointed, but he was also invested by the bishops with the symbols of dominion.   At a synod in 859, the same king, acting under the pressure of difficult political circumstances, enunciated the constitutional theory of consecration in these words: " He who is consecrated, anointed, and raised to the throne in accordance with the usages of the Church, can never be deprived of either his sacerdotal character or of his throne, except by the formal judgment of the bishops at whose hands he has been consecrated king, and to whose fatherly reproof and discipline even the king himself submits."[27]

The indelible character which the ruler acquired at his consecration is here very significantly extended into the constitutional sphere.   We must, however, note at once that mediaeval law never bowed to this theory.   Both before and after 859, anointed kings were deposed.   This fact can best be explained in a later section, where it will be shown how little the inviolability or irremovability of kings was upheld in the Middle Ages.   None the less, the notion that the anointed king is irremovable, once it had been advanced, could not be entirely displaced.   During the Investiture Controversy, for example, the adherents of Henry IV advocated the idea even more vigorously than Charles the Bald; for though Charles had at any rate admitted the possibility of deposition on the ground of a judgment by the officiating bishops, Henry IV's party upheld irremovability even in the face of the king's condemnation by the Church of Rome.

But the constitutional importance of ecclesiastical consecration was enhanced in yet another respect.   Charles the Bald in 859 had already recognized that the participation

---

[27] *MGH.*, *Capit.*, II, 451, no. 300, c.3: . . . " electione sua aliorumque episcoporum ac ceterorum fidelium regni nostri voluntate, consensu et acclamatione cum aliis archiepiscopis et episcopis Wenilo me . . secundum traditionem ecclesiasticam regem consecravit et in regni regimine chrismate sacro perunxit et diademate atque regni sceptro in regni solio sublimavit. A qua consecratione vel regni sublimitate subplantari vel proic a nullo debueram, saltem sine audientia et iudicio episcoporum, quorum ministerio in regem sum consecratus et qui throni Dei sunt dicti, in quibus Deus sedet et per quos sua decernit iudicia, quorum paternis correptionibus et castigatoris iudiciis me subdere fui paratus et in praesenti sum subditus."

of the Church in the king's inauguration into government was no longer confined to the act of anointing. Because of the community of interest between bishops and king, which has been mentioned above, the participation of the clergy tended to extend into the other ceremonies for the creation of a king, especially into the crowning and the enthronement. Consecration attracted into the ecclesiastical sphere acts of investiture which had hitherto been secular; it gave an ecclesiastical character to the whole process of investing the elected prince with the powers of government. This spiritualization of the most solemn constitutional ceremonies symbolized the ever-growing encroachment of ecclesiastical principles on the secular law of the State. We have seen above the way in which legitimist principles and royal consecration were inter-related, how princes whose title was dubious according to secular law, were driven to seek ecclesiastical recognition, and thus to increase the constitutional influence of the Church. Since in the late Carolingian period, scarcely any claims to the throne were uncontested, a rich field was offered for the growth of ecclesiastical influence in constitutional ceremonies. The middle and late ninth century, a period of disputed successions on the one hand, and of exalted theocratic self-consciousness in the Church on the other, witnessed the completion of the process which had begun in 751. The beginning and the end of the Carolingian dynasty were decisive moments in the history of ecclesiastical Divine Right in the West.

But once it had become customary for accession to the throne to be preceded by spiritual acts, the question necessarily arose, whether ecclesiastical consecration was not indispensable for the lawful acquisition of the powers of government. Because consecration was regarded as a guarantee against loss of dominion, as a means of strengthening a doubtful title, it was possible to infer that the exercise of governmental powers was absolutely dependent upon the previous conferment of consecration. If we were to read only papal or royal pronouncements in the early Middle Ages, it would indeed seem as if consecration was then regarded as a constitutive act. But we must not overrate the importance of such declarations. Strongly though they may emphasize the immediate divine origin of government, they still lack the precision of law, and are far from denying the twofold secular foundation of government, election and kin-right. Thus a king could perform governmental acts even before his consecration ; indeed, even as late as the end of the ninth and the beginning of the tenth centuries, consecration might be entirely omitted, without the monarch suffering thereby any diminution of authority. Clerical contemporaries, however, felt themselves aggrieved when Henry I of Germany refused consecration; and because he was not anointed he was described as " a sword without a hilt." Later the question lost practical importance, for we know of no case in the eleventh and twelfth centuries, in which a reigning king was not anointed. Consecration was now so clearly an element in the king's inauguration into government, that the monarch might even date his reign from his coronation instead of from his election, as though coronation alone established his right to rule. But even at this later period, it was still abnormal for a prince to succeed to the throne unless his consecration had been preceded by election, even if it were merely formal in character. In this respect, ancient Germanic constitutional law was strong enough to withstand the pressure of ecclesiastical consecration and investiture. Consecration does not bestow a right to the throne; it only strengthens by divine confirmation an existent right. Mediaeval coronation-ceremonies reflect these conditions. They begin with a symbolic act of election by the people, and only after that do the skilfully combined spiritual acts of consecration and investiture follow. At the same time, the ceremonial harmonized kin-right with the other elements, so that in the tenth century, the prince at his accession is addressed as follows: " Stand and keep the place which thou hast hitherto possessed in succession to thy father, and which is now conveyed to thee in virtue of hereditary right by the might of God, and at the hands of us, the bishops, by this our present deed. . . . May Jesus Christ confirm thee in this the throne of the realm."

Thus government seemed to result from a combination of

election, hereditary right, and consecration.[28] The elective element in this triad was usually paramount; only in the later Middle Ages did hereditary ideas begin to predominate in the coronation ceremonies of most kingdoms, while at the same time electoral rites gradually declined. There were even cases in which consecration received special emphasis, but in no case could it supply the place of both the other factors; at least, it never succeeded in making election superfluous. Consecration, it was believed, ought only to be conferred on such rulers as had already obtained the people's recognition; indeed, it was considered to be legally binding only if it were carried out, expressly or tacitly, with the consent of the people.

In the Empire, the highest secular authority in the West, conditions were very different from those in the monarchies where the national and dynastic foundations of government were preserved. In the Empire, election and kin-right gave way to consecration, and the latter ultimately became a genuinely constitutive act. This victory was not obtained without a struggle. Since the imperial dignity, after its revival in 800, was normally conferred only on a prince who was already a king, the view could gain ground that a certain position of authority—for example, that of the Frankish or the German king—was itself sufficient to entitle its possessor to the rights and the dignity of Emperor. On the other hand, the Empire, being Roman, could be regarded as a dignity conferred by an elective act of the Roman people,

---

[28] Ivo of Chartres, with his usual juristic acuteness, made the following definition: "Si enim rationem consulimus, iure in regem est consecratus, cui iure haereditario regnum competebat, et quem communis consensus episcoporum et procerum iampridem elegerat." Cf. Rudolf Glaber: " Totius regni primates elegerunt Ludovicum filium videlicet regis Caroli ungentes eum super se regem hereditario iure regnaturum." Among the Anglo-Saxons it is said: " frater eius uterinus electione optimatum subrogatus pontificali auctoritate eodem catholice est rex et rector ad regna quadripertiti regiminis consecratus." Frederick I declared when announcing his election to the pope: " principes et caeteri proceres cum totius populi favore . . . nos in regni fastigium elegerunt . . ., pari et eodem consensu cum benivola populi acclamatione . . . nos per sacratissimas . . . venerabilium episcoporum manus oleo sanctificationis regaliter unxerunt et in solio regni cum benedictione solempni collocaverunt. Nos vero in multiplicis regiae dignitatis ornamentis, quibus partim per laicorum principum obsequia, partim per reverendas pontificum benedictiones vestiti sumus, regium animum induimus " . . . in as much as we shall strive to uphold our coronation vows.

and this might mean either the citizens of Rome, or the people of the *Reich*.   The existence of such views meant that the constitutive importance of the crowning of the Emperor by the pope remained in dispute even as late as the fourteenth century.   Charles the Great himself had asserted his hostility to the conferment of the imperial dignity by an act of papal consecration, when he sought to introduce the custom that the Frankish king, whose position of power singled him out to be Emperor, should crown himself by taking the crown from the altar with his own hands as though from the hands of God.   Although Charles could not foresee the later extensions of the papal claim to crown the Emperor, he thus seems to have surmised that the highest secular dignity in Christendom would become dependent upon priestly pleasure, if it could be acquired only in Rome. He who holds the position of an Emperor, i.e., the effective overlordship in the West, alone possesses a legitimate claim to bear the Imperial title.[29]   It was for this reason, it seems, that Charles, when in 806 he partitioned his lands among his sons, gave none the title of Emperor; but when in 813 only one heir survived, on whom Charles's whole heritage now devolved, he passed on to him not only his own undivided powers, but also the imperial title, which implied a position of sole and undivided control.   The practice of self-crowning, which Charles desired to introduce, symbolized the independence of *Imperium* from *Sacerdotium*.   A period followed in which the practice of crowning by the pope and crowning by the king himself rivalled each other.   Then under Charles's successors, the papal claim won a decisive victory—a victory whose foundations Pope Leo III had laid by the surprise which he sprung on Charles the Great when he placed the crown on his head in the year 800.   The papal right to crown the Emperor, in spite of occasional vigorous opposition from the contrary theory, henceforth maintained its supremacy throughout the Middle Ages.   The right to confer a legal title to the Empire remained entirely in the pope's hands, and the legally decisive act was always the consecration of the Emperor in one of the principal churches of Rome.

[29] Cf. Pope Zacharias's judgment in 751; *supra* p. 29 n. 16.

In all this, the " Donation of Constantine " played its part.

The claim that consecration of the king was an effective legal act found weighty support in the precedents supplied by the imperial coronation. Nevertheless, the conviction that the clergy could confer a royal title never fully penetrated into those States which were ruled by kings. The Empire might be dependent upon the pope, but kingship derived from God and the people. The loss of rights which the Empire suffered in its relations with the papacy during the course of the ninth century, did not affect secular government in general, although according to mediaeval theory the Empire was the prototype of all lordship, and everything asserted about the *Imperium* in relation to the *Sacerdotium* otherwise applied equally to the *Regnum*.

The mediaeval Emperor, therefore, according to the prevailing view, received his imperial dignity only after a series of ecclesiastical proceedings. Thus in one respect the theory of succession to the Empire resembled the fully developed legitimism of modern times; in both, dominion is detached from the will of the people, and is a mandate from above, not from the community. In the modern theory of legitimism, this conception is based upon the inherited rights of the royal dynasty; in the mediaeval Empire, on the contrary, it was based upon the constitutive force of the priestly rite, whilst the claims of the city of Rome, e.g., of an Arnold of Brescia, made no headway. But the ecclesiastical principle could as little establish itself in full during the early Middle Ages as could the principle of dynastic legitimism. The popular basis of monarchy still remained powerful. Consecration had from the start to be combined with the elective right of the people, just as kin-right also had been combined with election. Because in Germany, the seat of the Empire, electoral principles were increasingly emphasized after the eleventh century, the most peculiar and most complicated throne-right in the West came into being there—a throne-right which resulted from the interaction of the rules applied in the German kingdom and those enforced in the Empire. . Consequently, the German king, dependent both upon his electors and upon the papal bestower of the crown, played little part in the development of legitimist Divine Right. This was left to the monarchs in the States of Western Europe who were transforming their realms into hereditary kingdoms.

Royal consecration, as we saw, was based upon theocratic conceptions of monarchy as an office, and it never abandoned its claim to be the visible symbol of office. But when consecration became a part of constitutional law, its relation to the clerical conception of office immediately shifted. The principal implication of that conception was that the ruler had duties to perform ; but consecration first and foremost implied the conferment of rights. Theocratic principles demanded that the character of every candidate for the throne should satisfy certain requirements ; but consecration gradually became nothing more than an inevitable accompaniment of every accession to the throne. Moreover, other profound differences between theocratic principles and the formal practice of consecration appeared. These were differences that had to be fought out between Church and State, and also between the various authorities within the Church itself. We turn now to consider these struggles in their own context, in order to sum up and round off our previous observations.

C. The Cleavage between the Theocratic Idea of Office and the Sacral Consecration of the Monarch

Since the later period of classical antiquity, a great revolution in the attitude of the Christian Church towards the State had gradually taken place. No longer did it tolerate good and evil rulers as a dispensation of God, to be endured like good or bad weather. On the contrary, it now actively participated in the inauguration of rule; it anointed and exalted the monarch as the Vicar of God. It consequently undertook some sort of responsibility for good government, and as a result it might in certain circumstances find itself obliged to censure a ruler whom it had anointed, but otherwise it declared the ruler's divinely established rights to be inviolable against illicit attacks.

All this was a step forward in the conquest of secular civilization by ecclesiastical principles. The Church now held sway over the most solemn moments known to mediaeval constitutional law—the accession of the monarch, the establishment of dominion. But if we look not so much at the fundamental ideas represented by the papacy at its greatest period, as at the actual course of events from the eighth to the eleventh centuries, then we realize that the introduction of royal consecration helped to exalt the power of the State more than it exalted the ecclesiastical hierarchy. It is true that the Church, in recognizing the divinely-willed nature of the State, and in sanctifying the wielder of governmental power by a religious rite, definitely reserved to itself the right of scrutiny; and if it could have held to its programme of according consecration only to princes who were tractable and worthy in its own estimation, it would have been on the surest way towards that suzerainty which it claimed over all secular authority. But it was out of the question for the Church to fulfil this programme. *Staatskirchentum*, with its subordination of Church to State, prevailed without a break until the eleventh century, and so long as it held good, consecration seemed to glorify the monarch rather than to tighten up the theocratic conception of monarchy as an office. It was no accident that both the practice of consecration and the sacramental theory of monarchy which was derived from it, established themselves just at that time; for both met the needs of the prevailing system of Church and State. We are not here concerned with the special motives which, as we have seen, made recognition by the Church particularly valuable to the monarch with a disputed title, for every type of kingship profited in some way from the introduction of consecration. On the one hand, it counterbalanced the loss of sacral dignity, which the kingship suffered as a result of the weakening of the pagan foundations of kin-right in the Christianized world. Through consecration the Christian God bestowed upon the person of " His Anointed " the mystical virtue which once had lain in the blood of the sons of Woden and of the *reges criniti*. When Charles the Great inserted the

formula " by God's grace " into the royal title, his act
signified, as we saw, both the submission of the State to
Christian conceptions of society, and the establishment of
monarchical power upon a transcendental and inviolable
legal basis. We need not repeat here that the secular
foundations of government were not thereby abandoned,
that the early Middle Ages knew of no right to the throne
based solely upon God's grace. On the other hand, the *Dei
gratia* formula was from the start an avowal of the relative
independence of monarchical power from the will of the
subjects. As a symbol of the insurmountable barrier between the divinely-ordained power of authority and the
subjects' duty of obedience, the Middle Ages could find no
expression more appropriate than the *Dei gratia* formula,
which proclaimed the indissoluble connection of authority
with the divine world-order. But above all else it was the
anointing that embodied this theocratic monarchical element
in constitutional law. Once consecration was introduced,
earthly authority was readily assimilated with the heavenly;
the disobedience of their subjects seemed to the Frankish
kings as sinful as the fall of Lucifer. The person of the
monarch, who reigned in God's place, acquired a partly
transcendental legal position, to which the defenders of
kingship against the Church effectively appealed in the
Investiture Controversy; unassailable, so they declared, is
the prince, " whose name was conceived at the beginning of
the world itself."[30]

Such a transfiguration of monarchy derived primarily
from the theocratic idea of office, which exalted the magisterial power into a unique position, whilst at the same time
humbling it before God. But it was the tangible rite of
consecration rather than the abstract ideas of preachers or of
treatises on the princely office that led to the sanctification
of the person of the king in the estimation of the people.
It was, indeed, this concrete ceremony that conferred or at
least strengthened the material rights of the ruler. But the
most important advantage that the State obtained from the

[30] Cf. *MGH.*, *Lib. de Lite*, I, 289: " Novum . . . est et . . . inauditum,
pontifices . . . nomen regum, inter ipsa mundi initia repertum, a Deo postea
stabilitum, repentina factione elidere."

royal consecration was the legitimation of its control over the national Church.

In an age when State and Church were united ·by the common ideal of the *Civitas Dei*, Charles the Great himself, as ruler over both, had been endued with the lustre of a high priest, openly addressed as *Rex et Sacerdos*, and even reverenced as the Vicar of St Peter, and vested with the " two swords." The idea of the " priest-king " originated in the theocracy of the later Roman Emperors, and was justified by the inevitable reference to Scripture. The stimulus to create this hybrid " *rex et sacerdos* " was provided by the passage in Genesis relating to Melchisedech, which in consequence of its mystical allusions to Christ possessed a high and acknowledged significance in the liturgy of the Mass. Early Christian art had the task of depicting this " hybrid " type; it sometimes gave the biblical king priestly garments, and sometimes garments like those of an Emperor. It diverted historical illustration into symbolism; beginning with a eucharistic-like act of an Old-Testament king, it eventually symbolized an Emperor with priestly functions. The result of artistic interpretation of this motif was that during the period of the " national Churches," the monarch was customarily arrayed in priestly vestments at his coronation.

Nevertheless, such theological efflorescences were not as yet of great importance; for royal control of the Church in the Germanic States did not grow out of theocratic ideas, still less out of the practice of royal consecration, but out of the constitutional situation during the Merovingian period, out of the system of " national Churches," and the rude Christianity of the Germanic peoples. When under Charles the Great the need was felt for a theological justification for the subordination of the Church to the monarchy, the position of the monarch in the Church as compared with that of the bishops was still so exalted that the remarkable simile of the period of the Church Fathers: " the bishop is to the king as Christ is to God the Father," could be revived in the eighth century. This conception, which gave the king the same hierarchical quality as the priest, but a higher ecclesiastical rank, served even later as the basis for the rights exercised by the monarch in the Church. He who accepted this conception, did not at first need to support the king's rights by subtle reference to consecration. Charles appeared as the " bishop of bishops," not in virtue of his consecration, but simply because of his character and position. But when the dominance of the laity in the Church began to be condemned as uncanonical, the State defended its right to govern the Church by reference to the sacramental character of consecration; and a time was to come when such a justification was very necessary, although very difficult.For in the meantime the Church had rejected the sacramental nature of consecration, and had turned against the whole system of "State Churches."

The hey-day of consecration as a sacrament coincided with the still unbroken dominance of the State over the Church, on the one hand, and with the close alliance between kingship and episcopate, on the other. The half-spiritual, half-secular character of " mediator," bestowed upon the " Anointed " by the bishops, corresponded to the constitutional situation of the tenth and eleventh centuries. But this priestly kingship could not last. The Church only needed to become conscious of itself and its power, only needed to replace the Carolingian ideals of a " State-Church " by the hierocratical ideals of Pseudo-Isidore, and the early mediaeval *Rex et Sacerdos* by the later mediaeval *Papa verus Imperator*, in order to discover in the sacrament of the coronation a bastard concept, at once uncanonical, barbarous, and 'fit only to be contemned.

After numerous anticipations in the ninth century, the pontificate of Gregory VII marked the great turning point. For him, there were no intermediate grades between laity and clergy; the monarch, like every layman, was below the priest and was subject to priestly authority, and in the Church of God no layman might rule.

Henceforth the Church rejected with increasing rigour the sacramental character of consecration. All suggestion of it became forbidden.[31] When in the twelfth and thirteenth

[31] " Sed garruli fortasse tumido fastu contendunt regem non esse de numero laicorum, cum unctus sit oleo sacerdotum. Hos manifesta ratio insensatos deridet . . . Aut enim rex est laicus aut clericus." (Hon. August., *Summa Gloria*, 9; *MGH., Lib. de Lite*, III, 69.)

centuries, the Church's sacramental doctrine was finally settled, royal consecration was for ever excluded from the seven sacraments. Pope John XXII could emphasize its worthlessness by pointing out that since it lacked any sacramental efficacy, it could be repeated any number of times.[32]

We can, however, understand that the archbishop of Canterbury, the prelate who crowned the English kings, remained of a different opinion from the pope on this point.[33] The exalted position of the spiritual princes who performed the crowning in the Western monarchies, depended after all in large measure upon their right to consecrate the king. If the effect of the royal " sacrament " was to put the king in possession of his royal privileges, the episcopate also gained much by its share in the coronation ceremonies. Consequently, it was not the Church in general, but only the centralized Church of Rome, that sought under papal leadership to nullify the spiritual significance of royal consecration. From Rome also came the outward reactions of Church reform upon the coronation ceremonies. As early as the beginning of the eleventh century at least one important step had already been taken towards differentiating the consecration of the Emperor from that of a bishop.[34] Still

[32] In a letter of the year 1318 to Edward II; cf. Legg, *English Coronation Records*, 72.

[33] In the thirteenth century, Bishop Grosseteste still wished to uphold the inner sacramental efficacy of the anointing; on the other hand, he expressly emphasised the fact that it bestowed no spiritual character. With regard to its legal efficacy, he was cautious in giving an opinion. *V.* his letter to Henry III of England: " Quod autem in fine littere vestre nobis mandastis, videlicet quod intimaremus, quid unccionis sacramentum videatur adicere regie dignitati, cum multi sint reges, qui nullatenus unccionis munere decorentur, non est nostre modicitatis complere. Hoc tamen non ignoramus, quod regalis inunccio signum est prerogative susceptionis septiformis doni sacratissimi pneumatis, quo septiformi '(munere) tenetur rex inunctus preminentius non unctis regibus omnes regias . . . acciones dirigere. . . . Hec tamen unccionis prerogativa nullo modo regiam dignitatem prefert aut etiam equiparat sacerdotali aut potestatem tribuit alicuius sacerdotalis officii." (Legg, *op. cit.*, 66.)

[34] Whereas the ruler had previously been anointed on the head, he was now anointed on the right arm and between the shoulders; and instead of chrism, ordinary oil was now used. The first pope to explain the reasons for these changes was Innocent III (c. un. §5 X 1,15): " Refert autem inter pontificis et principis unctionem, quia caput pontificis chrismate consecratur, brachium vero principis oleo delinitur, ut ostendatur, quanta sit differentia inter auctoritatem pontificis et principis potestatem."

more decisive changes followed after the Investiture Controversy. The papacy allowed to survive only the subsidiary and comparatively harmless clerical features of the Emperor's coronation, the use of Mass vestments and the like. The practice, mentioned above, of appointing the Emperor to an honorary canonry at St Peter's, actually remained characteristic of late mediaeval Imperial coronations, but during the twelfth century, the declaration: " Here the pope makes the king into a clerk," vanished from the coronation rite. In other ways also the boundary between the spiritual and the secular was more sharply drawn. In vain did the German Emperors, after the Investiture Controversy, demand a return to old customs—customs which no longer suited the times. The sacral character of the monarch had been admirably adapted to the early mediaeval alliance between crown and bishops; but in the centralized Church of a Gregory VII or an Innocent III, such semi-spiritual powers had to disappear in face of the strict differentiation between priestly and lay authority. The pope, after he became " Universal Ordinary," took the similes of the " two swords " and the " two lights " very much more seriously than the provincial bishops. He no longer tolerated the encroachment of " evil " customs at the coronation. Consecration was to give the king a place in the ecclesiastical hierarchy, but not as " head," only as an " arm " which obeys the priestly head, and wields the sword at the behest of the head. These ideas, and these alone, were what the ceremony of anointing symbolized after Innocent III's authoritative pronouncement in 1204.

We might here question whether the Church did not do itself an injury by revoking the sacramental significance of this ecclesiastical rite. Certainly the importance of royal consecration was reduced in the later Middle Ages; robbed of its ecclesiastical significance, its constitutional importance also suffered, and in Western Europe it lost ground as compared with hereditary right, and in Germany as compared with electoral right. Consecration remained constitutionally indispensable in the one case where the pope himself participated as the officiating prelate: namely, in the creation of an Emperor. But the Curia had no intention of strengthening the position of the bishops who officiated at the coronation in the various States of Europe. On the contrary, the pope himself in the latter Middle Ages definitely increased his influence over the proceedings by which the German kings were established in power; but his intervention affected the electoral proceedings, not the ceremony of consecration, and took the form of an examination both of the proceedings themselves and of the character of the candidate chosen. The theocratic idea of monarchy as an office here clearly parted company from consecration; the papal claim to approve the election shifted the centre of gravity to an earlier and more effective stage in the proceedings by which a ruler was set on the throne. It is no doubt true that consecration should in theory have expressed the Church's recognition of the suitability of the monarch, and therefore should have qualified him for rule; and the Old-Testament example of Samuel anointing the kings of Israel for their office never allowed the notion of the constitutive force of consecration to fade away entirely. But when consecration had once been subordinated in constitutional law to the election and acclamation of the monarch by the people, it was no longer a weapon worth considering by the protagonists of clerical claims. The German prelates, in whose hands the coronation lay, followed the pope's example, and transferred their influence to an earlier stage of the proceedings; they became less and less crowning prelates, and more and more electoral princes. Henceforth, the pope—and in Germany after the thirteenth century, the college of electoral princes also—exercised the right of establishing and deposing kings, and consecration played little part in the proceedings.

But the rôle of royal consecration in legal history, in spite of this deterioration, was not yet finished. Due and proper conferment of unction retained constitutional value for the monarch with a disputed title, both in the later Middle Ages and far beyond. For that purpose, however, each of the traditionally prescribed ceremonies, election in the customary place, the possession of the crown jewels,

and the like, was of no less importance than consecration.
All the same, we must bear in mind the curious persistence
of the early mediaeval notion of the sacramental character
of consecration.

It was Shakespeare who, with historical accuracy, attributed to Richard II the theory upheld by the defenders of
Divine Right:

> Not all the water in the rough rude sea
> Can wash the balm off from an anointed king.
>
> *(Richard II*, 3, 2, 54sq.)

This indelible character of the ruler anointed and crowned by
the Church still remained for the legitimists the surest
guarantee of his irremovability:

> No hand of blood and bone
> Can gripe the sacred handle of our sceptre,
> Unless he do profane, steal, or usurp.
>
> *(Ibid.*, 3, 3, 77sq.)

The transcendental legal title conferred by consecration
was so valuable to the rising hereditary monarchies of
Western Europe that they upheld the sacramental character
of the anointing in spite of the opposition of the Church.
Precisely because it was a symbol of the Church's subordination to the State, the sacrament of anointing had been dis-
credited by the Church. With the collapse of ecclesiastical
centralization and the advance of Gallicanism, the conception
of priestly kingship once more came to life; for once again a
symbol for royal control of the Church was needed.

The Church, the papal party had maintained, must not be
ruled by the laity; very well, then, the anointed king is a
" spiritual person," and as the " first prelate " of his realm,
as " episcopus extra ecclesiam," " évêque du dehors,"
" chef et première personne ecclésiastique,"[35] he once again
summons national councils of the Church in the fifteenth
century. The ideas of the " Anonymous of York ", almost

[35] These ideas, which came to the fore in France in the fifteenth century,
were never more fully expressed than in a joke made by Napoleon I after
his abdication: " Sa Majesté me plaisante sur ma croyance," writes General
Gourgaud (*Sainte-Hélène, journal inédit de* 1815 à 1818, II, 143): " ' vous
vous confessez! Eh bien, moi, je suis oint, vous pouvez vous confesser à
moi.' "

heretical in their own day, triumphed on the threshold of modern times.

Whilst in Germany, the principle of election, the conception of kingship as an office, and the influence of the Curia inevitably hindered the development of this mystical sacramentalism, in France, where the monarchy had become hereditary, the quasi-episcopal character of the Most Christian King was vividly reflected in the coronation ceremonies. All this, it is true, remained uncanonical, and drew its strength solely from a deeply rooted belief in the monarchy. But the most primitive superstitions once more flourished, and were woven round the person of the new *Rex et Sacerdos*, and the virtues which he derived from the holy oil with which he was anointed. The touch of his hand healed the scrofulous. Even in the age of Voltaire, a few years before the Jacobins enthroned the goddess of Reason, the last king of the *ancien régime* solemnly paraded through the serried ranks of scrofulous sufferers: " Le roi te touche, Dieu te guérisse."[36]

In England also, the king, in virtue of his Divine Right, developed an extensive medicinal practice. There the anointed king, as a worker of miracles, is exalted over the bishops and ranged with the saints because of his sacramental powers. His magical healing powers are a true sign of the pseudo-mysticism of absolute Divine Right—a mysticism which in spite of its religious affinities, was rejected by the Church. Its adherents sought to make the monarch a god or at least a demi-god. Thus the consecration of the ruler, which at the time of its introduction into the Christian West, had been tacitly or openly opposed to Germanic kin-right, finally ended as one of the most striking privileges of the ruling dynasty, and was included in the ritual of coronation as a symbol of Divine Right even more exalted than the king's hereditary rights. In this way, the interests of the kingship triumphed; the influence of the Church over the proceedings for setting up a king—an influence which had been implicit in the conception of monarchy as an office—

---

[33] On the whole subject, cf. Marc Bloch, *Les Rois Thaumaturges*, (Strasbourg, 1924).

was henceforth completely neutralized, and in spite of the Church, the monarchy upheld the royalist dogma of the holy unction.

Such, then, is the history of the sacramental element in Divine Right. In pagan times, there is no difference between the king's rights of blood and the support he derives from the gods; for the special virtues upon which a claim to rule is based lie in the blood which flows in his veins. Under the influence of Christianity, the divine sanction of kingship and the rights which the king inherits from his forebears are separated, and the introduction of clerical confirmation of royal rights modifies the value of Germanic ideas of legitimism. But since secular custom was successful in resisting the tendency to make lawful government partly or wholly dependent upon the conferment of unction, and since, on the other hand, the Church—as soon as its power and dogma were more fully developed—excluded royal consecration from its sacraments, a complete change took place. The hereditary monarchies of Western Europe were completely successful in incorporating ecclesiastical consecration into the ceremonial of accession to the throne; and henceforth the Divine Right acquired by anointing merely enhanced the Divine Right acquired by birth, strengthened it and gave it a religious character. In this way, the king's divine ordination and his hereditary rights were once again united in the eyes of the masses, just as they had been united in pagan times. The Church Universal consistently remained hostile to the sacramental interpretation of royal consecration. But if the Church refused to regard the act of consecration as anything more than a benediction of the king; the State knew how to make use of consecration to justify and strengthen the subordination of the Church to the State. The peoples of France and of England never forgot the lustre that surrounded the anointed and crowned head of their hereditary monarchs—indeed, their respect for kingship grew from century to century. On occasions of disputed successions, consecration—combined in some way with the rights of the legitimate blood—always proved its power as a constitutional factor in determining a ruler's right to govern. It is sufficient to recall the vigorous faith of Joan of Arc, who continued to address Charles VII, long after his accession, as simply the Dauphin, until he had been anointed with the chrism from the sacred ampulla at the right place. Charles's consecration at Rheims, because it expressed the judgment of God, proved to both the Maid of Orléans and the French people that his rule was lawful.

The glorification of the "king by divine grace" as a result of the influence of ecclesiastical ideas is by far the most important, but not the only way in which the rudimentary Germanic ideas of kingship were enhanced and enriched in the course of the early Middle Ages. Another source of enrichment was the traditions of monarchy handed down from antiquity; these also furthered the development of Christian kingship in the Middle Ages.

§4. THE EFFECTS OF THE PRE-CHRISTIAN CULT OF THE MONARCH

This chapter, in view of the present condition of research, can scarcely yet be adequately written, and the following remarks indicate the position at which specialized investigations have arrived, rather than complete those enquiries themselves. But at least the general result can be stated with certainty. What remained of the pagan kingship of the ancient world seems, until the twelfth century, to have been fused with and neutralized by Christian and Germanic ideas; but later, under the Hohenstaufen, a kind of humanistic disentangling of these ancient elements from the unity of Christian thought began, and a glorification of the monarch, which was definitely contrary to clerical views, made itself felt once again.

The old civilizations of the Near East and the eastern Mediterranean were the breeding ground of a sanctification, indeed, of a deification of the monarchy, which was radiated far and wide. When the Greeks and afterwards the Romans subjugated these lands, both gradually learned from the conquered peoples the practice of reverencing the monarch as the " son of God," the " Saviour," and so on.   Although in the West philosophical enlightenment and memories of the great days of the City-States strengthened resistance to such deification, one effect of the general orientalization that underlay so much of the later culture of the ancient world, was the penetration of the new " religion " into the lands of rationalistic thought; and the Emperor-cult of the West soon became hardly less unrestrained than that of the East.   Christianity combated the Emperor-cult with the legions of its martyrs, as soon as the two came into contact.   But, though the legends of the martyrs kept alive in the mind of the Church the memory of the cult as an abominable, heathenish belief, to which all were forced to submit, the Christian Church was not able to eliminate all traces of this Emperor-worship.   The Christianity that compromised with antiquity, the ἑλληνίζων χριστιανισμός which according to the ecclesiastical historian Socrates submerged true Christianity after the time of Constantine, gave scope to a strange survival of veneration for the monarch. The provincial priests who practiced the cult were not immediately suppressed by the Emperor after the reception of Christianity.   The temples of the *Divi* and the practice of sacrifice vanished, but the title of *Divus* itself remained for the deceased Emperor; the games in honour of Majesty, and other elements in the old cult, persisted.   The legal position of the Roman Emperor had been so thoroughly permeated with pagan sacerdotal ideas and forms, that the legal terminology of the Roman Empire could not but bequeath to the Christianized Empire of the fourth century and to mediaeval Byzantium a mass of wholly pagan or semi-pagan notions.   The Eastern Roman Emperors, made nominally Christian by baptism, were no longer divine, but they became all the more sacred.   Moreover, even the Fathers of the Church did not refrain from using the expression " adoration of the Emperor," and the law-books, the Corpus Iuris Civilis, of the " god-like " Justinian were still less restrained in their proclamation of the " divinity " of the monarch.   Henceforth, Byzantine imperialism, as is well-known, assiduously maintained the Emperor-worship of the East. The cult of Majesty, in words, forms, objects, and ceremonies, wrapped the court in priestly mysteries, behind which the Emperor's person, " a demi-god in purple and silk," shunned profane eyes; but whatever he touched enjoyed almost the veneration accorded to holy relics. Barbarians in the imperial service zealously learnt these practices, although some of the Goths and others could compete with the praetorian Emperors in nobility of blood. When the Huns, at a banquet of Byzantine and Hunnish envoys, boasted of their king as the former did of the *Basileus*, Wigilia reproved them by saying: " It is not right to liken a man to a god; Attila is only a man, but Theodosius is a god." This assertion enraged the Huns, and the Emperor's envoys were obliged to appease them with gifts, but not to change their own opinion.

The hallowed and ceremonious imperial life of Byzantium was sometimes rejected or ironically criticized in the West, but on the whole, its aloof haughtiness impressed the Western princes of the early Middle Ages, to whom Byzantium refused to concede either equality in rank or even the use of the purple vestments of majesty. The ancient and illustrious court-civilization of Byzantium, firmly established and rooted in tradition, had no equivalent in the Germanic States of the period; it necessarily became a model for them all, especially as, according to a belief which no one before the eighth century disputed, Byzantium retained its over-lordship, even if only nominal, over the whole of the old *Orbis Romanus*. If a consciousness of their independent rank and dignity gradually developed in the rulers of the West, and if finally in the year 800 the greatest of them took the title of Emperor, hitherto reserved for Byzantium, it was nevertheless inevitable that the pomp of Emperor-worship, even if simplified and adapted, should be trans-mitted from the East to the Latin world. The Curia of the bishops of Rome also imitated much of the ceremonial of the Imperial court in Byzantium. Thus the ancient oriental cult of the ruler conquered the world a second time, in a Christianized and modified form, by way of Byzantium. It was tolerated as being reconcilable with Christian culture, and so in fact it was; for this court ceremonial did not raise the person of the monarch out of the ranks of humanity and place him among the divinities; the Western Church never learnt to cringe before the monarch, and it was contrary to Germanic traditions that freemen should approach their *dominus* as slaves approach a δεσπότης.

Thus it meant little that the designation of the monarch as *sacer, sacratus, divus, sanctus* or *sanctissimus*—a designation derived partly from Byzantium and its law-books, and partly from the unbroken Roman traditions of the West— re-appeared first in the barbaric Latin of Merovingian charters, and then in the deliberate and formal theological parlance of the Carolingian court. Ancient Roman and Byzantine titles, such as these, were combined with ecclesiastical formulae, such as "*gratia Dei*," or "*a Deo coronatus*," to make up a new compound in which the diverse origins of the biblical and pagan elements are all the less apparent, because Byzantium had already anticipated this mixture of divine grace with Emperor-worship. A remarkable atmosphere of sublimity, legal, moral, and religious, developed around the person of Charles the Great; by their imperialistic ideas the theologians and humanists at his court prepared the way for a revival of the Empire in the West, and this revival in its turn strengthened the impulse towards an increased veneration of Majesty. Nevertheless, there was still a naïve intimacy in the paeans with which Carolingian poets, scholars, and Churchmen celebrated their prince, an intimate touch which sprang partly from the fealty of the freeman towards his lord, partly from the self-reliance and independent spirit of the Western prelates.

Besides, it was not easy for Germanic kings to exchange their homely garments for impressive Imperial pomp. In the tenth and eleventh, as in the eighth and ninth centuries, the most important princes of Western Europe opposed all idea of veneration for themselves. When the Byzantine ceremonial and the cult of the monarch penetrated into the West, particularly with the revival of the Western Empire, it almost inevitably resulted—as, for example, in the case of Otto III—in a weakling of the old foundations of the king's power. Until well into the twelfth century, the German Emperors, if we omit Otto III, made no attempt to reproduce the alien language of their ancient " predecessors. " Not until the accession of the Hohenstaufen was there any endeavour to imitate the imperial style and methods of ancient Rome. The best known, because the most lasting, result of Frederick I's tendency to imitate antiquity, was that under him the Empire became the " holy " Empire— a title which it kept until 1806—or rather the " sacred " Empire; for so the familiar phrase should really be translated, if we are to reproduce accurately the distinction between the *sancta ecclesia* and the *sacrum imperium*.

But, in the meantime, the word for " monarch-worship, " " *adoratio,* " had become unpalatable to mediaeval men, and they readily corrected the Greek texts on this point. The Church, especially from the time of Gregory VII, learnt to emphasize its view that the monarch is only a layman, and inferior to even the most insignificant priest or deacon in the all-important spiritual and religious aspects of life. The formulae of Byzantine " Caesaro-papism " were incompatible with the outlook of Western hierocracy, which attributed the origin of the State to evil lusts and the machinations of the Devil, to a $ἀνθρωπίνη\ χτίσις$. Nor did they suit the constitutional ideals of the West, which kept the secular sword distinct from the spiritual; moreover, they did not conform to the fundamental notion in the law of the mediaeval State: Fealty. The notion of Fealty, instead of placing the subjects under their lord unconditionally, united both by personal ties. The ruler might well obtain a supernatural sanctity in virtue of consecration by the Church, but this applied not so much to his person as to his office; it impressed upon him his theocratic duties; and the Church, which conferred unction upon him, insisted, at times very bluntly, that a distinction must be drawn between the holiness of the office and the unholiness of an unworthy official. Under the dominating influence of these ideas, the cult of the monarch in the West, still remained, as in the time of the Caesars, a stage behind that of the East.

Nevertheless, the old official style of the Roman Emperors, in which " *sacer* " meant as much as " imperial, " or at any rate, " imperial " meant as much as " *sacer*, " supplied to Barbarossa the weapons with which to protect his sovereign majesty against all attacks. Precisely at the time when the Curia, by its ambiguous allusion to the Empire as a *beneficium* held of the pope, raised a storm in the Diet of Besançon in 1157, and when the city of Rome was striving to revive the notion of the Empire as a republican magistracy, the new and flourishing school of Roman law at Bologna gave Barbarossa a chance of effectively protesting against such disparagement by simply resuming the titles of the Emperors of ancient Rome. For those titles, which had been in existence before the Germanic States had appeared and the papal theocracy had emerged, seemed to him and to the jurists of Bologna as imprescriptible as the Roman law itself. According to a plausible conjecture, Rainald of Dassel, who was placed at the head of the Hohenstaufen chancery in May, 1156, introduced the designation of the Empire as *sacrum* or *sanctissimum*, in order to emphasize the independence of the Empire from the papacy. The Emperor once again acquired *Numen*, which imparted oracular powers. The imperial palace, the court, the fisc, the law which the Emperor promulgated, the writs issued in his name, all were *sacer*. The *respublica* became *diva*, and the *Sacra Maiestas Imperii* meant not only that deceased Emperors were celebrated as *divi* or as *divinae memoriae*, but also that the living monarch bore once more the title of " *perennitas nostra.* " Whilst ecclesiastical consecration deified the monarchical office, the person of the monarch, the *Domnus Heros*, as a chronicler called it, was bathed by this revival of ancient practices in supernatural glory.

Barbarossa himself was evidently aware that this veneration ran counter to the teaching of the Church. He allowed contemporaries to attribute to him even in official texts a *sanctissima benignitas*; but he himself took care not to apply the designation " *sanctus* " to himself. Indeed, he is reported to have reproached his Byzantine equals with ignoring the difference between the sacredness of secular authority and the holiness of the religious power. Nevertheless, the adherents of the Emperor frequently overstepped the dividing-line between *sacrum* and *sanctum*; to them Barbarossa was *sanctissimus dominus*. The monarch's own feelings vacillated between the *hauteur* of conscious majesty and the lowliness of Christian humility. Thus, after the failure of his anti-papal policy, he acknowledged with his own mouth that " the dignity of the Roman Emperor has not deprived us of the characteristics of human nature, and our Imperial Majesty has not precluded error. " But at another time, he spoke of himself in official documents as being " guided by the Holy Ghost. " The Hohenstaufen poet Godfrey of Viterbo, addressing Henry VI, chanted: " Thou art a god from a race of gods," and Peter of Eboli called him " resounding Jupiter, the sun-god. " In all this there was nothing fundamentally new, but only an intensification of the revival of the ancient attitude already initiated under the Merovingians and Carolingians; and yet it betokened for the first time an open departure from Christian conceptions of society. It is understandable that this revival of the old imperial phraseology in the not always very skilful or appropriate expressions of chancery officials, chroniclers, and panegyrists seemed, to strict religious-minded contemporaries, to be sheer neo-paganism. Already John of Salisbury clearly perceived that the source of the new " *divi* " was the ancient cult of the monarch, and he saw the stain of this sin and heresy even in illustrious and pious princes. What would he have said at the further enhancement of the cult under Frederick II, whose birthplace was likened to Bethlehem, whose chancellor was compared with the Apostle, and before whose countenance the sun and moon were said to bow down!

This progressive adoption of the ancient deification of the monarch in the Middle Ages seems to have been more and more the deliberate accompaniment of absolutist tendencies. It is a phase of the incipient Renaissance. Whilst over almost all the West, the thirteenth century witnessed the growth of that idea of representative Estates which was to have so great a future, support for the monarchy and for the unification and concentration of the life of the State embodied in the monarchy was forthcoming from Roman law and its implications. Amidst the struggles of the period of Estates, the transformation of the Germanic monarchies into absolutisms based upon Divine Right was completed—transformation into a majesty which remained not only inaccessible on earth, but also *diva* after death.

In this development of the royal title, the other princes of the West did not long allow the Emperor to keep the start that he had won in the twelfth century. The kingdoms beyond the German frontiers took over from Roman law the attributes of the Roman *princeps*, in virtue of the dictum: " The king is emperor within his own kingdom." And a century after Frederick II's death, the Golden Bull of Charles IV bestowed upon the electoral princes the rights of majesty, " for they also are a part of our body."

Thus, precisely at a time when the Church was belittling and withholding its sacramental consecration, which had been characteristic of the early mediaeval period, Western monarchy hallowed itself with a new, non-clerical sanctity; the Emperors revived the traditional titles of their ancient " predecessors, " and the other monarchs inherited their share of the legacy. The person of the monarch became more and more removed from the common mass of the people. But the mediaeval view of society, so long as it endured, stood as a strong bulwark against these developments. The mediaeval world was not a congenial soil for any *Roi Soleil*; it gave no scope for fanatical Caesarism. Not only did the actual weakness of most monarchies in the Middle Ages hinder the growth of absolutist forms of government, but also the general legal convictions of the time resisted any tendency to release the monarch from the obligations and legal duties incumbent upon every man. We must now examine more closely this aspect of our subject.

II

The Limitation of the Monarch by Law

IRRESPONSIBILITY seems to be an essential right of the monarch in the finished doctrine of Divine Grace in the seventeenth century; it was, indeed, fundamental, and absolutism was deemed to be an integral part of Divine Right.

Our survey up to this point has shown that the doctrine of Divine Grace, so far as succession to the throne is concerned, was unknown in the early Middle Ages. An indefeasible hereditary right to the throne did not exist; an act of popular will was an essential element in the foundation of government, and consequently the concept of Divine Right could not in this period be based simply upon right of birth, as it was later, under the domination of the principle of legitimism. The derivation of government from God did not at this time exclude its simultaneous origin in a human act.

But it is also true, in a wider sense, that the early mediaeval monarch, however exalted his theocratic position, was always at the same time bound by earthly fetters. The prince was dependent upon others besides God, both in the establishment and in the exercise of his power. There was no legally absolute monarch, and even the rudiments of an absolutist doctrine had scarcely appeared.

We shall, therefore, describe next how far the ruler, according to the legal ideas of the early Middle Ages, was limited in the free exercise of his princely will, and was obliged to respect legal limitations outside his own control. Afterwards we shall show how individual subjects, the whole community, or else some authority set up by them, reacted to any overstepping of these limitations, and to what measures they resorted for resistance and protection against royal arbitrariness. We shall then be able to consider the first emergence of absolutist doctrines, which arose as a result of the evils caused by the exercise of the right of resistance, and which, challenging the validity of that right, asserted that to free the ruler from restraint was in practice the lesser evil. But the end of the early mediaeval period also witnessed the beginnings of those constitutional ideas which, keeping midway between revolution and counter-revolution, seek to realize the early mediaeval ideal of a monarch who, though limited by law, is none the less independent in his rights, and rules not only by Divine Grace, but also with the consent of the community.

§I. THE MONARCH AND THE LAW

Germanic and ecclesiastical opinion were firmly agreed on the principle, which met with no opposition until the age of Machiavelli, that the State exists for the realization of the Law; the power of the State is the means, the Law is the end-in-itself; the monarch is dependent upon the Law, which is superior to him, and upon which his own existence is based. The words of Tacitus typify the beginnings of the Germanic States: *Nec regibus infinita aut libera potestas.* Ecclesiastical literature offered rich material for the further development of this idea, although Germanic thought and Christianity, when they alluded to the Law which alone was sovereign,[37] and which was binding on all powers in the State, meant different things.

In the Germanic State, Law was customary law, " the law of one's fathers, " the pre-existing, objective, legal situation, which was a complex of innumerable subjective rights. All well-founded private rights were protected from arbitrary change, as parts of the same objective legal structure as that to which the monarch owed his own authority. The purpose of the State, according to Germani political ideas, was to fix and maintain, to preserve the existing order, the good old law. The Germanic community was, in

---

[37] Cf. Cicero, *De Legibus*, 3, 1, 2: " ut enim magistratibus leges, ita populo praesunt magistratus, vereque dici potest, magistratum legem esse loquentem, legem autem mutum magistratum." ˙

essence, an organization for the maintenance of law and order.[38]

But the purpose of the State, according to Christian ideas, was more progressive, active, and ambitious. The State must respect and enforce not the existing traditional law, but the law, never quite attained, yet ever to be striven for, of God or Nature, the law of Reason, and in a certain sense, the law of the Church also, especially its biblical and theological premises. The mediaeval Christian State is not merely a juristic institution, but expresses the ideal of active social betterment and civilization. Hence it binds the monarch to another law, and not merely to the existing order, but to one which has still to be created.[39]

The divine law, which the Church expected the State to enforce, and the customary law of the " folk " were, therefore, not necessarily identical in purpose. On the contrary, precisely because it is a new law, revolutionary, reforming, and civilizing, the divine law of the Church is often found opposed to folk-law. Consequently, the Christian kings of the Germanic States were often induced by the Church either to broaden the earlier Germanic conception of the State as an institution existing simply to preserve the law, or to replace it with the ecclesiastical notion of the State's duty to advance the welfare of its subjects. It was one of the most imperishable achievements of ecclesiastical jurisprudence to free the executive power of the State from its subjection to customary law. According to clerical thought, Christian magistracy was dispensed from its subordination to positive law, on condition that it put into practice the divine law preached and expounded by the Church. From

[38] Typical of this attitude is the following passage from one of Barbarossa's charters (1152): " Patrem patriae decet veneranda priscorum instituta regum vigilanter observare et sacris eorum disciplinis tenaci studio inherere, ut noverit regnum sibi a Deo collatum legibus ac moribus non minus adornare quam armis et bello defensare." (MGH., Const., I, 191, 12sq., no. 137.)

[39] As an example of the duty of the monarch to adapt secular law to ecclesiastical, cf. Isidore, Sentt. 3, 51, 4: " Principes saeculi nonnumquam intra ecclesiam potestatis adeptae culmina tenent, ut per eamdem potestatem disciplinam ecclesiasticam muniant. Caeterum intra ecclesiam potestates necessarie non essent, nisi ut, quod non praevalet sacerdos efficere per doctrinae sermonem, potestas hoc imperet per disciplinae terrorem." (Migne, PL., 83, 723B.)

the conversion of Rome to Christianity until well into the eighteenth century, the alliance between government and the divine law or the law of reason in opposition to traditional law was a powerful force in the development of jurisprudence; and the effect of this alliance was to free the monarch from the bonds of customary law. Thus the law of Nature, which was a criterion for the reform of positive law, and absolutism, which was freed from popular control, worked hand in hand. Already in the later Middle Ages, canonists and civilians expressed this fact in the dictum: " The monarch is below natural law, but above positive law."

Nevertheless, the contrast between the duty of the king to the positive law and his duty to the law of reason was by no means so marked in political life as the theoretical difference between the two laws might suggest. For one thing, customary law and natural law were often regarded as identical, since, on the one hand, traditional law was considered reasonable and equitable law, and, on the other hand, the law of reason was supposed to form a vital part of the legal traditions of the community from time immemorial. For another thing, the duty owed by the king to *iustitia* and *aequitas*, comprised both customary and natural law, and thus assimilated these two great systems, each of which, in different ways, prevailed within the Christian Germanic States. Moreover, the law of reason could be expressed only through the positive law, and the monarch, according to the ecclesiastical view, was in the main subject to positive law because it embodied divine law. Most important of all, however, was the fact that as a result of the close relations between Church and State in the early Middle Ages, both the spiritual and the secular powers shared the same means of enunciating and maintaining the law, and the objects of secular and ecclesiastical law were so very similar, that the Church had a large vested interest in the traditional law, and therefore respected it. And at the same time, a measure of agreement was established between Germanic legal ideas and the law of the divinely-ordained State. For the common basis of spiritual and secular administration meant that ecclesiastical as well as political power was bound to the actually existing law. The community of the faithful and the community of the people were represented side by side in the State assemblies, where both the spiritual and the secular authorities co-operated in carrying out the law.

"Law" was the living conviction of the community, which, though not valid without the king, was yet so far above the king that he could not disregard the conviction of the community without degenerating into lawless "tyranny." Even though the "common conviction" might inevitably violate the views of a minority, might even represent solely the opinions and interests of a small but powerful class, and even veil substantial injustice, the principle was nevertheless firmly established that no individual will, not even that of the king himself, ought to prevail against it. It is true that the Frankish kings, in their Capitularies, created much new law on their own initiative. But the new laws all remained technically folk-law—in the sense that the community "found" them, and the monarch "ordained" them.

For the mediaeval Germanic notion of law, in spite of its preference for the old law, did not in the ultimate analysis envisage any downright unalterable rules; it claimed only that no change in existing conditions should take place unilaterally, without the free assent of those whose rights were affected. The monarch ought never to interfere arbitrarily with well-established subjective rights, upon which, according to the opinion of the time, the whole fabric of the objective legal order was based. Moreover, the monarch, except in cases of urgent and general necessity, must maintain each individual among the people in the legal condition in which he found him. But if, on the other hand, the king intervened in the interests of the community, he must make no ordinance without the *consensus fidelium*. There is scarcely any important statute in which the mediaeval monarch omitted to claim that his decree had received advice and assent, i.e., that it was in harmony with the legal convictions of the community. Even in innumerable decrees of lesser importance, this was officially stated. It is through this *consensus* that every legal innovation and statute is brought into accord with the conservative principles of customary law. This notion of consent implies the fixed idea that the enacted law—whether old or new in substance —lives in and is accepted by the legal consciousness of the community, that it is therefore a part of the law of the people; for legally speaking, there is only one law, the law which the community acknowledges by custom or express declaration, and which the monarch ordains.

Certainly only loose rules existed in the early Middle Ages as to the method by which this *consensus fidelium* was to be obtained. Generally speaking, representation of the people by the *meliores et maiores* developed in the larger communities, but no particular individual possessed in all circumstances an effective personal right to membership of the consenting body. Consequently, the assent of any single subject, or of any definite college, or even of a specific majority, was never requisite for the proper promulgation of a law, a legal judgment, or a political decision. The ruler was not tied to the formal consent of any assembly. He could assure himself in other ways that his proceedings were consonant with the law of the people, even without consulting any counsellors at all, provided that no doubt arose as to the lawfulness of his act. Amid the fluid and fluctuating rules and usages of the early Middle Ages for securing assent and agreement, the single decisive principle stands out that the command of the prince created true law only if it was in harmony with the free conviction of the people. How the monarch satisfied himself of this, was in any particular case his own business; but nothing relieved him from the necessity of seeking assent in one way or another.[40]

[40] This fundamental point will be dealt with in the following chapters. For the moment it is only necessary to quote one example taken from the law of the Crusading States: if a knight or a burgher has obtained a judgment of the court, and the king or the queen seek to prevent the execution of that judgment, then they do wrong, " et si vait contre Dieu et contre son sairement; et il meysmes se fauce, et ne peut ce faire par droit. Car le roi jure tout premier, sur sains, de mantenir tous les dons des autres rois; après jure de maintenir les bons hus et les bones coustumes dou reaume; après jure de maintenir et de garder à dreit, contre tous homes, à son poer, auci le povre comme le riche et le grant coume le petit; après jure de maintenir ces homes liges à dreit contre toutes persounes, segont l'us de sa

In the Germanic monarchies, important legal rules of general application are protected by the king's command. The royal " ban " gave them the highest sanction, and in the event of their violation, attached to them the severest penalties. Nevertheless, no rule was valid simply because it was promulgated in the form of a royal decree, unless its inherent content was in harmony with the theory of law we have just sketched. Should a royal decree deviate from the true living law that passed current among the community, the king's power might force people to accept it as positive law; but it was regarded as " wrongful " law, and the people had the right to abrogate it. Cases are not rare in which a monarch subsequently declares even one of his own decrees to be invalid because ordained contrary to law, or in which such a decree is condemned by his successor.

Thus we are led to the question, how far the kings of the early Middle Ages acknowledged and personally bound themselves to the duty of respecting the law and of not ruling without the *consensus fidelium*.

§2. THE MONARCH'S PERSONAL DUTY TOWARDS THE LAW

The princes of the Middle Ages frequently acknowledged that they were bound by the law. Since in the Middle Ages no fundamental distinction was drawn between ethics, custom, and law, this limitation possessed, as we should say, not only a moral or natural validity, but also a validity in positive law. Cases are numerous in which a solemn princely vow constituted the essential condition on which a prince was raised to the throne or was permitted to continue a reign already begun.

Solemn promises by a prince before he began to rule were here and there customary as early as the period of the folk-

cort, per ces homes liges. Et c'il avient puis, en aucune maniere, que il vaise contre ses sairemens, il fait tout premier tort et reneé Dieu, puis que il fauce ce que il a juré. Et ne l'deivent soufrir ces homes ni le peuple; car la dame ne le sire n'en est seigneur se non dou dreit, et de ces homes faire son coumandement, et de reseivre ses rentes par tout et ces dreitures. Mais bien sachiés qu'il n'est mie seignor de faire tort; car se il le faiseit, donc n'i avereit il desous lui nul home qui droit deust faire ne dire, puis que le sire meyme se fauce por faire tort." (*Ass. Bourg.*, 1, 26: *Recueil des Historiens des Croisades, Lois*, II, 33sq.). The views here stated are typically mediaeval.

migrations, but apparently there were no durable rules with regard to such undertakings, until clerical influence gave rise to fixed traditions. This seems to have occurred first in the Visigothic kingdom. When, in the ninth century, the ceremonies for the inauguration of a king came under ecclesiastical influence in the Frankish kingdom, the solemn undertakings subscribed by the monarch before his coronation assumed a form which, with certain modifications, set the standard for Western monarchy. The German coronation-order of the tenth century provides us with an example, and there the royal oath took the form of interrogation:

" Let the lord archbishop question the prince in these words:
" ' Wilt thou uphold the Holy Faith transmitted to thee by Catholic men, and follow after righteous works? '
" He answers: ' I will. '
" ' Wilt thou be a protector and defender of Holy Church and its ministers? '
" He answers: ' I will. '
" ' Wilt thou rule and defend this the realm which is vouchsafed to thee by God, according to the righteousness of thy fathers? '
" He answers: ' In so far as I am able, with divine aid and the succour of all His faithful, I swear to act faithfully in all things (*fideliter acturum esse*). '
" Thereupon let the lord archbishop address the people: ' Will you submit yourselves to such a prince and governor, and uphold his rule with sure faith and obey his commands? ' Then the clergy and people standing by shall acclaim with one voice: ' Yea, yea, amen! ' "

The form and content of this royal vow varied; in particular, the duty of the monarch to maintain customary law, to uphold the legitimate rights of individuals, and to safeguard the possessions of the State, was frequently enjoined in more detail and definition. But the actual wording of the vows was not of first-rate importance, although at times care was taken to define the ruler's duties in concrete terms. The decisive fact was that the monarchy in the very act of its establishment solemnly placed itself under the law.

Although the obligations imposed upon the king rarely entered into details and specifications, the custom of exacting a coronation-oath was itself evidence of an attempt to preclude absolutism, and this purpose was emphasized by the place that was usually assigned to the oath in the coronation proceedings.

Only after the king had taken the oath was he " elected " by the acclamation of the assembled people. This was merely a formal election. When it followed the oath, it expressed the fact that the subjection of the monarch to the law was a pre-requisite for his acceptance by the people. This notion was effective for so long that modern constitutions still assert the rule that homage shall be done to the prince only after he has taken the oath to the Constitution. This rule is nothing else but a modern survival of the early mediaeval coronation oath, which impressed upon the consciousness of the people the dependence of the king upon the law. Yet the oath was not merely a symbol of royal duty; it was at the same time a legal act re-affirming this duty.

The coronation vows contained nothing to which the king was not otherwise bound. They simply re-affirmed the essential royal duty in which all the king's other duties were comprised: the duty to defend the law. Nevertheless, they performed an invaluable service, as concrete and solemn evidence that a particular king had submitted to the bonds of law, and were the basis of his personal responsibility for performing the duties incumbent upon a king. In taking the oath the king pledged his honour for the fulfilment of his vows.

Hence the vows usually preceded the acts of acclamation, anointing, crowning, and enthronement, and the rest of the proceedings in which the lawful right to govern was solemnly imparted, so that the king could not obtain full possession of the crown without having first taken the vows as a condition of his recognition. It was easy to consider the limitation imposed upon the king by the oath and the homage of the people as the elements of a contract, in which it was tacitly or expressly stipulated that one party was bound to the other so long as each upheld the contract; and this view was argued from a very early date. But even if Germanic views of the relationship between subjects and monarch were tinged by contractual ideas, which were strengthened by the growth of feudalism, the fact remains that the legal bond between the two is not accurately reflected by the notion of a governmental contract. The relationship between prince and people is not the same as that between partners in an agreement at private law. Rather both are bound together in the objective legal order; and both have duties towards God and the " Law " which cannot be traced back to a contractual idea.

Thus it cannot pass as axiomatic that a breach of duty by one party has in all circumstances the effect of freeing the other from his obligations. This, indeed, is in general the prevailing opinion of the Middle Ages. But we shall see that such a belief is possible without introducing any idea of contract, and that the crude contractual theory, which was asserted for the first time in the eleventh century, brought something alien into Germanic political theory. Early mediaeval ideas, on the contrary, admitted the doctrine that obedience is a duty even towards an undutiful ruler—not so much a duty arising from contract as a duty owed to God and the Law. And when, on the other hand, the right to resist an evil ruler came to be taught, it was not conceived of as primarily the right of a partner whose contract has been violated, and certainly not exclusively as a personal right of the subject against the ruler, but mainly as a duty of resistance owed by the citizen to the objective legal order which had been disturbed by the ruler and was now to be restored.[41] In either case, therefore, the contractual idea alone does not suffice; that idea provides an adequate basis neither for obedience nor for resistance.

These considerations bring us to the question whether

[41] For a typically satirical reference to royal disrespect for the law, cf. *MGH.*, *Script.* IX, 72: " Regibus hic mos est, semper aliquid novi legi addere anteriori. . . . Nam qui regunt leges, non reguntur legibus, quia lex, ut aiunt vulgo, cereum habet nasum et rex ferream manum et longam, ut eam flectere queat, quo sibi placeat . . . "—a statement attributed to the German Emperor in order to condemn him as a " tyrant."

there is any power that may compel the prince to perform his duty, punish his breach of duty, and free his subjects from their allegiance. What guarantee did the commonalty in the early Middle Ages possess that the monarch would respect the limitation of his power by law?

III

The Right of Resistance

IF the monarch is responsible to nobody, and no legal consequences ensue from a breach of his duty, the legal limitation of the monarch remains a mere theory, and in practice his arbitrariness remains unrestrained. The mediaeval coronation vows are among the most important precedents for constitutional monarchy. But even if an essential condition for the recognition of a new ruler was that he should be a *rex iustus*, that was no guarantee that a king who had once been recognized, could be held to the path of the law.

The powerful and energetic kings of the Middle Ages did, in fact, rule more or less absolutely. At no other period were active policy and progress in government so dependent upon the personality of the king as in the early Middle Ages, with their lack of a bureaucracy, and their poverty of initiative on the part of the Estates. The State was conceived of as passive and defensive in domestic as well as foreign affairs. Established for the maintenance of existing legal conditions, the State was not designed to pursue the active and aggressive policy which is characteristic of the modern State. The king who best represented mediaeval ideals was not the ruler bent upon extending his frontiers, but the righteous and pious prince who ruled not only unselfishly but also with proper regard for the limits of State-action. The monarch might, indeed, with the assent of the magnates, increase the substance and power of the State, and extend his authority in lawful ways. But the magnates, his counsellors, became his natural enemies the moment he pursued a policy of centralization; for the position of the aristocracy rested upon its share in the *regalia* and upon the weakness of the central power. So the king by every act of aggression at home necessarily disturbed well-established

81

" rights, " and had to proceed more or less despotically. The fortunes of the central power in the early Middle Ages fluctuated spasmodically according as power was grasped by the magnates, or a strong monarch regained full possession of it in the face of vigorous opposition. Even in the earliest period of the Middle Ages, therefore, an active policy was always bound up with a royal ruthlessness more or less frankly absolutist in character. The sole possibility of an increase in the authority and resources of the State depended upon the monarch's autocratic will.

If the monarch projected fresh undertakings abroad which required sacrifices, he had to put into motion the clumsy apparatus of negotiation and discussion with his magnates. A foreign policy not resulting from long-standing tradition was regarded as a private affair of the king or the royal dynasty, which concerned the nation as such either not at all or only with its own assent. All innovations, it was held, fell in general outside the State's scope of action; and the numerous powerful royal personalities of the period would have found this narrow interpretation of the State's purpose an intolerable restriction of their freedom of action, if they had not calmly disregarded such restraints. As a consequence, they were often condemned as " tyrants " by contemporaries and by posterity, and a monarch with absolutist tendencies often created difficulties for his successors *vis-à-vis* aggrieved and mistrustful magnates. Nevertheless, the ruthless acts of active rulers often laid down fresh foundations for the State for generations to come. Henry I of England, when he succeeded the tyrant William Rufus, had to begin his reign with a mighty vow to abandon absolutism in favour of the good old law; but Pipin and Charlemagne, as successors to the autocratic Charles Martel, could continue a strong policy of personal rule as absolute monarchs without incurring the same condemnation as the violent predecessor who had prepared the way for them.

In the early Middle Ages, however, this absolutism in practice never developed into absolutism in theory, and this, from our point of view, is the decisive point. In theory, agreement with the will of the people was always sought after; the doctrine of the limitation of the monarch by law remained perpetually valid. In the Middle Ages, neither the monarch's divine mandate nor the subjects' duty of obedience implied an unlimited right of the monarch to command, though the wickedness of the subjects gave him the right or duty to " chastise with scorpions. " Where the prince's power permitted him to act the despot in practice, it did so without the support of a theory, and was certain to incur theoretical condemnation. Whilst, therefore, we seldom hear the voice of an absolutist among the upholders of strong government, the doctrine of " *tyrannus* " and " *rex iustus* " was widely disseminated not merely in sermons and tracts, but even in documents drafted by officials of the royal chancery. Consequently, the theory of absolutism arose not from the mediaeval doctrine of Divine Right, but from a different world altogether—from the Romanist doctrine of government based upon contract.

Even the most powerful monarchs usually avoided giving their personal decisions the appearance of arbitrariness, and tried to legitimize them by obtaining the *consensus fidelium*, and by drafting their charters as far as possible in traditional forms. Knowledge of Roman law at first brought no change in these respects; an Emperor such as Barbarossa solemnly acknowledged the prevailing doctrine of the limitation of royal power. But when a monarch took it upon himself openly to abrogate the limits of customary law, and failed to find sanction in the legal sentiment of contemporaries and succeeding generations, formal condemnation of his actions was the result. It is possible for us to perceive in some mediaeval rulers whose actions were out of harmony with the convictions of contemporaries, the embodiment of a wholesome use of force; but contemporaries saw only their lack of right.

But to oppose force to the king's use of force was, according to the common legal creed of the Middle Ages, not only permissible but even in certain circumstances obligatory. " The excesses of the king require special measures, " it is said.[42] The *Sachenspiegel* expresses the right or duty to

[42] Matthew Paris, *Chron. Maior.* (*RBS.*, 57, 5, 689): " excessus regis tractatus exigit speciales."

reject the unlawful acts of those in authority when it asserts: " a man must resist his king and his judge, if he does wrong, and must hinder him in every way, even if he be his relative or feudal lord. And he does not thereby break his fealty." Some years before Eike von Repgow wrote these words, an English king had himself acknowledged the right of the community, in the event of his wrong-doing, to compel him by all possible means, including the withdrawal of the powers of government, to make amends.

But such views of the right of resistance were not unopposed. When, for example, the *Sachsenspiegel* was glossed in the fourteenth century under the influence of Roman law, the glossator found that Eike's theory of the right of resistance needed emendation. He observed that by " the king " whom the individual might resist if he did wrong, were to be understood only " provincial kings " like the kings of Bohemia or Denmark, not the sovereign *rex Romanorum*; him no one might resist, unless he had forfeited his realm.

These three examples illustrate for us three different varieties of the doctrine of resistance. Eike von Repgow asserts an individual right to resist the wrong-doing of those in authority. King John of England, on the other hand, concedes not to the individual subject but to the organized community the right to compel him by force to maintain the law, and to suspend him for a time from government, but not to depose him. Finally, the *Sachsenspiegel* gloss admits the right of resistance only in the case of princes whose position is less than sovereign, and not in the case of the Emperor himself; but, on the other hand, it considers the question of the Emperor's forfeiting his realm by due process of law, and so envisages the possibility of a judicial deposition.

If we examine these doctrines and the differences between them, it will soon become clear that here again, it was, on the one hand, the antithesis, and on the other, the synthesis, of Germanic and ecclesiastical ideas that stimulated historical development.

§1. THE GERMANIC RIGHT OF RESISTANCE

The right of resistance was an integral part of mediaeval Germanic constitutional ideas. We find it in its pure Germanic form, before it became alloyed with ecclesiastical theories, in the States of the folk-migrations, and in Scandinavia. The Nordic royal saga transmits to us this form of the right in a vivid episode from the history of Olaf Scotkonning (944?–1042).

When the king, contrary to the wishes of his people, was unwilling to make peace with the Norwegians, the venerable doomsman of Tiundaland addressed him thus: " This king allows none to speak with him and wishes to hear nothing but what it pleases him to hear. . . . He wants to rule over the Norwegians, which no Swedish king before him wanted, and as a result many men must live in unrest. Therefore, we countrymen will that thou, King Olaf, makest peace with the Norwegian king, and givest him thy daughter to wife . . . and shouldst thou not fulfil our demand, we shall fall upon thee and kill thee, and no longer suffer unrest and unlawfulness. For so have our forefathers done; they threw five kings into a well near Mulathing, kings who were as filled with arrogance against us as thou." The clash of the people's weapons, the chronicler continues, gave these words ominous applause, and the king recognized the will of the people, in accordance, as he said, with the custom of all the Swedish kings.

If we ignore in this story what seems to be peculiarly Nordic, the twofold appeal to customary law in the words of the doomsman still remains characteristically Germanic. First, there was the appeal to the royal tradition, which the present king is on the point of breaking, of deciding questions which affected the peace of the individual member of the folk, not in the heat of personal prejudice, but after hearing the opinions of the people. Secondly, there was the appeal to the equally venerable tradition of the people, of abandoning and slaying the king when he acted lawlessly.

The Germanic peoples very frequently claimed the right

to rid themselves of a king who for one reason or another was unsuitable. The history of the Visigothic, Lombard, and Anglo-Saxon lands, and also of the Frankish monarchy, is full of revolts and forcible depositions, but this violence was not entirely devoid of justification in legal theory. The " lawlessness " of a monarch above all, but also bodily or mental incapacity, cowardice or political ineptitude, defective kin-right or the lack of other legitimation, and even the anger of the gods as manifested in bad harvests or military failures, all these demeritscould suffice, in the common conviction, to justify or even to require the abandonment of the king.

A formal condemnation of the monarch by legal proceedings was unknown. The people simply abandoned their king; they absolved themselves from obedience, and chose a new ruler. This new election was the decisive step, and usually the only formal legal one; it marked the end of the dethroned king's reign. But, because a deserted king seldom remained without a following—witness the last of the Merovingians—a change in the occupancy of the throne was often accomplished in such a way that the newly-elected king took the field as anti-king against the old one. Thus the party which declared against the existing king's right to the throne, at the same time chose its military leader in the person of the anti-king; and in this case the oath to combat the old king was a part of the oath of allegiance taken to the new king.[43] Resistance to a lawless king need not, of course, necessarily aim at his dethronement. But the logic of events usually led to that, even when deposition was not at first contemplated by the rebels. If they wished to save their own skins, there was as a rule no choice for the party of resistance except to overstep the borderline, in itself very tenuous, between reform and deposition. Thus resistance developed at times into a struggle which from the

---

[43] Cf. for example, Walter of Coventry apropos of 1215: " Hii (the English barons) itaque etsi multi essent, tamen in se ipsis parum confisi confugerunt ad regem Francorum Philippum, elegeruntque Lodowicum primogenitum eius in dominum, petentes et obsecrantes, ut in manu robusta veniens eos de manu tyranni huius (King John) eriperet; sic enim iam habebatur " (*RBS*. 58, 2, 225).

start necessitated the downfall of either the king or the insurgents. The monarch whom they wished to be rid of might lose his life, especially if he took to arms or otherwise threatened the new order of things. But it never occurred to anyone at the time to pass an actual sentence of death upon the king, just as there was still no formal legal process of deposition.

In these informal proceedings, it is very difficult to distinguish the use of force from the exercise of customary right, or treasonable insurrection from the flaring-up of legal feeling. And yet, questionable as were the motives in most cases where the right of resistance was exercised, the general conviction that the community's duty of obedience was not unconditional was deeply-rooted, and no one doubted that every individual member of the " folk " had the right to resist and to take revenge if he were prejudiced in his rights by the prince. Even the Romanized parts of Europe had possessed similar notions in the traditions of the Roman Empire; but it is hardly possible to find evidence of the influence of this late Roman idea of resistance upon the Germanic States.[44] Mediaeval ideas of the right of resistance were rooted rather in the basic legal idea of the Germanic peoples: Fealty.

The subject, according to the theories of the early Middle Ages, owed his ruler not so much obedience as fealty. But fealty, as distinct from obedience, is reciprocal in character, and contains the implicit condition that the one party owes it to the other only so long as the other keeps faith. This relationship, as we have seen, must not be designated simply as a contract. The fundamental idea is rather that ruler and ruled alike are bound to the law; the fealty of both parties is in reality fealty to the law; the law is the point where the duties of both of them intersect. If, therefore, the king breaks the law, he automatically forfeits any claim to the obedience of his subjects. Manegold of Lautenbach remarks, in complete harmony with the spirit of Germanic law, that no oath of fealty was of any account unless sworn

---

[44] Cf. John of Salisbury, *Policraticus*, 3, 10: " Suos quoque imperatores, quos de more Romanus populus fideliter iugulabat, deificavit fidelius."

on such conditions as these.[45]   Only the " loyal " king has
loyal subjects.

The English barons in the fourteenth century gave this
idea a modern formulation when they stated that their oath
of fealty was due to the Crown rather than to the actual
wearer of it—that is, to the unchangeable symbol of lawful
magistracy rather than to the individual caprice of a particular monarch.   Fealty so defined might, therefore, in
certain circumstance be fulfilled on behalf of the Crown
against the king.   The mediaeval sense of right rejoiced in
the anecdote of the irascible Emperor who threatened an
official with high-handed justice: " I no longer regard you
as a senator, " he said.   " And I no longer regard you as
Emperor, " calmly replied the man so threatened.[46]   On the
other hand, it might happen that a monarch ruled badly
because he was deceived and cheated by his counsellors and
favourites.   Then a loyal opposition emerged, " faithful to
the king and the State, aiming not at deposing or dis-
honouring his majesty, " but at freeing him and the realm
from the tyranny of these counsellors.   In such cases, the
people boldly fought " for the prince against the prince."

Many an insurgent knew how to give his struggle for right
a high moral justification.   When Richard Marshall, earl of
Pembroke, was blamed by King Henry III in 1233 for having
attacked the royal demesne, the earl declared that he was
not the aggressor, for the king had denied him his right and
had first attacked his lands.   Therefore he was absolved
from his oath of fealty, and considered himself free to use

[45] *Lib. ad Gebeh.* c. 47, 48 (*MGH., Lib. de Lite*, 1, 392sqq.).   And cf.
Bruno, *Bell. Sax.*, 25: " Fortasse quia christiani estis, sacramenta regi
facta violare timetis.   Optime, sed regi.   Dum michi rex erat, et ea quae
sunt regis faciebat, fidelitatem quam ei iuravi, integram et impollutam
servavi; postquam vero rex esse desivit, cui fidem servare deberem, non
fuit."
[46] Matthew Paris, *Chron. Maior*, a. 1240 (*RBS.*, 57, 4, 59).   Cf. *ibid.*,
57, 5, 339 (a. 1252): King Henry III threatened : " ' infringam hanc et alias
cartas, quas praedecessores mei et ego temere concessimus.'   Cui magister
Hospitalis . . . respondit alacriter vultu elevato: ' Quid est quod dicis,
domine rex? Absit, ut in ore tuo recitetur hoc verbum illepidum et absur-
dum.   Quamdiu iustitiam observas, rex esse poteris; et quam cito hanc
infregeris, rex esse desines.'   Ad quod rex nimis incircumspecte respondit:
' O quid sibi vult istud, vos Anglici? Vultisne me, sicut quondam patrem
meum, a regno praecipitare, atque necare praecipitatum? ' "

force against the wrong-doing of the king's counsellors. " It would not," Matthew Paris makes him say, " be for the king's honour if I submitted to his will against reason, whereby I should rather do wrong to him and to the justice which he is bound to observe towards his people. I should set all men a bad example, in deserting law and justice out of consideration for his evil will. For that would show that we love our worldly goods more than justice." The difference between freemen and slaves according to secular law was precisely that the latter had to obey unconditionally the will of their master, whilst freemen tested the actions of their lord by the standards of the law, and shaped their course accordingly.

This conditional nature of fealty stood out clearly, once ecclesiastical law had developed the conception of obedience. Bishop Wazo of Liège (1042–1048) bluntly expressed the difference a generation before the Investiture Contest, when he said to the king: " To the pope we owe obedience; to you we owe fealty." True, the question how far an unlawful decision of the superior authority was to be obeyed was also raised within the ecclesiastical hierarchy. But, on the whole, the contrast between the ecclesiastical and the secular authorities was considered to lie in the fact that the former, being in the last resort infallible, was worthy of unconditional obedience, whilst the latter, being fallible, was not to be accepted without conditions.

The history of mediaeval rebellions—for example, the almost incessant revolts against the king by the local princes of Germany in the tenth and eleventh centuries—cannot be properly understood unless we recognize that, behind the chaos of selfish antagonism and anarchy, there was a confused and obscure legal belief that anyone who felt himself prejudiced in his rights by the king, was authorized to take the law into his own hands, and win back the rights which had been denied him. A strange, anomalous, and undefined right, with which no other constitutional right is comparable! It was the ultimate law of necessity, which came into operation only when the source of all rights in the community—the king's justice—failed; a subjective right which could emerge only if the objective legal order was convulsed and overturned. Nevertheless, for that very reason, the right of resistance was deemed by mediaeval opinion a true and necessary " right."

The renunciation of allegiance by a single magnate or by a whole party was judged more mildly and found support more easily than seems conceivable in the modern community with its stricter notion of the obedience due from subjects. For the right of self-help was a familiar conception among the Germanic peoples. The blood-feud, and even private feud in general, did not stop or start at the royal throne. Both the old and the new form of feud depended upon the fact that the coercive powers of the State were considered insufficient or unreliable, and were repudiated or evaded, with the result that redress by self-help was able, as the only substitute, to claim some legal sanction.

A hybrid of right and force, self-help had its own rules of procedure—for example, those of the vendetta—but it did not recognize the authority of any supreme judge. From the beginning of the Middle Ages, the central government struggled to get rid of or to limit the right of private action. But the Middle Ages passed without armed self-help disappearing—at any rate in Germany. Not until the arrival of the centralized, bureaucratic State was the lawful avenging feud uprooted. Feudalism could not dispense with self-help when the legal order was violated; it was considered a necessary safety-valve. When confidence between lord and vassal, king and knight, was irrevocably broken, the right of self-help placed both parties in the last resort upon an equal footing, and left the issue to be decided by force of arms. To seek redress for a denial of justice by the judge was from antiquity a fundamental right among the Germanic peoples. But when the supreme judge upon earth, the king, denied right, there was only one lawful way of obtaining redress—namely, judgment of battle. The king was no exception to the general rule. Eike of Repgow, as we have seen, equated king and judge in so far as the default of either imposed upon the subjects the necessity of self-defence.

It is of course true that in the Middle Ages, as now, success alone in the end determined whether a revolt was wicked or glorious; and the rebel was described as a hero or as a miscreant according to his success and the party bias of the chroniclers.   It is, indeed, the essence of the judgment of God, that he who makes good, thereby proves his right. But whether or not the individual was always able to justify his resistance to the satisfaction of subsequent generations, contemporaries were almost always willing to grant the possibility that a rebel was acting in good faith, under the pressure of necessity.   How many famous warriors of the Middle Ages fought at one time for their king, and at another time with equal devotion fought against him to enforce some " right "!

Before a new conception of the State was introduced by the monarchies of modern times, and obedience was established as an overriding duty, the mediaeval monarch who embarked upon an active aggressive policy had to reckon with the possibility of overstepping the narrow limits of his personal authority and destroying a " custom " that he had promised to observe.   Every such encroachment on well-established subjective rights might evoke from among the aggrieved parties a Michael Kohlhaas, who " revenged " the breach of his rights at the cost of the peace of the realm. It was as an " army of God " that the English barons in 1215 went into the field against their king, four and a half centuries before Oliver Cromwell.[47]   As early as the ninth century, there were instances of rulers who expressly authorized resistance to their misdeeds.   At times, magnates did homage to the king with an explicit reservation of the right to disobey him, if in future he did not act as was right. To make this reservation in writing was, indeed, unusual; it was damaging to respect and confidence.   But tacitly it was included in every act of homage.   For when wrong-

---

[47] Cf. for example, Ralph Coggeshall (*RBS.*, 66), 171: " exercitus Domini et sanctae ecclesiae "; Walter of Coventry (*RBS.*, 58), 2, 220: " Constitutis autem ducibus exercitus quos vocabant marescallos exercitus Dei "; Matthew Paris, *op. cit.*, 2, 586: " constituerunt Robertum . . . principem militiae suae appellantes eum marescallum exercitus Dei et sanctae ecclesiae."

doing by the king was manifest, it was not the rebel who was regarded as the miscreant, but the king who by his actions had destroyed his right to rule.

> Sciat quod obsequium sibi non debetur,
> Qui negat servicium, quo Deo tenetur.[48]

Nevertheless, the old Germanic law, before it came under the influence of ecclesiastical ideas, never postulated a formal condemnation of the king as a necessary preliminary to his punishment or deposition. There was no judicial procedure for convicting him of his misdeeds. This might be to his advantage or to his disadvantage. On the one hand, only a notorious misdeed, an open breach of the law by the king, could authorize the rebels to speak in the name of the law. On the other hand, public opinion was not slow to credit an unproven accusation of royal wrong-doing. The wild rumours which the Saxons accepted as solemn lawful grounds for their revolt against Henry IV were worse than the chicanery which a defendant would have had to face in a regular court of law. In this way, every single member of the " folk " was allowed to make his own conscience the judge over the king.

Since the king who was abandoned was not deposed by any formal judgment, what he lost was not so much his royal dignity as his right to exercise the powers of government; he could, therefore, be restored to government by a simple renewal of recognition, as informal in character as his deprivation. In such cases, a formal procedure of restoration was as little necessary as previously there had been need for a formal act of deposition.

In Germany, after the Frankish period, attempts at dethronement were relatively seldom successful, compared with what occurred in the other States of the West. Among the many risings during the Ottonian and Salian periods which resulted in a repudiation of the monarch, but not in his deposition, the most important was the revolt against

---

[48] *Song of Lewes*, v. 707 sq.; cf. *ibid.*, v. 731 sq.:
  Si princeps erraverit, debet revocari,
  Ab hiis, quos gravaverit iniuste, negari,
  Nisi velit corrigi.

Henry IV, which ended in the establishment of a regular even if unsuccessful anti-kingship.

Saxony was the classical land of resistance in the 60's and 70's of the eleventh century, just as England was in the thirteenth century. Historians such as Lampert of Hersfeld, and Bruno, give the clearest picture of the right of armed resistance to the king, as it was conceived in Germany before the intervention of the pope and the impact of clerical influence.

The first movement against Henry IV which Lampert narrates, occurred in Henry's seventh year, immediately after Henry III's death in 1057. The Saxon princes believed that they had suffered wrong under Henry III. The moment seemed to them auspicious for obtaining redress. They proposed to wrest the government from Henry IV. As the ground for this proposed act of violence, they alleged that Henry IV would probably (!) follow in his father's footsteps. A candidate for the anti-kingship was brought forward; fealty was sworn to him, and military support was promised against Henry IV, who was to be overwhelmed at the first opportunity. The death of the anti-king designate, " the standard-bearer of the revolt," terminated this first Saxon rising.

But in the year 1066, when Henry IV had attained his majority and was personally responsible for the government, a general conspiracy of the princes took place, and at the Diet of Tribur he was given the choice between renouncing the government and banishing from his court his counsellor, archbishop Adalbert of Bremen. This demand of the princes, which ended successfully in the " deposition " of Adalbert, was in Lampert's eyes not merely a palace revolution, but a wide movement with a sound legal basis, since the princes had a claim to a place in the royal counsels, and the supremacy of a single prince in counsel was " a tyrannous usurpation of monarchical powers. " The king, therefore, was, in their view, not free in the choice of his counsellors, in so far as undue favour to one counsellor could in the eyes of others make the favourite an unlawful power at the side or in place of the king. To prevent this was permitted, and indeed, incumbent upon the community.

When we come to the third Saxon rebellion, that of 1073, Lampert of Hersfeld is once again able to bring forward solid legal grounds for the revolt. He refers to the threat by the king to the hereditary liberties of the Saxons, whom he desired to treat as bondsmen; and he adds to this *publica gentis causa* an allusion to the breaches of the law which the king had committed against individual magnates. The rebels were thus fighting for the freedom of their homeland and for their " laws. " They perceived a divine sign—an infallible proof of their right to resist—which now summoned them to " shake off the yoke of lawless rule. " Among the demands of the conspirators was the requirement that the king should dismiss his corrupt counsellors of low birth, and leave the business of government to the princes, to whom it belonged by right. The Saxons are also said to have demanded the removal of scandals in the king's private life, on the ground that they were contrary to canon law and disgraceful to the royal dignity. If the king did not recognize the justice of these general grievances and of the Saxon grievances in particular, they would meet force with force. They had sworn fealty to him, but only on condition that he used his royal position to build up and not to destroy the House of God; that he ruled justly, lawfully, and in accordance with custom; and that he granted every man his status, dignity, and right, safe and inviolable. Should he transgress these conditions, they were no longer bound to him by oath; on the contrary, they would be justified in levying war against him.

Here already Lampert is introducing terms and ideas derived from the ecclesiastical theory of resistance; but in essence his position is still Germanic in origin. It is in a different, more modern form, the same idea as the Nordic saga put into the mouth of the doomsman of Tiundaland.

Very notable also are the words which Lampert attributes to the king's envoys. The Saxons, they said, were setting a bad example; the other princes of the *Reich* must disapprove of their method of action, which none of the German races, " neither in their own nor in their fathers' memory had ever ventured to pursue. " They ought to leave alone all questions touching the king's majesty, which "is always secure and inviolable even among barbarians." But even the king's representatives who challenged the constant recourse to the right of resistance, and upheld the opposite principle of the king's inviolability, frankly conceded that the Saxons had taken up arms in " an honourable spirit, " and that their cause was just. They therefore suggested that a national assembly should be called, in which the king should clear himself of reproach and abolish abuses in accordance with the judgment of the assembled princes. According to Lampert, therefore, the envoys differed from the Saxons only in their belief that peaceful means of obtaining redress from the king had not been exhausted. Whether Lampert's report is exact does not concern us here; his account is itself authentic evidence of the ideas current at the time.

It is typical of the amorphous character of the Germanic right of resistance, even at this late date, that the Saxons had no desire for a judgment by the princes, such as the envoys proposed. A general verdict by the princes, the assembled representatives of the community, could not, in their opinion, decide between them and the king. For their quarrel with the king rested upon individual grievances; therefore they must pursue their cause " *privata virtute.*" They rejected the possibility of a court which should judge the king, or anything of the sort, and relied upon the old amorphous right of self-help against wrong. The king must satisfy them instantly; otherwise they would not " await the verdict of other German races or of the princes, " but would coerce the king. Lampert would not have composed this manifesto for the Saxons, if he himself, despite his status as a monk, had not considered the Germanic notion of extra-legal self-help, the " necessity of rebellion, " to be practical politics. Moreover, when Lampert mentions the preparations made by the opponents of Henry IV to set up an anti-king, no formal act of deposition is prescribed, but merely a fresh election.

On the other hand, Lampert's account reveals the fact that the right of resistance, which as a result of the Investiture Contest acquired an unprecedented strength, immediately evoked a reaction among Henry IV's adherents. The doctrine of royal rights received fresh emphasis; the views not only of the enemies, but also of the defenders of the irresponsibility of the monarch found expression in Lampert's writings. It was inevitable that the right of résistance, now that frequent exercise and theoretical definition gave it an appearance of a permanent element in " folk-law," should be attacked by the Henricians, and by them be stripped of its legal character, and branded as unlawful.

But friend and foe alike now drew their arguments largely from the arsenal of ecclesiastical theory. After Gregory VII had intervened in the struggle between the German rebels and their king, and had taken the lead in 1076 by formally and solemnly declaring, in virtue of his spiritual power, that the king was unfit to rule, it became increasingly difficult in practice to distinguish the Germanic theory of resistance from the ecclesiastical theory, all the more since secular and clerical ways of thought had already on previous occasions combined, when possible, to bring the monarch to account. Nevertheless, the very possibility of uniting the secular with the ecclesiastical theories of resistance was itself a fact which emphasized the diversity of the two theories, before the Investiture Contest, both in origins and in methods. One example of this we have already seen: namely, the indulgent consideration usually shown towards kin-right by the upholders of the secular right of resistance in the Frankish kingdom and the feudal States. Such consideration, as we saw, was foreign to the ecclesiastical theory of resistance. We shall, however, soon discover still more important differences between the secular and the clerical idea of rebellion; and for the moment it is their union, at the time of the Investiture Contest, with which we are concerned.

This union was not merely the result of a gradual penetration of Germanic thought by clerical ideas. On the contrary, the lack of fixed legal forms and methods which characterized the Germanic right of resistance, together with its uncertain position midway between right and force, inevitably led to an attempt to invest the legal grounds for action and criminal proceedings against the monarch with a stricter and more regular procedure. At this point, however, the ecclesiastical theory of resistance was available, with a political theory of a higher and more mature kind, and a court of incomparable authority was found in the spiritual power. The union of secular and ecclesiastical theories transformed the crude law of self-defence, and the Germanic practice of abandoning the king, into a positive duty of disobedience clearly defined by canon law, and set up an impartial tribunal and a regular legal procedure.

§2. THE ECCLESIASTICAL RIGHT OF RESISTANCE AND THE DOCTRINE OF PASSIVE OBEDIENCE

The right of resistance on religious grounds has its origins in the needs of an ecclesiastically organized minority amid an indifferent or hostile society. The consciousness that it was upholding a higher ethical standard and a higher sense of responsibility guided the early Christian community in its relations with the pagan State; it engendered a peculiar duty of resistance, which under similar circumstances had previously inspired the Pharisees of the Jewish nation under Roman rule.

The Christian right of resistance was based upon the command which was exalted into a standard of Christian life in the two biblical texts: " Render to Caesar the things that are Caesar's, and to God the things that are God's, " and " We ought to obey God rather than men. "[49] The limits of political obedience were exactly prescribed for the early Christians. When the law of the State conflicted with the law of God, then obedience was to be refused. The State is lord of the body, but not of the soul's welfare. Man cannot serve two masters. If the State demands idolatrous worship, the Christian must resist. He should sacrifice his life to God rather than make sacrifice to the Emperor in the way required by the State. When the Emperor cult was imposed as a civic duty, the result was to raise up martyrs as blood-witnesses to the religious duty of disobedience.

[49] *Mark*, xii, 17; *Acts*, v, 29.

But, on the other hand, nothing was so deeply rooted in primitive Christianity as the doctrine of passive obedience, the prohibition of actual rebellion against the appointed authorities. The words of Paul: " Let every soul be subject unto the higher powers. For there is no power but of God. . . . Whosoever therefore resisteth the power, resisteth the ordinance of God " . . . laid down in principle the rule for the Christian's attitude towards the pagan State.[50] But just as the Pharisees had built up the religious theory of resistance, so also they had already contrasted the doctrine of passive obedience with the right of resistance, in essentially the same way as the Christians. The principles of passive submission and of resistance were regarded as equally worthy, and a conflict between the two doctrines proved to be inevitable from the moment when a monotheistic community found itself subject to pagan rulers. The martyrs solved the paradox in practice by refusing to subscribe to the Emperor-cult, whilst allowing themselves to be put to death by the very Emperor whom they refused to worship as a god, because he was the divinely ordained authority. By this saintly compromise they promoted the spread of the Christian spirit; " the blood of the martyrs proved to be a seed." But such a solution was thinkable only so long as the Christians formed a minority in the State. Tertullian asserted in good faith that even if they had the power for active resistance, Christians would not, according to their principles, do otherwise than passively suffer the wrongs inflicted by the authorities. But the moment when the State itself became Christian, this policy, or rather this negation of any policy, was no longer possible. Passive resistance, no doubt, had always remained the sublimest expression of the Christ-like humility of the professed Christian; for the Church, the martyrs, her passive heroes, have always been an example of the way in which the duty of resistance should limit obedience to the State, and resistance itself should be limited by the duty of obedience. But after the fourth

---

[50] The principal Biblical authorities for passive obedience are *Matthew*, v, 21 sq., 38–48; xxii, 17–21; *Mark*, xii, 14–17; *Luke*, vi, 27–36; xx, 21–25; *Romans*, xiii, 1–7; *Titus*, iii, 1, 2; 1 *Timothy*, ii, 2; 1 *Peter*, ii, 13–18.

century, the attitude of the martyrs no longer provided an adequate foundation for the relations between the Christians and the State.

When the Emperors themselves became Christian, and Christianity rapidly developed into a State religion, it acquired an interest in the State. Henceforth a bad ruler could not simply be endured as God's scourge, like a plague or a famine. This attitude did not die out, but alongside of it another now became necessary, an attitude which raised the question of an active right—or rather let us say an active duty—of resistance. For the Church was never primarily concerned with the right to resist, to which anyone expectant of advantage might resort, but rather with a moral and religious duty which everyone must accept even at the cost of personal sacrifices. What was at issue, in theory, was the upholding of divine command against human command. If the magistrate, the vicar of God, sins against the commands of God, the question is not how the subjects may react, but how they ought to react.

A conspicuous and unequivocal case for the exercise of an active duty of resistance by the subjects against the ruler arose directly from the fact that the State had become Christian. If in the Christian community only he who is himself Christian can exercise the functions of the magistrate, and if from the fourth century, the full enjoyment of civic rights is dependent upon baptism, then these requirements apply in special measure to the ruler, the source of all magisterial function. A pagan or a heretic cannot represent the Christian State. A heretic ceases *ipso facto* to wield an unconditional power of command. No Christian can owe him the simple obedience of a subject, even though he has sworn him the most sacred oaths; the oaths are void, for it was to a Christian ruler that they were sworn, and the ruler who has fallen into heresy has no claim to them. This principle was almost undisputed in the Middle Ages. Even the bluntest defenders of the inviolability of princes did not directly contest it; and Henry IV in a manifesto declaring his own irremovability expressly recognized that if he were a heretic, he should or must be deposed.

The principle is especially important because it established a limit to the duty of obedience which in theory could not be easily denied. The possibility of a justified revolt was thereby admitted. But in view of the difficulty of lawfully convicting a monarch of heresy, other instances of the right of resistance became in practice more significant. Even an orthodox king could violate the commands of God and of the law of nature in other ways. Should the subjects passively acquiesce, or should they compel him to make redress? Not a little depended on the answer to this question. Essentially the question was whether the conditions of the Christian State should at any given time depend simply and solely upon the unstable views and personal caprice of the ruler. Should care for good government be left entirely to Providence? Or has the people the right and the duty of carrying out the tasks of the Christian *Civitas Dei* even in opposition to a lax government? Which is the higher good: peace and obedience at any price, long-suffering trust in God, with prayer as the only remedy against an evil magistracy, or a revolt of the conscience, and the reformation of unjust authority by the people or by the Church?

No unequivocal decision on these basic questions of Christian politics could be drawn from the New Testament; indeed, both possibilities could be supported from the Scriptures. It was merely a question whether the " command of of God, " which is to be obeyed unconditionally even against the magistracy, was given a slightly larger or a slightly smaller place in the substantive canon or customary law. The leaders of the Church themselves favoured different decisions according to the differences of their characters and circumstances.[51] But on the whole, the Church decided, in

[51] The right of passive resistance was always regarded without qualification as an immutable law of nature, based on the principles: " subditi non possunt cogi ad malum " and " obedientia non est servanda praelatis in illicitis." Honorius Augustod., *Summa Gloria*, 27 (*MGH., Lib. de Lite*, 3, 75, 23) paraphrases Luke, xx, 25, with the words: " Dum (reges) ea precipiunt, quae ad ius regni pertinent, est eis utique parendum; si autem ea, quae christianae religioni obsunt, imperant, obsistendum." But what are the things which *obsunt religioni*? It is here that the essential difficulty arises. And does *obsistendum* mean active or only passive resistance? This is the point at which argument becomes violent.

accordance with the logic of its own development towards world-dominance, more and more in favour of an active duty of resistance.

This view could without difficulty be combined with the Germanic right of resistance. Although, as we shall see, it went beyond the latter in one important point, it shared with Germanic law the principle that the bad king deprives himself of the capacity to rule, and that by his own misdeeds or ineptitude he *ipso facto* forfeits his royal rights. The unjust king ceases to be a king in the eyes of God; for king and right are inseparable ideas. The ruler dethrones himself by his own misdeed; he becomes *tyrannus*, usurper, a man using force without authority. There were two classes of tyrant; the one *quoad titulum*, by unlawful accession; the other *quoad executionem*, by unlawful governance. Even a ruler who succeeds to the throne in the way prescribed by law, is in the latter case to be regarded as a mere wielder of force. His dominion, as the saying goes, is no longer in God's stead and by God's grace, but exists only by God's tolerance, as a punishment for the sins of the people,[52] to be suffered for the time being, but for which judgment is reserved, either on this or the other side of the grave.

The fundamental idea in this ecclesiastical, law-of-nature doctrine of tyranny, as in the Germanic conception of the forfeiture of the right to govern, was that the prince passes judgment upon himself by his own actions. The verdict of men, which decides that the ruler has forfeited the throne, or at all events, that he may be resisted, has only a declaratory, not a constitutive character. Unjust government is in itself void, and the verdict merely discloses the fact.

But in the method by which the declaratory judgment was reached, the ecclesiastical doctrine of resistance introduced a very important advance over Germanic practice. In the Germanic theory of resistance there were no fixed forms, and the verdict was left to the legal convictions of the community, or rather of each individual within the com-

[52] Cf. Augustine's words: " Non est enim potestas, nisi a Deo, sive iubente sive sinente," which were used by the canonist Rufinus as the starting-point for his important theories on good and evil rulers; cf. Carlyle, *Mediaeval Political Theory*, II, 150 sq.

munity. In the Church, on the contrary, there was an established judicial authority, which was competent to recognize the ruler's guilt, and so a formal judicial process against the king was possible.

For the ruler, like every other Christian, was subject to the penal and disciplinary powers of the Church. This fact was universally admitted until the time of strife between Church and State, and even then it was only half-heartedly contested by a few royalists. A party professedly Christian could not genuinely doubt that the Church's judgment and the imposition of spiritual penalties upon the king were permissible if he acted unlawfully. The only question was whether spiritual discipline should have political and legal consequences, and whether the subjects ought to make the verdict of God's Church their own, and themselves execute justice upon the tyrant.

On this matter opinion was sharply divided, and inevitably a major controversy was engendered.

The older tendency, in which the tradition of the martyrs was continued, denied that force and coercion were permissible against the possessor of authority. Even for a Nero it exacted the recognition due to the lawfully authorized magistracy. It permitted resistance against the tyrant in matters of conscience, but in these alone, and even then only passive resistance. All else was left to the intervention of God. "'Mine is the vengeance, I will repay,' saith the Lord."

But the other view, which steadily gained ground, and which represented the true current of mediaeval thought, built up, on the basis of a common responsibility for the establishment of a Christian commonwealth, the duty of preventing the tyrant, who was an intruder into God's community, from doing harm. It established the duty of depriving him by positive law of the right to rule which he had forfeited by natural law, and, ignoring the secondary question of his personal fate, it preached the duty of helping to build the *Civitas Dei* under the leadership of a true *rex Christus* with a reformed authority. It was thought possible to combine this doctrine with the Pauline precept of obedience to all authority, but this was in fact impossible without a certain amount of sophistry. To mediaeval thought, with its nominalist belief in the reality of ideas, it seemed that the ruler who undermined his own authority by his misdeeds, automatically passed from the category of *rex* into that of *tyrannus*, and thereby ceased to possess authority. In this way, unconditional respect for lawful authority remained in theory compatible with resistance to tyranny. Nevertheless, this typically mediaeval play of ideas, which brought active resistance into superficial conformity with the Scriptures, and so appeared to legitimize it, was little more than a mockery in the actual struggles of the time, when, for example, it was used in the Investiture Contest as a cloak for anarchy.

In this way there grew out of the early Christians' apparently weary renunciation of the ideal of improving the State, an active reforming zeal which was not checked by the command of dutiful obedience to the State, but which on the contrary often proclaimed the sacred duty of rebellion against the ruler.

Already in the fourth century, these new notes were sounded in the words of a Christian bishop, Lucifer of Cagliari, and reached the ears of the Roman Emperor. But it was not until five hundred years later that the Emperor of the West, Louis the Pious, was stripped of the insignia of his office when he was subjected to the Church's penance, because a penitent could not be ruler. Already, therefore, it was clear that ecclesiastical punishment of the individual entailed disqualification for his duties as prince. His capacity for rule was suspended, and only after the performance of the penance which the Church imposed was the prince able to regain this capacity to rule. How did all this come to pass? The main cause was the advance of the theocratic idea of monarchy as a vocation from God, with all its implications regarding the legal position of princes. With the progress of this idea, princes became responsible holders of office, who rendered account before God and also —especially after the emergence of royal consecration—in certain respects before the Church. A royal command in order to claim obedience, should, according to the view of the Frankish bishops, prove itself to be inherently " reasonable. "[53] This demand, as a matter of fact, was not far removed from the outlook of secular law. But the innovation was that the bishops as the " thrones of God " should constitute a court of justice over the king.· The union of the secular and the spiritual duties of the ruler, which had been prepared by Charles the Great, was strengthened under his son, in such a way that the principal sign of the king's official character was his responsibility for his offences. During the reigns of Louis the Pious and his sons, the kingship was more profoundly humbled before the Church than in any previous century.

In the first place, the Ordinance of 817, which was drafted by the clergy, set forth a formal procedure for penalizing a " tyrannical king. " If one of the under-kings committed an injustice, he was to be privately admonished three times —the Gospel precept thus being satisfied. But if this had no effect, he was to be summoned before his brother the Emperor, and was to be warned and reproved by him in fatherly and brotherly fashion in the presence of the third brother, who was to act as witness. Should this reproof bring no improvement, then the common council of the realm as a court of law was to sit in judgment upon him. Doubtless the penalty of deposition was here envisaged, though it was not actually mentioned.[54] The Ordinance says nothing of the possibility of deposing a tyrannical

[53] *Conc. Laur.* (853), c. 3:. " Si quis potestati regiae . . . contumaci ac inflato spiritu contra auctoritatem et rationem pertinaciter contradicere praesumpserit et eius iustis et rationabilibus imperiis secundum Deum et auctoritatem ecclesiasticam ac ius civile obtemperare irrefragabiliter noluerit, anathematizetur."

[54] *Ordinatio Imperii* (817) c. 10 (*MGH.*, *Capit.*, 1, 272, 20 sq., no. 136): " Si autem, et quod Deus avertat et quod nos minime obtamus, evenerit, ut aliquis illorum (the under-kings) propter cupiditatem rerum terrenarum . . . aut divisor aut obpressor. ecclesiarum vel pauperum extiterit aut tyrannidem . . . exercuerit, primo secreto secundum Domini praeceptum (*Matthew*, xviii, 15) per fideles legatos semel, bis et ter de sua emendatione commoneatur, ut, si his renisus fuerit, accersitus a fratre coram altero fratre paterno et fraterno amore moneatur et castigetur. Et si hanc salubrem admonitionem penitus spreverit, communi omnium sententia, quid de illo agendum sit, decernatur; ut, quem salubris ammonitio a nefandis actibus revocare non potuit, imperialis potentia communisque omnium sententia coherceat."

Emperor; it is concerned only with the under-kings. But the principle of penal procedure against kings was none the less thereby proclaimed, and it was destined to be developed.

Louis the Pious, as well as his son Charles the Bald, solemnly recognized their subjection to the judicature of the Church, and this recognition greatly advanced the power of the ecclesiastical doctrine of resistance. The subsequent revolt against Louis the Pious in the year 833 is especially instructive, because although the abandonment of the Emperor in accordance with Germanic custom, and his condemnation in accordance with canon law both led to the same result—namely, the deposition of the Emperor—the two traditions differed fundamentally in the methods by which this result was achieved. Politically, the attitudes of the Church and of the lay nobility were identical, but legally they were quite distinct.

The princes, among whom the bishops figured in their capacity as magnates, simply deserted the Emperor without any regard for legal forms, withdrew their obedience, and treated his place as vacant; they acknowledged a fresh ruler, and this was the only formal legal step that they took. But subsequently the bishops in their capacity as rulers of the Church solemnly divested the Emperor of his office by a formal criminal procedure, because of his sins and " because he had neglected to perform the duties entrusted to him "; and they referred to the earlier informal abandonment as a verdict of God upon his incapacity to rule. Louis himself, as a penitent, laid down his royal insignia in the Church of St Médard at Soissons. It was not the first time that the Church had, by its disciplinary and penal powers, divested a monarch of his capacity to rule, but in fundamental significance no other instance approaches it.

The proceedings at Louis's restoration in 834 and 835 were similar in character. No formal legal act was needed in order to reverse the effects of the lay magnates' exercise of their right of resistance. Louis simply received obedience again, and proceeded to reign. The people, who in the fateful hour of his fall, had run away from him " like a torrential river, " now flowed back to him again with an equal disregard for any preliminary legal formalities. On the other hand, a formal ecclesiastical act was necessary in order to reverse the legal consequences of the ecclesiastical judgment; and this act took the form of the official termination of the penance, the re-instatement of Louis into lawful possession of the State of which he had previously been deprived, and the re-conferment by the bishops of the royal office which earlier had been " right unworthily administered by him." So Louis became " Emperor by the renewed grace of God."[55]

The political alliance between ecclesiastical and secular principles of resistance, as it is manifest here and elsewhere in the disorders of the ninth century, was due to the desire of secular potentates that their rival's removal should be regarded as a judgment of God; but it was by no means the rule in more peaceful times. On the contrary, the Church, though maintaining and developing its own formal and legal doctrine of resistance, could co-operate with the monarchy in order to restrict the sporadic right of resistance derived from popular Germanic tradition.

On the one hand, it became the practice of the Church to collect together all historical instances of the clerical punishment of kings, and to impress them upon the memory of posterity. The grandchildren and the great-grandchildren of Charles the Great provided plenty of opportunities for spiritual reproof and disciplinary action, and clerical leaders such as Nicolas I and Hincmar of Rheims (in spite of other differences between the policy of the great pope and that of the great archbishop) were united in strengthening the right of the Church to intervene against unjust rulers. On the other hand, it was one of the Church's principles to defend the " Lord's Anointed " against the self-help of those who resisted the king on account of alleged defaults of justice which the Church had not recognized. From such an alliance of kingship and Church sprang, for example, the declaration in 859 in favour of Charles the Bald, that an anointed king must no longer be deposed by secular power,

---

[55] " Divina repropitiante clementia imperator augustus "; cf. Simson, *Jahrbücher des fränkischen Reichs unter Ludwig d. Frommen*, II, 91.

but solely by a formal judgment of the bishops who had anointed him.

Thus the German and French kings of the tenth and eleventh centuries could usually find in the bishops reliable support against the insubordination of the magnates. This was the result partly of the Church's need for political support, but also of the principle that an attack upon the king not authorized by the Church was an unjustifiable rebellion, and that authority had to be made secure against the threat of self-help. In the period of the national Churches, therefore, a strong government could usually come to terms with the clerical theory of resistance without much danger. But the time came when the Church, striving after freedom from the State, once again and far more effectively than in the ninth century, entered into an alliance with the upholders of the secular right of resistance.

It was part of the practical wisdom of clerical policy to employ the severity of spiritual discipline against rulers only when their power was otherwise weakened, and when in some measure they were isolated. Pseudo-Isidore and Gregory VII could indeed assert that, as early as the fourth century, canon law had given the Church the power to interfere in affairs of State, but if we except the ninth century, this assertion remained little more than a theory between the fourth and eleventh centuries. The attitude of Gregory the Great towards the Emperor; his express renunciation of any resistance to unjust imperial commands; his refusal of any conflict between Church and State, for long remained typical. With the disintegration of the Carolingian Empire, the papacy sank into a lethargy from which it was to be aroused only by the Reform Movement at the turn of the eleventh century. The first generations of Cluniac reformers worked under the protection of the State, until in the days of Henry III the earliest stirrings of the movement towards resistance began in the rewakened Curia. Henceforth, the independence of the papacy grew rapidly and became menacing. But Gregory VII was the first pope who dared to take extreme measures against a monarch. He could do so because the king in question was already opposed by a great part of his subjects. The revolt of Saxony and the rising of the princes against Henry IV gave the papacy the chance not only to put into practice the boldest clerical theories of resistance, but also to develop them by actual application.

On this basis, Gregory VII, in spite of the fact that he had entered into political alliance with the upholders of the secular right of resistance, created something new. To the chaotic vagueness of the Germanic tradition of resistance, he opposed one great, even if alien principle: the subordination both of princes and of people to the papal monarchy, to the infallible judgment of a supreme, super-human justice. He gave to the world the unprecedented spectacle of the deposition of a monarch by the pope. He solemnly freed the subjects from their duty of obedience to the king. Henceforth, the right of resistance was to be strictly regulated; at the call of Christ's Vicar, the people were to combat their princes. The questionable state of affairs, in which everyone to whom the king denied justice took his own remedy by force, was to give way to a higher order of things. The tribunal of God was now to bind souls even in this matter; the people were commanded by the pope to rebel as the executors of a universally valid judgment. The secular power and its subjects must dissolve their constitutional relationship at the behest of the superior ecclesiastical authority; the oath of fealty must be broken at the pope's command. " For, " as Innocent III said, " the oath was not instituted in order to become a bond of injustice." Yet even here the judgment of the pope was not considered genuinely constitutive in character, but merely declaratory. It simply declared the facts; it gave to doubting minds the assurance that King Henry really was king no more, because he had, as a result of his sins, automatically forfeited his right to govern.

Once Christendom possessed a definite authority with power to bind and loose consciences, and to condemn tyrants, it is no wonder that even tyrannicide, with which Lucifer of Cagliari had already toyed, found a spirited eulogist in the twelfth century in the greatest political thinker of the period, John of Salisbury. The right of the ecclesiastical princes to judge the king whom they had crowned, which Charles the Bald had already conceded to his bishops, was again emphasized in the twelfth century. Helmold, in his account of the downfall of Henry IV (1105), makes the archbishop of Mainz say to his colleagues of Worms and Cologne: " How long are we to hesitate, brothers? Is it not our office to consecrate the king, to invest the anointed? Is it not right that what can be conferred by the decrees of the princes, should also be taken away by their authority? We invested him because he was worthy; why do we not divest him now that he is unworthy? " Such ideas lead on to the right of the electors to judge the king, a right which is found fully developed in the German legal theory of the thirteenth century, and of which we have still to speak.[56] In this way, the ancient but obsolescent right of the bishops to judge the king whom they had crowned was indirectly revived under the influence of the papal right to depose.

Meanwhile, how far had the militant Church of Hildebrand and his adherents travelled from the passive Christianity of early times! It was now inspired by the spirit of the Pataria, of the revolutionary movement of Lombardy—to the silent horror of aristocratic and fastidious reformers. One of the greatest among them called Gregory VII a " holy Satan, " and Gregory's fiery, bitter preaching of the right of resistance was divorced from the Gospel of Christ by a gulf which seemed to be unbridgeable. The call of the hierarchy for war on the State never succeeded in gaining the confidence and sympathy of Christendom in the measure necessary for complete victory. In the heat of party passion, the Church of the eleventh century lost not so much the purity of its motives nor the sublimity of its aim, as discretion in its choice of ways and means. Moderation, wisely maintained for a thousand years, veneration and reverence for the wielder of the power of the State, were all broken down as the result of papal policy.

In face of this destruction of political tradition, the

[56] *Infra*, p. 124.

defenders of kingship strengthened the bulwarks of monarchy by developing a doctrine, originally alien to the
Germanic peoples: the doctrine of the irresponsibility of the
head of the State. The doctrine of passive obedience had
never died out in Christendom; now, because it corresponded
with the most urgent needs of the political community, it
was developed on a new basis. Long confined to a passive
rôle in theological and moralizing literature, this ancient
Christian doctrine was now revived as a political theory in
the writings of the royalists against Hildebrand, " the false
monk " who had strayed far from the Gospel, in the direction of almost unlimited war-mongering.

The more boldly both secular and clerical revolutionaries
pressed their " rights," the more firmly the monarchical
principle—dependence upon and fidelity to a hereditary
lord, defying even the severest incitement—took root among
the people, notwithstanding the widespread popularity of
the right of resistance. The people of the ninth century
called the place at which Louis the Pious met his downfall,
the *Lügenfeld* or " the field of lies "; the people of the
eleventh century saw a judgment of God in the cutting-off
of the hand with which the anti-king Rudolf had sworn
fealty to Henry IV. They felt profound doubts in certain
instances even about resistance blessed by the Church,
without denying its admissibility in general. The genuine
authoritarian feeling of the people usually suspected that
rebellions by the magnates against an anointed and crowned
king were simply odious party intrigues. Even on an
occasion like the deposition of the incompetent Charles the
Fat in 887, when the overthrow of the king was obviously
to the benefit of the State, a not inconsiderable portion of
public opinion adhered to the fallen Emperor.

Now the Germanic right of resistance, the whole theoretical
basis of which, so far as it required any, was the constantly
renewed obligation, which the king accepted, to rule in
accordance with law and the counsel of the magnates, could
be contested in certain concrete cases, but could not, from a
purely Germanic standpoint, be refuted in principle. On
the other hand, the ecclesiastical right of resistance rested

upon a literary, half-theological, half-juristic basis, and could be contested with its own weapons, by written arguments and authorities, by religion and by reason. Every thesis constructed evokes its antithesis; and so the new theory of the irresponsibility of the monarch was evoked by the opposite theory of resistance and particularly by its abuses. The new theory for the first time completed the doctrine of Divine Right, and turned not only against the ecclesiastical doctrine of resistance, but against all theories of resistance. This new theory was not identical with the doctrine of passive obedience, but was related to it as the reverse of a coin is related to the obverse. The doctrine of passive obedience had as its aim the welfare of the individual subject's soul, and the unassailability of the monarch was only a corollary. The doctrine of the irresponsibility of the monarch, on the contrary, emphasized the exaltation of political authority and its wielder; the monarch was to be above all criticism. Even in this theory, it is true, the prince must be a just man and a churchman, if he wished to be blessed; none of his acts remained unexpiated before God. But the dignity of the State, the need of the community for order, and in addition the moral education of the people, demanded the abandonment of coercive measures against the monarch, even if he were unjust. This doctrine could therefore never be divorced from that of passive obedience, though it was distinct from it, since its principal aim was not so much the personal moral duty of the subject as the constitutional safeguarding of the supreme power in the State. In the works of theologians, indeed, the personal moral standpoint was emphasized simultaneously, and the inviolability of the monarch as a purely political claim emerged only in modern times. But in order to appreciate the historical development rightly, we must concentrate upon the changes by which, after the ninth century, the legal element was sorted out from the medley of constitutional and religious motives, and placed in the foreground.

Out of the Christian duty of passive obedience, and out of the conception of the divine consecration of the monarch, a doctrine was built up which rejected as unchristian all the violent conclusions of the doctrine of tyranny. There were, of course, also theologians who adopted a middle position, and believed that the passive obedience of the martyrs could be reconciled with the papal claim that the subjects should shun intercourse with an excommunicated monarch. The monarch's life, at any rate, was safe, according to this view; but how did the prohibition of intercourse agree with the command of rendering unto Caesar the things that are Caesar's? Suspension of intercourse with the excommunicated monarch deprived him of any possibility of ruling. The half-way standpoint was therefore untenable in practice; it was necessary to decide for or against the responsibility or irresponsibility of the king. The theory of irresponsibility could, indeed, be united in one respect with the papal theories—namely, in attacking the undisciplined right of resistance; and such an alliance of Church and monarchy against the Germanic right of resistance characterized the ninth century. But the defenders of kingship did not stop at this point; they maintained that the person of the Lord's Anointed was altogether inviolable. Even this doctrine had already been advanced in court circles in the ninth century, perhaps by complacent bishops. The king himself could choose, the courtiers proclaimed, whether or not he wished to stand his trial in any plea in the secular or ecclesiastical courts; he could not be impleaded unless he deigned of his own free will to answer. No matter what he did, he must never be excommunicated by his own bishops nor judged by alien ones.

Though the mediaeval prince was never said to be absolute in the sense that he could do or omit to do whatever he pleased, it is obvious that he was absolute in practice if he was answerable for his deeds to no earthly court. The later doctrine of the Divine Right of kings was thus already foreshadowed—that fully developed Divine Right of which absolutism was to be an essential part. The position which secular authority thus obtained was modelled upon that of the supreme spiritual power. In the Church, papal infallibility and exemption from every jurisdiction were claimed, and unconditional obedience was demanded from the laity.

But henceforth the Church found by degrees that it had to deal with a State which claimed an equally absolute untouchability for its own supreme authority. The early Christian duty of passive obedience was thereby transformed into a counter-revolutionary right of the State.

Like its irreconciliable opponent—the ecclesiastical theory of resistance—this new doctrine was engendered in the course of the widespread discussion of political ideas in the ninth century, and like the former, it reached provisional completion in the eleventh century. Even during the intervening period, it was not entirely forgotten, as Thietmar of Merseburg shows.[57] But it was the defenders of Henry IV, such as Wenrich, who were the most earnest in proclaiming that absolute veneration for the head of the State was better warranted by Scripture and religion than the duty of resistance preached by the Roman Church.[58] They referred their antagonist Gregory VII to the example of Gregory I, the most pious pope of the ancient Church, and maintained that the innovation of deposition outraged the commands of God.[59] Each party accused the other of heresy. For the Catholic Church, which from the ninth to the seventeenth century remained the protagonist of the right of resistance against the authority of the State, had for its part violently and wrathfully opposed such a capping of Divine Right with irresponsibility. Already Hincmar of Rheims was clear that it was devilish blasphemy to maintain that the monarch was subject to spiritual judgment only when he pleased.

Even to popular thought there was something artificial

[57] Cf. his remarks (v, 32) on the revolt of Henry of Schweinfurt in 1003: " Dicat aliquis, non ignorans causam tantae presumptionis, necessario eum hoc fecisse. . . . Quibus reciproco non ullam in hoc seculo esse dominationem nisi a Deo; et qui se contra eam erigat, divinae maiestatis offensam incurrat."

[58] MGH., Lib. de Lite, I, 290: " Porro de ordinatis a Deo potestatibus omni studio suscipiendis, omni amore diligendis, omni honore reverendis, omni patientia tolerandis, tanta ubique sapientia disputat, ut vel pro eorum inportunitate vel perversitate seu etiam infidelitate occasionem forsitan querentibus omnem ubique hesitationis locum omnino excludat."

[59] Ibid., II, 540: " Veteris . . . et novi actus historias relegentes et bonos principes invenimus et malos, sed nunquam repperimus conscripto iudicio ab aliquo sanctorum fuisse condempnatos. De ipsis enim sapientia, quae Christus est, dicit: Per me reges regnant. Per ipsum ergo solum condemnandi sunt, per quem solum regnare noscuntur. Si quis vero id, quod soli Deo reservandum est, voluerit condemnare, numquam evadet punitionem."

and in a way intolerable in the doctrine that the prince, no matter how he conducted himself, was to escape expiation and remain unassailable. The democratic teaching of Christianity, which subjected all men alike to the Church, better corresponded, in its convincing simplicity, to the common man's sense of justice. He might distrust the individual rebel, but the exclusion on principle of every right of resistance did not accord with his mental outlook. Did the commonwealth, then, exist only in order to be ruined for the sake of one man? Were the people to endure unspeakable sufferings without resistance? What protection was there, in that case, against the measureless despotism of one man, and against the slavish degeneration of the others?

Only complicated processes of thought and painful experience of the effects of rebellion could justify to the masses the absolutist doctrines of a Thietmar of Merseburg or a Wenrich. Only the arrogance of the coalition of pope and princes in the Investiture Contest, and the anarchy that sprang from its struggle with the monarchy, had the unsought-for result of endowing the opponents of the right of resistance with a certain degree of popularity. For the moment, the absolutists represented the more mature political idea. But, because they offered no substitute for the right of resistance, and promised no protection against the encroachments of royal despotism, the future could not really belong to them. Certainly the writings of the Henricians indicated a more refined and more subtle idea of sovereignty than the early Middle Ages possessed. The humiliation of the monarch no longer seemed to them a " *reparabile damnum.* " Historical development in general was to justify them in this view; royal irresponsibility in the course of time was exalted into an axiom, whilst the right of resistance was deprived even of the appearance of being a part of customary law. The dictum of one of the Henricians, bold for its period as it was, ultimately prevailed: " Power given by God is too exalted to be censured." The positive law of the State is admittedly not of absolute but of relative value, and revolution has at times proved itself to be a necessary liberating force. But it is best able to do this if it is first stripped of the appearance of legality, for where revolt is legalized and put on a par with the law, it must bring all law into the melting-pot. Thus the strong modern State could never have come into existence without the presumption that the monarch is irresponsible and irremovable.

But a long time elapsed before this separation of right and force emerged, and the hybrid right of resistance was abandoned. In the late mediaeval States with their representative assemblies, the spirit embodied in the famous Aragonese legal formula flourished for generations; namely, that the subjects would obey the king only so long as he performed his duties, " and if not, not. "[60] For a long time, the noble who allowed a wrong done him by the king to pass in silence, was deemed a coward. But what above all else kept the old ideas alive, was the Church's tireless opposition to royal irresponsibility, and the effects of this opposition were visible for centuries. Simon de Montfort could still fortify himself for his constitutional struggle with Henry III by reading Bishop Grosseteste's *De Principatu regni et tyrannicidis*. Not merely the Church's quest for power, but still more its sense of duty was still playing a part; and the Church had on its side the manifest truth that the prince also is but a man. Nor can it be disputed that the Church, so long as proper constitutional arrangements were lacking, met a certain political need, and responded to the popular love of freedom, by calling princes to account. Furthermore, the Church's jurisdiction over the monarch, if compared, for example, with the raw despotism of the Merovingian period, represented at first a higher ideal of civilization. Motives were very mixed in the mediaeval struggle between Church and State; the rights and wrongs of contests can scarcely be distinguished. Just as both parties could find support in St Augustine; just as Wenrich could extol the divine foundations of the State, whilst Greogry VII could denounce its sinful origin, without either of them violating

---

[60] Balaguer, *Instituciones y reyes de Aragón* (1896), 43, calls this phrase " y si no, no," the key and content of the political system of Aragon. It may have been based upon the Visigothic maxim: " Rex eris si recte facis, et si non facias, non eris " (cf. Balaguer, *op. cit.*, 48).

the Christian tradition, so it is impossible to say which side
had the better right.   Both *sacerdotium* and *regnum*, in the
course of their struggles, helped to prepare the way for the
modern sovereign State, and the Investiture Contest played
an important part in the history of the ideas upon which that
State was based.

There was one circumstance, however, which decided that
in the early Middle Ages, the idea of absolute sovereignty
found less support than that of the monarch's responsibility.
The age was not as yet capable of putting considerations of
Realpolitik into the foreground.   The re-discovery of the
Politics of Aristotle, in the thirteenth century, for the first
time freed thought a little in this respect.   It is true that a
doctrine so fundamental as that of the sovereignty of the
State derived from a number of different sources, and we
have found hints that even in the early Middle Ages the
utilitarian reasons for the irresponsibility of the monarch
were not entirely unrecognized.   But moral or equitable
arguments were still far more important than considerations
of utility.   Even the Henricians had to rely upon ideas of
personal ethics, on the sanctity of the sworn oath, on the
Christian duty of forbearance, and the like.

The weakness of such a position was that it had the Church
against it, and the Church surely knew better than its
opponents what Christian duty was.   The Gregorians could
assert that they equally respected secular authority, and
that their respect was purer in form since they deprived the
unworthy ruler of the capacity to discharge the function of
government as God's Vicar.   It was precisely to express
this distinction between the untouchable office and the
fallible person of the ruler that the theory of tyranny was
devised.   If the unworthy monarch were *ipso facto* no longer
ruler, who dare forbid the Church to declare this fact
authoritatively?

The defenders of Henry IV were always conscious of this
weakness in their position.   For that reason, they preferred
to maintain the argument that the papal proceedings against
Henry IV were not conducted in due form—an argument
which would obviously have been superfluous, if ecclesias-

tical proceedings were altogether ruled out. As a result of this unavoidable defect, the king's supporters had to leave the back door open for the view that papal action against the king, so long as conducted in due form, must be accepted as lawful and legally binding.

§3. THE RIGHT OF RESISTANCE IN ITS RELATION TO POPULAR SOVEREIGNTY AND GOVERNMENTAL CONTRACT

It is clear from what has now been said that the champions of monarchical right could not avoid feeling themselves at a disadvantage in the theological controversies which centred around the ecclesiastical right of resistance. In these circumstances, some of the Italian opponents of Gregory VII, who are perhaps to be sought among the schismatic cardinals, strove to win a new fighting position by moving out of the theological into the juristic sphere. Thus, about the year 1080, someone with legal knowledge inserted into a forged decretal of Leo VIII the assertion that " the transfer of power from the people to the monarch is irrevocable ," and that " the people cannot take away the power of a king once established ." Even if his elevation to the throne takes place as the result of a free act of the community, once the act has been performed, freedom gives way to necessity. This assertion the fabricators of the forged decretal justified by reference to Justinian's *Institutes*, where they found the so-called *Lex Regia*, by which the Roman people were said to have transferred their power to the monarch.[61]

In later centuries, Roman law proved to be a veritable arsenal for absolutism in its fight against Germanic customary law. It played this same rôle—at times exaggerated but still of undeniable importance—on its first appearance in the constitutional struggles of the Middle Ages in the early days of the Investiture Contest. The study of Justinian's law, which was just awakening to new life, and was probably stimulated by Gregory VII's command to search the libraries for ancient legal authorities, thus operated as a

---

[61] *Inst.* 1, 2 ; cf. the so-called " Privilegium maius " of Leo VIII (*MGH.*, *Const.*, I, 667, no. 449, § 4) : " Iam enim dudum populus Romanus imperatori omne suum ius et potestatem concessit."

potent force in the struggle over the relations between monarch and people. For long, indeed, it was not considered as important as either Germanic or clerical ideas. Nevertheless, the way had been found by which, in time to come, the defenders of absolute monarchy would be able to deprive the people of every right of resistance by a legal interpretation of what was considered to be the original governmental contract.

This use of the *Lex Regia* to prove the royalist case involved a leap into a new sphere, and a departure from the moral, natural-law and theological ways of thought which the controversy usually assumed. Or it would have done so, if it had not looked so much like an evasion. For no publicist of the eleventh century ever thought of defeating the theological premises of his opponents by such means. Even supposing that the transfer of dominion by the people were irrevocable so far as the people were concerned, God and His Vicar the pope could not in this way be prevented from depriving the unworthy ruler of his powers of government; for dominion still sprang from both a secular and a divine mandate. The right of the Church to intervene against an unjust authority was not destroyed by the *Lex Regia*; the *Lex Divina* was still superior to the most sacred and irrevocable human *Lex*.

Moreover, the contention of the royalist lawyers did not remain unanswered even within the sphere of positive law itself. Here also the thesis evoked its antithesis, and since in this contest the point was not so much to convince opponents as to disprove their arguments, the *Lex Regia* argument was soon turned by the party hostile to the monarchy into its exact opposite. The very argument brought forward by the defenders of absolutism now begot the idea which proved to be the bitterest enemy of the monarchical principle: the idea of popular sovereignty. This idea entered into mediaeval Germanic public law as something alien—as foreign, indeed, as the theory of absolutism itself. In the eleventh century, both these notions appeared only once, and then vanished again beneath the weight of theocratic ideas. Only in the later Middle Ages did the juristic method of controversy rival the theological, and with the increasing importance of Roman law, the dispute over the governmental contract became more and more the centre of the whole controversy about monarchical and popular right. This is the importance of the dispute over the *Lex Regia* in the eleventh century: almost insignificant as far as the Investiture Contest is concerned, it was to prove its worth in subsequent constitutional struggles that were to continue without respite from the twelfth to the nineteenth century.

It was the German monk, Manegold of Lautenbach, who first recognized, at the beginning of the eighth decade of the eleventh century, the vulnerable spot in the *Lex Regia* as used by the absolutists, and who, turning the tables on them with crude violence, went armed with the doctrine of popular sovereignty into the field against his king.

If the people transfer power to the monarch for a definite governmental purpose, what then is to prevent the people from revoking that power and giving it to a better governor, if the king fails to fulfil that purpose? Why must the transfer of power to the king be irrevocable?[62] Exactly as though he wanted to anticipate the inflammatory, democratic power that this idea held for later generations, Manegold deemed no simile too vulgar to prove that the position of the king by Divine Grace was in reality merely that of a dismissible functionary of the community. Can the sovereign people be prevented from treating the monarch in the same

[62] Manegold *ad. Gebeh.* 30 (*MGH. Lib. de Lite,* I, 365): " Neque enim populus ideo eum super se exaltat, ut liberum in se exercendae tyrannidis facultatem concedat, sed ut a tyrannide ceterorum et improbitate defendat. Atqui, cum ille qui pro coercendis pravis . . . eligitur, . . . pravitatem in se fovere, . . . tyrannidem, quam debuit propulsare, in subiectos ceperit ipse . . . exercere, nonne clarum est, merito illum a concessa dignitate cadere, populum ab eius dominio et subiectione liberum existere, cum pactum, pro quo constitutus est, constet illum prius irrupisse? " *Ibid.,* cap. 47, 391: " Cum enim nullus se inperatorem vel regem creare possit, ad hoc unum aliquem super se populus exaltat, ut iusti ratione inperii se gubernet et regat . . . At vero si quando pactum, quo eligitur, infringit . . ., iuste rationis consideratione populum subiectionis debito absolvit, quippe cum fidem prior ipse deseruerit, que alterutrum altero fidelitate colligavit." *Ibid.,* cap. 48, 392: " At vero, si ille non regnum gubernare, sed regni occasione tyrannidem exercere . . . exarserit, adiuratus iuramenti necessitate absolutus existit, liberumque est populo illum deponere, alterum elevare, quem constat alterutre obligationis rationem prius deseruisse."

way as the farmer treats the swineherd who, if unfaithful, so far from being fed for the rest of his life, is chased from the farmyard without wages?[63]

The period was not yet prepared to accept violent ideas of this character; they are but the first lightning-flashes of a still distant storm. In this regard, the opinion of Manegold's antagonist Wenrich, that the Lord's Anointed must not be treated like a bailiff, was much closer to the popular convictions of the eleventh century than Manegold's coarse fanaticism. The monarch might forfeit his claim to obedience as a consequence of his misrule; but he was not simply the dismissible employee of the community; on the contrary, so long as he reigned, he was the Vicar of God, the guardian of the community, and the master of all; he is *maior populo*, the *populus* is not *maior rege*. The radicalism of popular sovereignty was not shared even by those who shared Manegold's opposition to Henry IV. Paul of Bernried, for example, admitted in the most emphatic manner the validity of the right of resistance, but in his estimation it was the old Germanic resistance, the lawful rising after renunciation of the lord by his vassals, and not a measure taken by the true masters, the people, against their officer, the king.

Nevertheless, Manegold's theory was closer to the mediaeval practice of resistance than the opposite doctrine of the irrevocability of the transfer of dominion by the *Lex Regia*. And in one important point, Manegold himself gave a mediaeval form to his classical pattern; contrary to what we might have expected, he changed the *Lex Regia* into a *pactum*. According to Manegold, the prince also had a contractual right to dominion, just as the servant has to his wages; a self-sufficient, inviolable right, so long as he does his duty. The sanctity of this compact, therefore, over-

---

[63] Manegold, *op. cit.*, cap. 30, 365: " Ut enim de rebus vilioribus exemplum trahamus, si quis alicui digne mercede porcos suos pascendos committeret ipsumque postmodo eos non pascere, sed furari, mactare et perdere cognosceret, nonne, promissa mercede etiam sibi retenta, a porcis pascendis cum contumelia illum amoveret? . . . tanto dignius iusta et probabili ratione omnis, qui non homines regere, sed in errorem mittere conatur, omni potentia et dignitate, quam in homines accepit, privatur, quanto conditio hominum a natura distat porcorum."

shadows the sovereign will of the community; the agreement to submit to the ruler cannot be revoked unilaterally by the people; the people is free of its undertaking only if the prince fails in his contractual duty. The monarch's own personal right to dominion is thus guaranteed even in Manegold's view. Even here it was not the sovereign will of the people, but the ruler's violation of his legal duty, that gave grounds for the exercise of the right of resistance. It was not the community's right, but the general limitations imposed by the law that restricted the king's freedom of action. Consequently, in spite of popular sovereignty, the general mediaeval view of the State is preserved by Manegold in all its essentials. But, at the same time, governmental authority is brought well within the orbit of contract.

This contractual idea emphasized an element in mediaeval public law which actually enjoyed a great deal of recognition, but which, as we have seen above,[64] must not be exaggerated at the expense of other elements. The tacit contract which the ruler concluded with the people at the beginning of his reign, in as much as he and the people promised each other protection and submission respectively, was emphasized from the eleventh century at the latest, by the fact that the fealty of the subject was compared and even identified with the homage of the vassal. Although this did not mean that the relationship between monarch and subject was wholly feudalized, in the law of the land the mutual relations of the two were assimilated to the contract between lord and vassal.[65]

The influence of feudal law upon these relations must not be over-estimated. The idea of fealty, in which the reciprocal duties of monarch and subjects, and the right of resistance were rooted, received, it is true, its most complete expression in feudal law. But this idea already existed before and outside feudal law. Nevertheless, certain developments of the idea of contract were due to the in-

[64] Cf., *supra*, p. 78.
[65] Cf. for example, the oath of fealty sworn in England to Edmund I (940–946): " ut omnes iurent . . . fidelitatem Eadmundo regi, sicut homo debet esse fidelis domino suo." (Liebermann, *Gesetze der Angelsachsen*, I, 190.)

fluence of feudalism. In the security-pacts such as the Capitulary of Kiersy, for example, which Charles the Bald concluded with his powerful subjects, the right of resistance was certainly put upon a contractual basis. In feudal law, moreover, such ideas as the lord's breach of fidelity and the vassals' right of resistance received a definitely legal form on the basis of contract. The undefined right of resistance sanctioned by the law of the land was clarified and strengthened as a result of the definitely legal form of the aggrieved vassal's right of renunciation. Denial of justice by the lord authorized his vassals to raise the feud against him, and set both parties against each other as independent powers. The *bellum iustum* was often ended by a renewed contract, the terms of which reflected the fortunes of war. Here in feudal life, still more unquestionably than in the wider field of politics, the subordinates were authorized to coerce their superiors to maintain the law, a law which was originally based upon contract. Thus, in the public law of the Crusading States, which was drawn up in strict accord with feudal law, the right of resistance received an especially clear legal formulation.[66] Even in England, where the right of feud was extirpated particularly early by the energetic Anglo-Norman kings, the barons raised the mediaeval right of resistance to its peak when, in 1215, they applied the idea of large-scale reprisals against the feudal lord in order to protect public liberties from the monarch.

In the same way, the opponents of Henry IV in the Investiture Contest could rely upon the contractual idea in order to argue that the breach of contract committed by Henry IV freed the subjects from their duty of fealty. But when Manegold introduced the theory of popular sovereignty into the controversies of the day, he detached the contractual idea from its historical background. He drew his comparison not from the contract of the vassal, but from that of the servant, and in his theory the ruler degenerated into the rôle

---

[66] Cf. *Ass. Haute Cour*, Ibelin, 206 (*Recueil des Historiens des Croisades, Lois*, 1, 331): " Et se l'ome attaint son seignor en court, que il a mespris vers lui de sa fei, et il en requiert à aveir dreit par esgart ou par conoissance de court, je cuit que la court esgardera ou conoistra, que l'ome est quitte vers lui de sa fei, et a son fié sans servise tote sa vie."

of employee, whilst the people were exalted into that of employer.

§4. THE TRANSITION FROM REPRESSION TO PREVENTION

Thus, from the ninth century onwards, the popular right of resistance was brought into the literary combat between the ecclesiastical theory of resistance and the doctrine of passive obedience. The paucity of mediaeval public law was revealed in these constitutional controversies no less clearly than in the political struggles themselves. The lack of definite limitations on the monarch, the existence of restrictions, which, on the one hand, were much too vague and wide, and on the other hand bound him too narrowly and minutely to law and counsel, equally encouraged both the absolutist tendencies of the ruler and the anarchy of unregulated resistance. The publicists who contended for or against the responsibility of the ruler ended up on both sides in a legal maze; the struggles of the day fluctuated, as we saw in the case of the Saxon rebellion, between the blind destruction of royal power, and the unwarranted abrogation of the rights of the people. The fruitlessness of the strife, the dangers inherent in the right of resistance, and yet its indispensability in the struggle against absolutism, all became clearer as the centuries passed. The more the European States developed, the more futile the existing ideas of the ultimate regulation of the relations between monarch and people seemed to be.

In the later Middle Ages, historical interest turns away from the struggle over the monarch's responsibility or irresponsibility, away from the right of resistance, towards the new institutions which the States of Western Europe evolved in order to secure a better functioning of the central power by means of a clearer definition both of its freedom of action and of its obligations; i.e., to the organization of Estates of the realm. Even if the lands in which representative Estates were developed did not yet do away with the right of resistance, the creation of representative institutions meant above all else a change from merely repressive limitation of monarchical power to preventative measures. It is

not our task here to trace the origin of the organization of
Estates; but we still have to show how the beginnings of
preventative measures grew out of the early mediaeval right
of resistance. At first, indeed, the repressive right of resistance seemed as though it would succeed in establishing
itself in the constitution and in developing still further.
The Church, as we have seen, had helped to transform the
amorphous popular right of resistance, unregulated and
inchoate, into a system of a superior and more durable kind.
It set a regular judge over the king, and built up a regular
procedure of punishment and deposition. Just as Germanic
kin-right and the pagan rites of royal consecration had
passed through the filter of ecclesiastical ideas, were in part
attacked and in part modified by the clerical theory of kingship as an office, and yet ultimately in large measure preserved their own essential forms, so also the popular Germanic right of resistance gained much from ecclesiastical
theories, strengthened itself with their aid, and yet in the
end repulsed in large degree the alien influences which
sought to confine it within fixed legal forms.

In Germany, the idea of a formal legal procedure of
punishment and deposition, which had originated in the
Church, for long triumphed over the lack of formal methods
inherited from the Germanic past. Not, of course, in the
early Middle Ages, though even then people argued, moral-
ized, and pleaded on clerical lines about the grounds for
resistance. But although armed with clerical arguments,
they drew back at formal deposition, and preferred, like
their forefathers, simply to throw over a politically unsuitable or unpopular king. After the Investiture Contest,
however, an imperial theory of deposition within the limits
of the imperial constitution grew up side by side with and
modelled upon, but also in opposition to, the papal theory of
deposition. This late mediaeval development may be indicated here only in the briefest fashion. The German law-
books of the thirteenth century proclaimed as an established
fact that there is a judge over the king. The court of the
Princes of the Empire, under the presidency of the Count
Palatine, could, they maintained, inflict deposition or even

sentence of death upon the king. Similar theories were also not unknown in thirteenth-century England. People were inclined to see in the sword which the " earl palatine " bore before the English king at the coronation a legal symbol of the earl palatine's judicial power over the king, if he erred.[67] There is even mention, in contemporary additions to some texts of Bracton's famous law-book, of a judicial court of magnates set over the king.[68]

The ingenious political idea of a *judex medius* between the monarch and the people was more elaborately developed in the Aragonese constitution than elsewhere. Whilst in Merovingian times the magnates were not seldom called upon to arbitrate between rival kings; whilst in thirteenth-century England, people and king, seeking an impartial tribunal to decide their constitutional conflict, once invoked the arbitration of a foreign ruler; in Aragon, an independent judicial office was created to arbitrate between king and people. In Germany, on the other hand, the doctrine of the German law-books never found literal application, and no monarch was ever executed by the " golden axe " which they prescribed. But in spirit the practice of the thirteenth, fourteenth, and fifteenth centuries was not far removed from that doctrine. Even if the whole body of the princes of the Empire under the presidency of the count palatine, did not in fact claim and exercise the right to judge the king, a certain small group of princes did. It was the electoral princes who, by formally deposing the German king in 1298

[67] Matthew Paris, *Chron. Maior.* (1236), III, 337 sq.: " Comite Cestriae gladium sancti Aedwardi, qui Curtein dicitur, ante regem baiulante, in signum quod comes est palatii, et regem, si oberret, habeat de iure potestatem cohibendi, suo sibi, scilicet Cestrensi, constabulario ministrante, et virga populum, cum se inordinate ingereret, subtrahente."

[68] " Rex autem habet superiorem, Deum scilicet. Item legem, per quam factus est rex. Item curiam suam, videlicet comites et barones, quia comites dicuntur quasi socii regis, et qui habet socium, habet magistrum, et ideo si rex fuerit sine fraeno, id est sine lege, debent ei fraenum ponere." The second passage, after the statement that there is no remedy against the king, except to petition " ut factum suum corrigat et emendet," adds " nisi sit qui dicat, quod universitas regni et baronagium suum hoc facere debeat et possit in curia ipsius regis." Bracton himself, however, knows no judicial precedure against the king, " cum breve non currat contra ipsum." On the question of the authenticity of the two famous additions, *v.* Pollock and Maitland, *History of English Law*, I (2nd ed.), 516, and Bracton, ed. Woodbine, I, 333.

and again in 1400, proclaimed that those who had elected the king could reject him. So dangerous a judicial power was not originally, of course, an attribute of the electors. But the electoral princes' claim revived the old idea, familiar to us already between the ninth and twelfth centuries, that the princes who gave seisin of the State to the monarch retained a right to supervise his official conduct, and in case of need were competent to depose him. In England also, Richard II was deposed by a formal legal process quite unknown at an earlier date.[69]

However, the establishment of a constitutional in place of an ecclesiastical procedure proved to be a mistake. In Germany, where the usurpation of judicial powers by the electoral princes meant that electoral principles were pushed to extremes, and the sovereignty of the Emperor was destroyed, the old idea of the extra-judicial abandonment of the king again came into the foreground in the middle of the fifteenth century. Even in England, the legally undefined right of resistance did not die out. The idea of setting up a court over the king proved to be completely fruitless and anarchical. The anarchical type of revolt, which in certain circumstances was a necessary means of self-help, became a repulsive hypocrisy when decked out with all the formalities of law and procedure. The early mediaeval right of resistance could not recover its strength in this way; it constantly reverted to its old undisguised formlessness.

But there was another, more hopeful way of giving resistance a comparatively orderly legal form. Mediaeval kings, as we know, almost always submitted to the view that

---

[69] Even at the deposition of Edward II in 1327, the only formal legal act was the election of Edward III, and only thereafter was Edward II's incapacity set forth in Strafford's six articles, whilst an attempt was made to wring a " voluntary " renunciation of the throne from Edward II. In 1399, on the contrary, a formal process of deposition was introduced, and the election of Henry IV followed after the deposition and " voluntary " renunciation of the throne by Richard II. Cf. Lapsley, *The Parliamentary Title of Henry IV*, EHR., XLIX (1934), 423–449, 577–606; Richardson, *Richard II's Last Parliament*, *ibid.*, LII (1937), 37–47; Lapsley, *ibid.*, LIII (1938), 53–78; Clarke, *Mediaeval Representation and Consent* (1936), cap. 9; and *Fourteenth Century Studies* (1937), nos. 3 and 7; Chrimes, *English Constitutional Ideas in the Fifteenth Century*, 106–114.

resistance against their violations of the law was permissible, but owing to the unspecified nature of royal duties and promises, this submission tended to be of little value in the practical decision of individual cases. The legal position, however, was quite different if the king expressly bound himself to certain definite obligations under penalty of forfeiture of obedience. This had already occurred in the Frankish period; the reign of Charles the Bald, weak but fertile in proclamations as it was, in this respect was epoch-making. In the year 856, for example, the king bound himself to definite obligations, and conceded his subjects the right to refuse him obedience if he failed to fulfil his commitments. The right of resistance thereby became a a contractual penalty, and precisely for that reason acquired something of a preventative character. In the thirteenth century, this legal idea found more frequent expression in connection with the emergence of representative Estates, in Hungary, in Aragon, and above all, in England. We shall examine this transformation of the right of resistance a little more closely in the country where it was most fully developed—in England.

What is the essence of Magna Carta, in virtue of which it has become a landmark in history? Not the fact that a king once again, as so often, admitted certain legal duties, and promised to fulfil them. Equally little the fact that once again the magnates, with weapons in their hands, extorted such an admission from an unwilling king. The only fundamentally new thing in the treaty which John Lackland concluded with his barons at Runnymede, is the establishment of an authority to see that the king carries out his obligations, and, if he fails, to coerce him. But this coercion does not take the form of criminal proceedings directed against the king's person and culminating in a sentence of deposition, but of extra-judicial pledge-taking, saving the king's person and right to govern. Such coercion is in accordance with both the Germanic and feudal rules of self-help, and the greatness of this constitutional experiment lies in the combination of these two elements. Even when disturbed by the illegal acts of the monarch, public life was to continue as peacefully as possible; neither deposition nor regicide was to be resorted to; but no injustice, no absolutism was to be tolerated. A provisional government was to put the king into tutelage for the duration of his wrongdoing, to bring him back to the right path by coercion, and make him fit to govern again. But all this was to be no sudden revolutionary measure worked out afresh from case to case, but a part of the constitution authenticated in writing and prepared for by administrative measures. For when the king admitted the right of his subjects to resist him if he violated his duty, his acceptance was expressed in specific, not merely general terms. He himself decreed the coercive machinery which his subjects were to set in motion against him in such a case; and this machinery is specified in §61 of *Magna Carta* (1215), where it states:

" Since, moreover, for God and the amendment of our kingdom and for the better allaying of the quarrel that has arisen between us and our barons, we have granted all these concessions, desirous that they should enjoy them in complete and firm endurance for ever, we give and grant to them the underwritten security, namely, that the barons shall choose five-and-twenty barons of the kingdom . . . who shall be bound with all their might, to observe and hold and cause to be observed . . . the peace and liberties we have granted . . . to them by this our present Charter, so that if we . . . or any one of our officers shall in anything be at fault towards anyone, or shall have broken any one of the articles of the peace or this security, and the offence be notified to four barons of the aforesaid five-and-twenty . . . the said four barons shall repair to us . . . and petition us to have that transgression redressed without delay. And if we shall not have corrected the transgression . . . within forty days . . . the said four barons shall refer the matter to the rest of the aforesaid five-and-twenty barons, and these five-and-twenty barons shall, together with the community of the whole land, distrain and distress us in all possible ways, namely, by seizing our castles, lands, possessions, and in any other way they can, until redress has been obtained as they deem fit, saving harmless our own person, and the persons of our queen and children; and when redress has been obtained, they shall resume their old relations to us. And let whoever in the country desires it, swear to obey the orders of the said five-and-twenty barons for the execution of all the aforesaid matters, and along with them, to molest us to the utmost of his power; and we publicly and freely grant leave to every one who wishes to swear, and we shall never forbid anyone to swear. All those, moreover, in the land who of themselves and of their own accord are unwilling to swear to the twenty-five to help them in constraining and molesting us, we shall by our command compel the same to swear to the effect aforesaid."[70]

Here, in Magna Carta, a royal decree established not merely the ideal limits of royal power, but set up an authority to ensure that the king observed specific limits, an authority which was entrusted with all the powers of the State. The central committee was given support by the local authorities, and a flexible method of procedure was provided. The offending king was to be suspended by the executive authority of the twenty-five, who included the Mayor of London, and so the *communa terre*, instead of waiting patiently for the restoration of a law-abiding king, could compel him to respect the law. Precisely because of this coercive power, no change in the occupancy of the throne was needed. The constitutional scheme set out in *Magna Carta* excluded any extreme proceedings against the king; it gave him security against deposition, just as it guaranteed the people against misrule.

The sixty-first article of *Magna Carta* deserves the fame which all centuries have accorded to it, and which not even recent attempts at depreciation have seriously shaken. It incorporated the right of resistance in the written public law of a nation, and the creation of a committee of resistance gave it the vitality necessary for institutional development. Neither ecclesiastical legal doctrines, nor the theory of popular sovereignty, nor the idea of governmental contract have any credit for this achievement. The right of resistance, popular or Germanic and feudal in origin—and **we** have seen above how far customary law and feudal law may in this regard be considered identical—itself gave birth to this new development. The idea of a constitutional method of securing the nation against the misrule of a monarch

[70] Cf. McKechnie, *Magna Carta*, 577.

remained alive in England, and for half-a-century English-
men understood the essentials of this security in the same
way as the authors of the Great Charter, until broader constitutional ideas developed out of English conflicts, and the
place of the committee of resistance was taken by parliament.

For the later history of the right of resistance showed how
crude and raw were the beginnings of rules for constitutional
resistance which are found in *Magna Carta*. For the very
reason that the barons proposed to seize governmental
power from the king during his wrong-doing by means of a
rival executive, they created no system of regular co-operation in government by the Estates, but merely a scheme for
intervention in occasional emergencies. This beginning of
constitutional monarchy was therefore nothing more than
the constitutional organization of self-help. This self-help,
when exercised by the " community of the land " necessarily
took on at once the character of an unlimited, destructive
rule of force. The machinery of §61, ingeniously planned
as it was, could not work as planned, because, in practice,
it was scarcely distinguishable from revolution. Prevention
expressed itself here merely in the fact that repression was
given a constitutional form. The ridicule by foreign critics
of the twenty-five " over-kings " was therefore not without
justification. Half-a-century later, Henry III, after his
capture at Lewes, was accepted only on sufferance. The
Lord Mayor of London did homage to him in these words:
" Dominus, quamdiu vos volueritis esse nobis bonus rex et
dominus, nos erimus vobis fideles et devoti." The idea of
limiting the king was fruitful and auspicious in respect of
its content, but its form was still ineffective and old-
fashioned; on the whole, it is best regarded as a legacy to
the constitutional State of the modern period from the
mediaeval right of resistance which was overreaching its
powers.[71]

[71] The fundamental idea of §61 of Magna Carta embodied a " creative
principle " for the whole constitutional future of the realm. But the true
authors of Magna Carta, the barons, had so little idea how to begin to
impose their plan that, in the very same year, they went on to desert John
by the old, informal method of insurrection. They elected an anti-king,

Only the later development towards regular co-operation between the Crown and the Estates solved the difficulties with which Magna Carta struggled in its own way. The growth of the Estates of the realm resulted in control of the monarch without the necessity for a committee of resistance; ministerial responsibility made royal irresponsibility possible without submerging the nation under the weight of absolutism. The beginnings of the organization of Estates of the realm dates only from the end of the thirteenth century,[72] but a decisive step was taken in 1215 when the king recognized the emergency-power of the people as a constitutional safety-valve against the monarchy, and accepted it as something permissible and even necessary.

We have now seen the direction which development took. The right of resistance was only the acute symptom of an organic ill in the early mediaeval body politic. The indistinct boundary between the rights of the king and those of the people engendered the sudden fluctuations between absolutism, which was almost essential in practice, and an immoderate limitation of the king in theory. Where passions and human ineptitude, where abnormal political situations and blunders affected the relations between ruler and people, this chronic disease became acute. The personal factor, which can always lead to conflicts in the State, could not be eliminated, but at least defects in organization could be remedied.

At first, as we have seen, it seemed to be an improvement when the amorphous, unregulated Germanic right of repression was clothed with legal forms. The Church sought to

and sought to drive the king out permanently. So short was their memory of their own work that, in 1216, the anti-king could maintain that the barons of Magna Carta had threatened King John with a permanent withdrawal of obedience. The fact was that the " committee of twenty-five," which was supposed to fulfil the rôle of a *iudex medius*, lacked both the necessary authority and a non-party basis. For this reason the parties in 1263 turned to the outside arbitration of Louis IX.

[72] Cf. McKechnie, *op. cit.*, 549, on the difference between the opposition of 1215 and that under Edward I: " Instead of using, as was afterwards done with steadily increasing success, the king's own administrative machinery and his servants to restrain his own misdeeds, the barons preferred "—as if they had any choice!—" to set up a rival executive of their own, with wide but ill-defined powers, and connected with the older executive by no constitutional bonds."

define the right of resistance in this way, and other attempts at setting up a regular judge over the king were not lacking. But ecclesiastical intervention against unjust authority in the State was thinkable only during the period of the mediaeval " City of God on earth, " and the growing self-consciousness of the State necessarily led to the rejection of such an " extraneous " supervisory tribunal. But the idea of establishing repressive authorities within the State was in practice doomed to failure; their existence insulted and undermined the sovereignty of the king, and merely created a new form of anarchy.

If, therefore, no real progress could be made by improvements in the methods of repression, the views of those who completely rejected the right of resistance were very much more auspicious. Nevertheless, the upholders of unconditional obedience inevitably shook the main pillar in the structure of Germanic society—the universal legal order valid for both the monarch and the people. Consciously or unconsciously, they led on towards the absolute State, and endowed Divine Right with its most important theoretical postulate: irresponsibility. They got rid of legalized rebellion, but set up in place of it the legalized will of the prince, and thereby shattered the whole fabric of the mediaeval State.

There was only one third way, very difficult to open up, which found its theory last of all, but which for that reason possessed a far greater future than either the right of resistance or absolutism. This was the path which led towards constitutional monarchy. It consisted not in improving the methods of repression, but in bringing the *consensus fidelium* into a definite form. Only here could true progress be found. The age-old and never extinct notion that prince and people together constitute the State, and that their unity alone can give it cohesion, had to be put into practice in such a way that the possibility of conflict between the right of resistance and absolutism was reduced to a minimum. On the one hand, the limitation of the monarch's powers must be clearer and more definite; on the other, the government must be guaranteed by the constitution more freedom of action and scope than the rigid basic ideas of Germanic public law allowed. Whilst absolutism sought to destroy the theoretical validity of repressive action, constitutionalism sought to abolish it in practice by transforming repression into prevention. In the communities organized on the basis of representative Estates the attempt was made to realize this advance over the earlier mediaeval State. Not only the community or its representatives had much to gain from this advance, but the monarchy also avoided the strain of the perpetual struggle against self-help, which had often menaced its very foundations. The history of the English parliament is the most important chapter in this development of the Estates. We have seen how at the beginning of its history, there stands the Great Charter, with its experiment in transforming the repressive right of resistance into a means of prevention, an experiment which would have to be counted among the ineffective improvements in the right of resistance, if it had not been followed by, and had not led up to, an improvement in the methods of obtaining the *consensus fidelium*, in the form of the assembly of Estates, or Parliament.

We must end our study with this glance at the forms of absolute monarchy and of constitutional monarchy. The early Middle Ages only vaguely foreshadowed the age-long struggle which was to ensue between these two types of State—a struggle which goes to make the drama of modern political history. But by developing the ideas of Divine Right and of the Right of Resistance, the early Middle Ages forged the weapons to be used by all future parties in this contest.

I

The relationship between monarch and subject in all Germanic communities was expressed by the idea of mutual fealty, not by that of unilateral obedience (p. 87). Fealty was binding upon the subject only so long as the monarch also fulfilled his duty (p. 88). In this respect the fealty of the subject was akin to that of the vassal (p. 121).

The king is below the law (p. 70). It is his fundamental duty not to alter the pre-existing legal order without the consent of his subjects, to protect every individual in his lawfully-acquired rights, and not to encroach upon them arbitrarily (p. 73).

If the monarch failed in these duties—and the decision of this question rested with the conscience of every individual member of the community—then every subject, every section of the people, and even the whole community was free to resist him (p. 83), to abandon him, and to seek out a new monarch (p. 86).

But the king is not simply a removable servant of the people, as the doctrine of popular sovereignty, which was first formulated on the basis of the rediscovered Roman law about the year 1080, maintains (p. 119). It is true that the monarch holds his mandate in part from the people, in virtue of election or acclamation (p. 12). But certain other factors, of equal or greater force, operate in the establishment of government: (i) the hereditary title derived from kin-right (p. 13), and (ii) divine consecration, which in pagan times is almost identical with kin-right (p. 14), but which in Christian times is distinct from it (p. 128), and may even be opposed to it (p. 31).

The king is superior to the people (p. 7). Even if the people may in certain circumstances withdraw obedience from a particular ruler, they cannot deprive kingship of its inherent independent rights, and cannot abolish the monarchical principle *per se* (p. 10). And though the community could in emergencies set kin-right aside, and deprive a whole dynasty of its right to the throne, even then a legitimist connection with the old line was sought as soon as possible (p. 17), and also a special divine sanction (p. 35).

II

On to this secular element in mediaeval monarchy, the ecclesiastical theory of magistracy was grafted. Anticipated by the Early Fathers (p. 28), it was fully developed under Gregory VII (p. 108) and Innocent III (p. 31). According to this theory, the monarch is an officer of God, His deputy, bound to His commands and to divine and natural law (p. 71). The people must give him passive obedience (p. 98). To violate the Lord's Anointed is the gravest of sins (p. 44). The king is indisputably sovereign, since he holds office by God's grace (p. 43), and being sovereign, he is the guardian of his people (p. 7), and is responsible to God and His Church alone (pp. 106–7).

But this official character, which exalts the king over his subjects, humbles him before his divine Master, and the responsibility which he bears before God is not a matter appertaining exclusively to the next world; the Church is authorized to declare the judgment of God; it possesses the power to bind and to loose (p. 104). Consequently, it is competent to decide when a prince, because of his unjust deeds, has ceased to be God's deputy, and therefore has ceased to be a person vested with authority on earth (p. 109). It deprives the tyrant of the mandate which belongs only to the just king (p. 101). The spiritual authority frees the people from their duty of obeying such a king, and indeed denies them the right to obey him (p. 108).

No independent personal right protects the monarch from this ecclesiastical judgment (p. 102). In so far as constitutional and legitimist titles form a bulwark against the dependence of the monarchy upon the Church, they are contested by the Church; the principle of canonical fitness or "idoneity" in particular militated against kin-right (p. 30). The theocratic idea of kingship as an office soon came into conflict with the sacramental implications of royal consecration, which bestowed upon the Anointed a semi-priestly position, and the idea of office was therefore actively opposed to the mystical tendencies of Divine Right. According to orthodox ecclesiastical views, the monarch must neither be authorized to rule over the Church nor be removed beyond the discipline of the spiritual power (p. 115).

The secular and ecclesiastical theories of resistance were by no means always in harmony, since they rested upon fundamentally different concepts (p. 71). But in a given case, they were capable of combining politically against a particular monarch (pp. 96, 109, 114).

III

An individual, informal right to resist the ruler can be found throughout the centuries from the time of the folk-migrations onwards, but with the development of feudal law, it was strengthened by association with the vassal's right of *diffidatio* (p. 122). The ecclesiastical theory of resistance is to be distinguished from this Germanic and feudal right of resistance, which was based upon the idea of mutual fealty (p. 87); in the former, the idea of a formal legal condemnation of the *rex iniquus* or *tyrannus* was conceived. Since the monarch, as a Christian, is subordinate to the spiritual tribunal, even though he has no secular court over him, a formal judicial process against the king is gradually built up; and the beginnings of this procedure lay in the spiritual punishment of sin. Later, the idea of a formal legal judgment of the king is adopted in secular spheres. We find it in the thirteenth-century German law-books, with their theory of the " count palatine, " and elsewhere (p. 124).

In the early Middle Ages, prior to the development of the institution of Estates, the community, when it has to resist the monarch, is represented only by a vague and undefined body of *proceres, maiores et meliores*, etc. And when the king is to be opposed and resisted, every member of the people is equally free to participate, as much or as little as he will. The right to resist is as indefinite and inchoate as the right to consent. The individual conscience decides; it is the only tribunal that judges between monarch and subject. Only with the development of assemblies of Estates did a definite representation of the community begin to play some part in the exercise of the right to resist. But the formal judicial process against the king always remained distinct from the amorphous, extra-judicial right of resistance, which belonged to every subject against every authority, whether king or feudal lord; the new theory of the rights of the count palatine, for example, in no way replaced the old general right of resistance.

IV

The theory of absolute Divine Right developed only with difficulty from out of these Germanic and ecclesiastical concepts. It changed the moral duty of passive obedience (p. 98) into a legal claim on the part of the king to unconditional obedience (p. 110). It transmuted the sacramental consecration of the king into a mystical tabu that made the monarch inviolable and a quasi-spiritual person (p. 59). It exempted him from the authority and disciplinary powers of the Church (p. 112), and at the same time manifested him to the people as a " real and incarnate God on earth " (p. 63), as a *vice-Deus* against whom every rebellion is blasphemy (p. 112). It rested finally upon legitimism, the inborn right to rule, which freed its possessor from all human dependence (p. 25).

Already in the Middle Ages, Roman law was used to support these absolutist tendencies; on the one hand, because it was regarded as a proof of the irrevocability of the transfer of government from the people to the monarch; and on the other, because it formed the link between the ancient tradition of deification of the ruler and the new cult of the veneration of Majesty (p. 66). Thus it furthered the severance of the king's rights both from theocratic and from customary bonds; but, the influence of Roman law was at first slight (p. 118).

V

There was no less difficulty in opening up the way for the

development of democratic radicalism. The fact that it originated in the wake of the absolutist theory showed that the one extreme called forth the other, whilst both alike stood in contrast to Germanic and ecclesiastical ideas. The doctrine of popular sovereignty emerged from the compact which the true sovereign, the people, concluded with the king as its officer. The people might, according to Manegold of Lautenbach, dismiss an unsuitable king (pp. 119–20).

The absolute Divine Right of the king, and popular sovereignty, were thus two deviations from the main current of mediaeval political thought, distinct and incomplete experiments which confronted each other under the aegis of of the mediaeval world of ideas. Only the dissolution of the mediaeval scheme of thought gave them an independent standing. But already it was evident that these ideas, once they were freed from the tutelage of mediaeval theocracy, and had grown to their full stature, would face each other in irreconcilable antagonism, without prospect of accord. Wherever absolute Divine Right had its advocates, popular sovereignty would always find its champions, and *vice versa*. For however one-sided each of these two doctrines was, each undoubtedly expressed an effective argument against the other, and the one inevitably evoked the other. Their conflict is insoluble, because each selected one element from the Germanic and ecclesiastical constitutional ideas of the early Middle Ages, which each magnified, exaggerated, and pushed to the extreme.

VI

Over both these extremes, constitutional monarchy emerged victorious. Like absolutism and popular sovereignty, constitutional monarchy itself was rooted in the early Middle Ages, but unlike them, it was not an exaggeration of one current of thought alone, to the exclusion of all others. On the contrary, it sought, by reconciling the extremes, to enforce the central idea of the early mediaeval State more vigorously and more permanently than the Germanic and ecclesiastical doctrines of divine right and of the right of resistance had succeeded in doing. Constitutional monarchy implied a synthesis of the monarchical principle with the limitation of the monarch by the law. It allowed the king to accomplish the most important constitutional acts of State only in co-operation with his subjects, i.e., with popular representatives and ministers; but it gave to such acts so strong and unchallengeable a validity, that no right of resistance could be admitted. It united the independence of the sovereign with the notion of the sanctity of the law (or the constitution), together with the people's rights rooted in the constitution; a complex combination, difficult to grasp, but which was latent in both Germanic and ecclesiastical political thought, and which the Middle Ages brought into a more definite and practical form when the transition to an organization of the State on the basis of representative Estates was made. In this way, the right of resistance was transformed from a repressive into a preventative force (p. 123). Effective constitutional machinery was, indeed, first brought into being during the period of representative Estates, but the prospect of welding together the rights of the king and of the people into an organic unity was already present when this new arrangement of European society was still in preparation.

From this point of view, the essential elements of early mediaeval constitutional ideas must be set forth in the following order:

A. The rights of the monarchy were derived not only from the king's independent, hereditary and divinely-sanctioned title, but also from an act of the community—from kinright and consecration on the one hand, and from popular election on the other (pp. 12, 25–26).

B. The monarch is above the community, but the law is above the monarch. In the language of the Germanic peoples, this means that, although the promulgation and enforcement of the law belongs to the king, the declaration of what the law is, belongs to the community; in the language of the Church, it means that the magistracy is the source of positive law, but positive law is valid only in so far as it is in harmony with divine and natural law. In

both views, the monarch was regarded as being below law
(p. 72).

C. If the theoretical limits of autocracy are clearly defined
in this way, it is none the less true that the sovereignty of
the people is excluded. The people participate in the
appointment of the king, but the monarch's power is not
simply a mandate conferred upon him by the community.
The people share in the making of the law, which is above the
king; but, in the opinion of the Church, the people also are
bound by the law of God and the Law of Nature, which alone
are sovereign, and which demand obedience to authority;
whilst from the standpoint of Germanic law, the people lack
the essential constituent of sovereign power—the ability to
enforce the law (pp. 73-75).

To the early mediaeval mind, king and people together,
welded into a unity which theoretical analysis can scarcely
divide, formed the State. Neither the rule of a monarch
whose powers were limited by law, nor the active legislative
co-operation of the community expressed in the *consensus
fidelium*, was regarded as " sovereign " in the modern sense.
Sovereignty, if it existed at all, resided in the law which
ruled over both king and community. But any description
of the law as sovereign is useful only because it emphasizes
the contrast with later political ideas; otherwise it is better
avoided. The blunt " either-or " of later times—*either* the
king is unlimited *or* the people is sovereign—is an impossible
dilemma from the standpoint of the early Middle Ages.

We have, indeed, found the beginnings of both these
propositions within our period. But they fell outside the
framework of early mediaeval thought. None the less, the
balance which modern constitutional monarchy has created
is, in a form adapted to modern conditions, a reversion to
early mediaeval principles. The *consensus fidelium*, the
participation of the community in government, was greatly
improved when organized on constitutional lines, but the
fundamental relation between the rights of the king and the
rights of the people, as it existed in the early Middle Ages,
proved capable of sustaining even the most complex modern
forms of political organization. It was certainly more

adaptable and successful than the negation of it under the domination either of absolutism or of popular sovereignty, whose conflicts marked the beginnings of the political and constitutional struggles which were settled only when the extremes were reconciled in the modern constitutional system.

Thus the early Middle Ages offer us a vantage-point from which to follow the historical evolution of kingship. We have traced the mutual relations of political theory and political life, and in doing so we have found it necessary, from the point of view of method, to distinguish sharply between the State of the early Middle Ages and the State of the later Middle Ages, organized upon the basis of Estates, although the one grew out of the other.

There were still other weighty reasons which obliged us to regard the beginning of the thirteenth century as a turning-point in the history of constitutional ideas. The re-discovery of Aristotle's *Politics* stimulated the growth of a learned political philosophy during that century. The old theological and customary traditions, together with the flourishing jurisprudence of the Glossators and Canonists, were fused by scholastic philosophers into a new unity; the whole aspect of mediaeval political doctrine was changed. In the imposing political thought of the later Middle Ages, we find again all the familiar features of the early mediaeval world of ideas, but now in different associations, and, more-over, in the guise of conscious, learned doctrines and systems, whereas in the early Middle Ages, formal political theory on the whole played a subordinate part. It is from the transactions of political life itself, from royal and papal charters, from capitularies and synodal acts, from chronicles and tracts, and often from unconscious revelations of the general attitude of mind, that we get an insight, as direct and uncoloured as the past itself, into the constitutional ideas of the period. Difficult as it is to formulate these ideas, and to express them in accordance with modern categories, we must not evade this difficulty, for it is from such sources that we obtain the most reliable evidence of popular ways of thought in the mediaeval world.

Even that spiritual and intellectual revolution which gave birth to the constitutional conflicts of later centuries—the revolution that began, after a few preliminary stirrings in the ninth century, with the interaction between Germanic and ecclesiastical ideas during the Investiture Contest—is most readily studied in the early Middle Ages. It is possible to see how Germanic and ecclesiastical political ideas, starting from totally different premises, came into conflict, though each contributed to the formulation both of Divine Right and of the Right of Resistance. Often hostile, the two traditions still more often co-operated. Above all, it is clear that the ecclesiastical conception of monarchy suffered from a self-contradiction which it bequeathed to later generations; within the doctrine of the Church, the right of active resistance and the duty of passive obedience contended one against the othe with almost equal strength.

And yet, in the last analysis, it must be recognized that this antagonism is necessary, permanent, and inevitable, because it is rooted in human nature. Even the magic of modern constitutional monarchy has not abolished the possibility of conflict between the rights of the government and the rights of the people. No matter how ingeniously balanced the constitutional relations between the ruler and the community may be, there will always be times when limits which are respected in normal circumstances, will in moments of strain and stress give way to final decisions that are based not on legal methods and legal rules, but on the realities of power. Not a few pages in the political history of the West bear the marks of this violence—of violence which may abolish positive law, but which can only replace it with a new and lasting law under the sign and seal of a higher and more creative ideal of Justice.

Appendix

Notes on the following topics occupy pp. 296-444 of the German edition. It has not been possible to reproduce the contents of these Notes here, but for the convenience of readers who may wish to pursue further any of the topics, a list of the titles of the Appendices is here appended:

THE SECOND PART
LAW AND CONSTITUTION IN THE MIDDLE AGES

I

LAW

FOR us law needs only one attribute in order to give it validity; it must, directly or indirectly, be sanctioned by the State. But in the Middle Ages, different attributes altogether were essential; mediaeval law must be " old " law and must be " good " law. Mediaeval law could dispense with the sanction of the State, but not with the two qualities of Age and Goodness, which, as we shall see, were considered to be one and the same thing. If law were not old and good law, it was not law at all, even though it were formally enacted by the State.

§1. LAW IS OLD

Age has at all times been important for subjective rights, especially for rights of possession, and in certain circumstances, prescription can have the force of law. But for the validity of objective law, Age, in the present era of enacted law, is of no account. For us, law, from the time of its promulgation to that of its repeal, is neither old nor new, but simply exists. In the Middle Ages, it was a different matter altogether; Age was then the most important quality even of objective law. Law was in fact custom. Immemorial usage, testified to by the memory of the oldest and most credible people; the *leges patrum*, sometimes but not necessarily proven by external aids to memory, such as charters, boundaries, law-books, or anything else that outlived human beings: this was objective law. And if any particular subjective right was in dispute, the fact that it was in harmony with an ancient custom had much the same importance as would be given to-day to the fact that it was derived from a valid law of the State.

It is true that for law to be law, it had to be not only

old, but also " good. " The controversy among modern jurists, as to whether great age creates or merely reveals the binding force of customary law, would have been meaningless to mediaeval minds. For age cannot create law, and long-usage does not prove a practice to be rightful. On the contrary, " a hundred years of wrong make not one hour of right, " and Eike of Repgow in the *Sachsenspiegel*, for example, emphasized that slavery, which originated in force and unjust power, and was a custom so ancient that " it is now held for law, " was only an " unlawful custom. " The existence of an unlawful or " evil " custom for so long a time shows that usage or age cannot make or reveal law. In Eike's estimation, slavery, though ancient, was a modern abuse as compared with the universal liberty which prevailed " when man first established law. " Prior to the centuries of abuse, there were a thousand years of law, perhaps even an eternal and imprescriptible law. It was through the notion of imprescriptibility that ecclesiastical ideas entered into Germanic concepts of law. The law of nature of the Golden Age, in the ultimate analysis, stamped as unlawful every legal system resting upon the inequality of man. Even if in this example the popular legal ideas of the Middle Ages (with which we are alone concerned in this study) are coloured by learned jurisprudence, the fact remains that the law's inflexible resistance to institutions justified solely by long usage is characteristic of mediaeval legal thought as a whole.

Not the State, but " God is the source of all law. " Law is a part of the world-order; it is unchangeable. It can be twisted and falsified, but then it restores itself, and at last confounds the evil-doer who meddled with it. If anyone, a member of the folk, or even the highest authority in the State, made a " law " which conflicted with a good old custom, and this custom were proved beyond doubt by the evidence of venerable witnesses or by the production of a royal charter, then the newly-made law was no law, but a wrong; not *usus*, but *abusus*. In such a case, it was the duty of every lawful man, of those in authority as well as the common man, to restore the good old law. The common man as well as the constituted authority is under obligation to the law, and required to help restore it. The law being sacred, both ruler and subject, State and citizen, are equally authorized to preserve it. These facts, as we shall see, lead to extremely important conclusions in the constitutional sphere; but we shall also see that ideas as wide in scope and as ill-defined as the mediaeval idea of law, gave rise to great confusion in practical life.

But let us first throw more light upon the peculiar consequences that followed from the fact that Age was a necessary attribute of law.

When a case arises, for which no valid law can be adduced, then the lawful men or doomsmen will make new law in the belief that what they are making is good old law, not indeed expressly handed-down, but tacitly existent. They do not, therefore, create the law; they " discover it. " Any particular judgment in court, which we regard as a particular inference from a general established legal rule, was to the mediaeval mind in no way distinguishable from the legislative activity of the community; in both cases a law hidden but already existing is discovered, not created. There is, in the Middle Ages, no such thing as " the first application of a legal rule. " Law is old; new law is a contradiction in terms; for either new law is derived explicitly or implicitly from the old, or it conflicts with the old, in which case it is not lawful. The fundamental idea remains the same: the old law is the true law, and true law is the old law. According to mediaeval ideas, therefore, the enactment of new law is not possible at all; and all legislation and legal reform is conceived of as the restoration of the good old law which has been violated.

At this point we must turn our attention to the second attribute of law, which for the Middle Ages is closely related to, if not identical with the first:

§2. LAW IS GOOD

Philologists still disagree whether the old Germanic word for law: *é*, is connected with *aequus* or with *aevus*, with " equity " or with " eternity. " For the mediaeval mind, the two would be almost the same thing; for what exists from time eternal is equitable, and what is equitable must somehow be traceable back to the eternal order of things. The old law is reasonable, and reasonable law is old.

Nevertheless, there are solid reasons for preferring the connection of *ê* with *aequus*. For the fundamental characteristic of mediaeval legal thought—without a knowledge of which the historian is bound to make many wrong inferences —is that it draws no distinction between law, equity, *raison d'État*, and ethics. Where we moderns have erected three separate altars, to Law, to Politics, and to Conscience, and have sacrificed to each of them as sovereign godheads, for the mediaeval mind the goddess of Justice alone is enthroned, with only God and the Faith above her, and no one beside her. Prince and people are kneeling at her feet, while she holds her sword and her scales in eternal and inviolable impartiality above their heads; confronting her, and inciting the kneeling figures to rebellion, is the hellish, hostile spectre of Injustice.

The legal philosophy of the Fathers of the Church was based upon that of the Stoics, in which the theory of natural law, with its mixture of law and ethics, was handed down from the ancient world to the Middle Ages; and the reason why this philosophy found so much sympathy in the Middle Ages is to be found in the fact that mediaeval thought failed to arrive at that divorce between law and ethics which in modern times has been carried—by Fichte in particular—to the length of a dialectical contrast between the two.

But whilst the contrast between ancient ideas and the living customary law of their own world, on the one hand, and the study of Roman law on the other, taught mediaeval scholars to work out the notion of positive law as something different from and complementary to natural law, this distinction had no effect on the popular mind. The law, in its majestic, inviolate simplicity, seemed to the people to be one great whole, which like Righteousness, was " God's hand-maid, " " giving to everyone what is his own." Here we are concerned only with this popular belief, which underlay the broad living law of the Middle Ages, not with the ideology of the scholastics and jurists, and its implications; and so we have simply to establish the fact that the ideas which moulded popular legal practice drew no distinction whatever between positive law and ideal law. Law is the Right, the Just, the Reasonable. Divine, natural, moral law is not above, nor beyond positive law, but rather all law is divine, natural, moral, and positive at one and the same time—if, indeed, all these differentiations, which had no place in mediaeval thought, may be introduced into the one, undifferentiated, all-embracing idea of law.

" Right and just," " *juste et rationabiliter*, " is one of the favourite combinations of words in mediaeval legal phraseology, and it reflects the unity of " positive " and " moral " law. For us, the actually valid or positive law is not immoral but amoral; its origin is not in conscience, God, nature, ideals, ideas, equity, or the like, but simply in the will of the State, and its sanction is the coercive power of the State. On the other hand, the State for us is something holier than for mediaeval people—at any rate if the State is one which we recognize and can love, which is a part of ourselves, and is our spiritual home. If not, then it is a different matter; if, for example, we repudiate a law forced upon us by foreign rule or by the rule of the mob, then we become rebels against the State in the true mediaeval sense of the right of resistance. We mean, of course, that both law and State are rooted, for us also, in feelings which are more than legal and more than political. But we are able to discriminate; and even the hated law of the most hated State is for us fully valid positive law until the day when we can, by rebellion, destroy both together. For us, the heirs of scholastic jurisprudence, law is only secondary; the State is primary. To the Middle Ages, law was an end in itself, because the term " law " stood at one and the same time for moral sentiment, the spiritual basis of human society, for the Good, and therefore for the axiomatic basis of the State. For the Middle Ages, therefore, law is primary, and the State only secondary. In other words, the State is only an instrument for putting the law into effect; its very being is derived from the law, which is superior to it. Law is prior to the State; the State exists for the law and through the law, not the law through the State.

For us, " moral, " " natural, " " ideal " law does not have its place primarily within the legal sphere at all. Only when positive law expressly invokes moral sentiment, is ethics deemed to be a part of the legal world, employed as a buttress for the edifice of positive law. The positive law enacted by the State ideally should cover all the realities of life; and it is only when a gap in the positive law has been discovered that equity or the moral judgment of the judge is invoked, in order to fill the gap; or the head of the State is empowered to mitigate the strict law by the exercise of grace. Then, and then only, in the modern world, does the moral law emerge from the inner realm of conscience, and take its place in the law-courts—invoked, authorized, controlled, and supervised by positive law. In this way, moral law becomes one of the elements in positive law, so that formally there is still only one single law in the State— positive law, and none other. But, according to modern constitutional and legal ideas, the State can change this positive law at any time. The State is sovereign; therefore it can even decide how far moral right is to be law.

According to the modern view, there is only one way in which the ideal law, Antigone's law of the Gods, can lawfully or constitutionally prevail over the positive law, the law of the State: by the enactment of new positive law. This occurs when the State is convinced that moral notions, hitherto outside the law, call for the revision of positive law. But in this case there is no direct replacement of the positive by the moral law; instead, the State remoulds its positive law, which, as sovereign, it can do at pleasure.

We do not need to discuss how far fiction is latent in this modern legal theory. It is enough for us to observe that the conception is one of a unified and closed system, based upon the sovereignty of the State and on the exclusive validity of the law established by the State; namely, the positive law.

The mediaeval conception is in complete contrast. Here the law is sovereign, not the State, the community, the magistracy, the prince, or any other person or body which we should contrast with the law. The State cannot change the law. To do so would be to commit something like matricide. In the next section we shall begin to consider the results of this potent belief upon mediaeval legal practice; here we need only explain once again the reason for this superiority of the law. Its basis is the lack of differentiation between ideal and positive law. Law which is identical with the Good is naturally prior to and superior to the State. The mediaeval world was filled with theoretical respect for the sanctity of the law—not for the prosaic, dry, flexible, technical, positive law of to-day, dependent as it is upon the State; but for a law which was identified with the sanctity of the moral law. The reader presumably will quickly convince himself not only that the modern divorce of law from morality was a technical advance and a sound sobering-down, but that in actual fact the law has gained in sanctity as a result, just as in a different sphere, the cold, legally enforced obedience of modern times is more potent than the highly-coloured, warm, equivocal fealty of mediaeval times. We are, therefore, not to infer from the impressive sublimity of the mediaeval idea of law that in practice the law was particularly sacred. We shall not attempt here to depict from the standpoint of the history of civilization the value and practical influence of the lofty mediaeval idea of law; neither its creative, civilizing, and spiritual power, nor even its harmful tendency towards obscurantism and cant. We content ourselves merely with a demonstration of the practical inconvenience of an idea so vague and ambiguous, and for the moment our purpose is to portray and elucidate the idea itself.

Language often preserves the ideas of a vanished ·epoch, and transmits them in their obsolete logic to posterity. This is true of the German tongue, which still reminds us of this former unity of law and morality, since it relies on orthography alone to distinguish what is " right " from what is " law. "[1]

---

[1] Cf. Vinogradoff, *Common Sense in Law*, 61: " . . . in most European languages the term for law is identical with the term for right. The Latin *jus*, the German *Recht*, the Italian *diritto*, the Spanish *derecho*, the Slavonic

It can now be understood in what sense the attribute of goodness, was, in the mediaeval view, indispensable for law, and we turn next to a third dictum:

§3. THE GOOD OLD LAW IS UNENACTED AND UNWRITTEN

We are now better able to understand why the old law and the good law are intimately bound up with each other, and are, so to speak, identical. Modern law is always, in one way or another, enacted by the State. Mediaeval law simply exists; it was accepted by mediaeval opinion not as being enacted by men, but as part of the Just and the Good, which are eternal. We have remarked above that modern law is the law of the land from the day of its establishment until the day of its repeal; previously it was future law; subsequently it will be obsolete law; in both cases, therefore, it is not really law at all. Modern positive law never has the attributes of age and goodness, neither before its enactment nor during the period of its validity nor after its repeal. Mediaeval law, on the other hand, being neither enacted nor annulled, was not so much actual as timeless. Only good law was real law, no matter whether human law-givers or judges recognized it or ignored it, no matter whether it were positive or " only " ideal law. The attitude of law-givers and judges towards the law was only like a shadow that fell over it; it might obscure the law, but could not set it aside.

But if the law is not recognizable as something enacted, and if, since there are long-standing abuses of law, it is not recognizable by mere age; if its main attribute is goodness, and consequently if age also counts, how then can it be recognized with certainty? Where will the law be found?

It will be found, in the first place, where all morality resides—in Conscience. And, indeed, since law comprises all the rights of the community, it will be found in the common conscience of the people, in their sense of legality, or in that of their representatives, the chosen doomsmen.

pravo, point both to the legal rule which binds a person and the legal right which every person claims as his own. Such coincidences cannot be treated as mere chance, or as a perversion of language likely to obscure the real meaning of words. On the contrary, they point to a profound connection between the two ideas implied. . . ."

For them neither learning nor law-books are necessary, but only the possession of the " normal " legal sense of the community, the fact that they are *sapientes, prud'hommes*, lawful men.

But, in the second place, the law will be found in old tradition. All good and true law was, according to universal belief, somehow contained already in the legendary law of a sage law-giver, of a venerated and exceptionally wise and powerful king.

We observe, then, a two-fold source of law. From the point of view of jurisprudence, it would be interesting to consider this dualism in more detail; but the Middle Ages gave no thought to the problem, and naïvely took it for granted. There was no argument over the questionable theory of *Volksgeist*; it was assumed that one and the same law resided in the breast of the doomsmen and in ancient tradition; that the doomsmen found in their memory what the ancients had created; that they therefore were testifying to good and true tradition, and that this tradition, in spite of all possible obscuration, lived on without perishing. Through this mingling of the sense of legality with tradition, the good law and the old law were merged as the good old law.

The association of law with a mythical law-giver seems to contradict our assertion that law is unenacted and unwritten, but the contradiction is only apparent. For the law-giver is thought of not so much as an arbitrary law-maker as rather a specially strong and clear revealer of the True and the Good. God is the only law-giver in the fullest sense of the term. The law reveals itself, so to speak, in the wise rulers of early times. Even they do not create it; they bring it into day-light, and put men under its dominion. Even they, like all men in authority, are under, not above, the law. But because they are in some sense prophets or heroes, they surpass the mass of humans in their closeness to God, and as they possess superhuman powers, they themselves may well be venerated as makers of law. Our statement that the law is not enacted by the wits or will of men, is confirmed rather than contradicted by this belief. Moreover, the law of the mythical law-giver was not even written; on the contrary it was exceedingly plastic and ill-defined; all that is good had a place in it; all that is bad was a later deviation from it and a corruption of it, and must be removed.

On the other hand, law was recorded even in the Middle Ages. There was no written law, but there was recorded law. This fact requires careful consideration; for at this point, we stand at the historical dividing-line between customary law and statute law.

Sooner or later, some piece or other of law will be recorded, as an aid to memory in doubtful cases, in order to stabilize tradition and to keep it unambiguous. The possessor of a subjective right, as we should call it, may, for example, have his right corroborated by the *publica fides* of the ruler or of a notary. The community may solemnly and officially put into writing some of its legal rules, so that they may be accurately preserved for posterity. Or some private person may on his own initiative write down what he knows of "objective law"—to use a strictly modern term, where mediaeval people would have spoken simply of the "good old law." These are the three forms of law-recording known to the Middle Ages: charters, folk-right (i.e., the authentic law of some community), and law-books; three sources of different quality, but in the mediaeval estimate not of such widely different quality as they must seem to us.

All these recorded portions of the law are, of course, surrounded by and subordinate to the living legal sense of the community, or the law transmitted by word of mouth, and this alone contains the whole of the law. The recorded law is not statute law (apart from private contractual law, which naturally was fixed then as now by the will of the contracting parties), but is simply recorded customary law, as we call it; and it is never more than a fragment of the whole law which lives exclusively in the breast or conscience of the community.

The character of modern statute law is very different. Modern statute law, by its very nature, must be written law, for the whole of the law is contained in the verbally defined commands of authority.   It is a code, which makes claim to systematic completeness, and consequently anything outside this fixed law which is still to be law must somehow be deducible from this code.   Even the living evolution of law out of the legal sense of the community—for example, the decisions of our high-court judges—is formally and technically only possible in so far as the constitution, or legal code, sets up an authority empowered within limits to interpret the law.   In this way, all legal development is brought under the heading of the application and particularization of the law.

The contrast between customary law and enacted law may be summarized thus: in the latter, the whole law is comprised in a written code; in the former, it lies in the living legal sense of the people.   Recorded customary law is, therefore, never more than a fragment of the whole law.   We shall now consider the effect of this difference upon mediaeval legal practice.

§4.   OLD LAW BREAKS NEW LAW

With us, new positive law naturally overrides older law. That is the reason for and purpose of its enactment.   It would be a mockery if the older law, vested with the sanctity of greater goodness, were to claim to exist in spite of the more recent enactment.   The mediaeval principle would for us be as nonsensical as for my ancestor to inherit from me. But a mediaeval man would use a different comparison, and say that when old law overrides recent law, a stripling gives way to a venerable old man; or rather, the intruder gives way when the lawful possessor returns home.

It is, of course, possible, even in modern circumstances, for a new law to contain a legal error; in that case still another new positive law will be made, a third law which restores the first one.   But in all these three cases, the valid law is that which is for the time being enacted by the State. According to mediaeval ideas, on the contrary, the first law simply continues to exist whilst obscured by the second, and is restored again with the third enactment.

What, in general, does " older law " mean?   Under the

dominance of unwritten custom, it is for the most part not possible to establish the age of a law in the same way as it is in the case of codified, dated, statute law. When law is called " old, " it is rather a description of its high quality than a strict determination of its age. The law which is held to be better, is, until proof to the contrary arises, always declared to be the older. Numerous instances of this exist, and one has already been cited from the *Sachsenspiegel*.[2] On other occasions, the law of a recently deceased and unpopular monarch is contrasted with the ideal law of a mythical law-giver, is revoked as being new and bad law, and the law of the mythical law-giver is restored. But if the latter should conflict with certain desirable innovations, then the law of the mythical law-giver is represented as being perhaps obscured and perverted by a corrupt tradition, and therefore capable of improvement. In short, so far as possible, everything, without open violation of legal theory, is done to serve the practical needs of the moment.[3] In any event, the attribute of venerable age is always claimed wherever possible for the law which it is desired to have.

It was particularly easy to bring the awkward theory that the old law overrides the new into harmony with the fact that even the Middle Ages in practice needed new law, if neither the " old " nor the " new " law was dated with certainty. There were, nevertheless, some difficult cases; but even these were mastered by practical needs, which were never allowed to be completely fettered by theoretical considerations.

In the year 819, for example, in a question of marriage-law the Franks detected disagreement between the rules of customary law and those laid down in the *Lex Salica*. Were they to repudiate and reverse the current usage as an evil

---

[2] *V. supra*, p. 150.

[3] An example of this is Henry I's declaration in 1100: " Omnes malas consuetudines quibus regnum Angliae iniuste opprimebatur, inde aufero ... Legem Edwardi regis vobis reddo cum illis emendationibus quibus pater meus eam emendavit consilio baronum suorum." The laws of Edward the Confessor, i.e., the good customs of the Anglo-Saxon period, are to be restored with the addition of the amendments or " improvements " made by the Normans.

innovation in view of the express testimony of the ancient folk-law, which was the law of their fathers? On the contrary, the Franks simply decided that the marriage-custom was to be treated " as our forbears have treated it heretofore, " and " not as it stands written in the *Lex Salica*. " We might, perhaps, suppose that the basis of this decision is the rule that customary law breaks enacted law. But this explanation is not necessarily the right one. That legal principle, it is true, was characteristic of the period which stands historically and logically intermediate between pure mediaeval customary law and pure modern enacted law. In later modern law, the principle is nonsensical, because customary law has become theoretically a part and parcel of enacted law, and prevails only within the limits imposed by enactment. In early mediaeval law, on the other hand, such a principle was inconceivable, because enacted law was nothing but recorded customary law.

But even if the *Lex Salica* were not regarded as enacted law, it would seem that being old and recorded law, it ought to override less ancient and unrecorded law. The Franks, however, apparently did not look at it in this way. They perceived no conflict between the unfettered legal feeling of their own day and the recorded custom of their forbears. An ancient custom, actual and conscious in a living tradition, triumphs over a " dead " Latin record, over a written legal dictum which the Franks of 819 may have conceived to have been introduced into the *Lex Salica*—God alone knew how—perhaps as a result of a slip in writing, of interpolation, or possibly of a wrongful custom adopted by the author of the *Lex Salica*, who might err, in so far as he did not follow divine inspiration. It seems, at any rate, that practice knew how to find a way out, without violating theory.

But such an evasion was more difficult when the recorded law had a more authentic character than folk-law, as was true in the case of royal charters. Here theory was in fact at times master over practice.

It was impossible to set aside an ancient royal charter which was unexpectedly brought forward, provided that its authenticity was unquestionable. Even if it lay like a block in the path of current legal practice, and controverted already well-established legal facts, still it was law and remained law, and destroyed the validity of later royal charters in which the earlier charter was not expressly excepted. Think, for example, what mediaeval princes from King Pipin onwards decreed and conceded, in the belief that they must restore the good old law, when they were confronted with documents like the Donation of Constantine!

Here a distinction must be made between legal rules concerned with the affairs of individuals, e.g., the right to possess a field, and those concerned with the affairs of all or at any rate a large number of people, e.g., the rules of inheritance or services due to the ruler. In cases of the first type, the legal position can be changed contractually; in cases of the second type, the legal position, according to mediaeval theory, is unalterable, though in practice the community freely determines what is right. Royal charters produced in litigation were almost always such as interested parties brought forward. In such cases an older charter overrides a more recent one, unless the later charter expressly states that it is issued with knowledge of the earlier grant. One cause of this was the lack of any proper registration of royal grants; the ruler issued charters with *publica fides*, but he was very much less reliable than a modern land-registry, and consequently it was comparatively easy to obtain a charter from him surreptitiously under insufficient and partial knowledge of the facts. Where a legal relationship was altered by agreement, therefore, the interested party had to secure himself against the contingency that a royal charter existed concerning the previous legal position—and who could know that such a charter did not exist and might not be discovered?—by procuring a royal charter which expressly revoked any older charters to the contrary. Even then there was no unqualified guarantee that the king, in granting his charter, was fully cognisant of the facts; grounds might still be adduced to prove the legal validity of the position testified to by an old charter as against that testified to by a more recent charter. But the value of a more recent charter would be hopelessly compromised if it omitted to revoke older charters, and any new right is quite valueless if there is no documentary support for the new legal position, when there is an authentic charter witnessing to an older legal position, which must then be accepted as being what ought to be. But where ancient and more recent charters conflict, the maxim holds good: *ut praecepta facta, quae anteriora essent, firmiora et stabiliora essent.*

Such situations reveal one of the chief weaknesses in mediaeval legal life: its gross insecurity, its groping in the fog, as soon as an ancient charter comes to light—often resulting in rage, contempt, and openly-expressed suspicion on the side of the aggrieved party. Here we touch upon the domain of the mediaeval forger. It is clear enough from what we have now said, why mediaeval forgers foisted their fabrications on the oldest possible monarchs; not only because it was more difficult to devise tests of authenticity for very ancient charters, but also because the older a charter appeared to be, the stronger and more secure from nullification it was. Hence forgers went back as far as Constantine and Caesar.

Hitherto we have distinguished, for reasons of practical convenience, between charters which concern only particular rights and those which concern general law. This distinction must now be abandoned, for it is quite unmediaeval. For the Middle Ages, there was no distinction between objective and subjective law; every stone of the legal edifice, of the objective law as the sum-total of all subjective rights, was equally sacred and valuable, according to the lofty theories of the period. The small-holding of the bondsman as much as the boundary-stone of the realm; the goods of the merchant as much as the judicial system of the people— all are equally sacred and valuable. But that was not all. " Private persons, " as we should say, when they obtained charters from the Crown, showed a particular preference for acquiring rights of a general character, or what we should call public rights.

Supposing such a charter, genuine or false, came to light, and was found to conflict with the actual public law (as we should say) of the period in which it was brought forward, then a difficult question arose: could it be set aside as a forgery, because of this conflict? Or could the return to the conditions set out in the re-discovered charter be restricted to the grantee himself, without disturbing the general legal position? Or must it really be given general retrospective effect? Here, in matters of general concern, considerations of politics, power, and opportunity naturally often decided the attitude adopted towards the charter. As an example, it is sufficient to recall the Austrian *Privilegium Majus*, the true basis of which was not its justification in law, but the power of the House of Hapsburg.[4] But the general principle with which we started, that older law breaks the more recent law, was never contested, and could, indeed, be as little denied as the statements that good is good, and bad is bad. Now from this there follows another principle:

§5. LEGAL INNOVATION IS RESTORATION OF THE GOOD OLD LAW

Let us for a moment consider the mediaeval outlook as a whole. It knew nothing of the idea of progress, of growth and development; it did not regard human affairs biologically (in spite of the metaphor of the body politic inherited from antiquity), but as being morphologically fixed. It knew only a static, graded existence. Timeless fixity, not the process of Becoming, but What Should Be, ruled its conception of human life. This assumption of educated thought in the Middle Ages was easily combined with popular

---

[4] The forgery of this and other charters was, as is well known, the duke of Austria's answer to the Golden Bull of 1356, which excluded the Hapsburgs from the ranks of the imperial electors. The *privilegium maius* emphasized Austrian independence, and by claiming the novel title " palatinus archidux," Rudolf IV implied that he possessed a rank higher than that of the electoral princes, while at the same time he laid claim to every right which the Golden Bull had conferred on the electors. The Emperor Charles IV was not deceived by the five charters brought forward by Rudolf—they included one attributed to Nero and another attributed to Julius Caesar—but in view of the political strength of Austria, the *privilegium maius* was accepted as a genuine charter, granted by Frederick I in 1156. The forger had, in fact, based his fabrication on the so-called *privilegium minus* of that date, but this also, it has been shown, is not free from interpolations. The text of the two documents should be compared; cf. *MGH., Const.*, I (1893), nos. 159 and 455.

Germanic custom, which accepted law as old and lasting, as static and to be preserved in its fixity. Popular Germanic tradition and the moral culture propagated by the Church combined to create a fixed, defensive, unprogressive idea of law, based on a changeless eternity.

Yet even in the Middle Ages, life constantly created fresh facts and situations; and since these new departures had to be brought into line with the current idea of unchangeable law, change and innovation in law were possible, and, indeed, necessary, provided that they took the form of real or alleged restoration. Neither upheaval nor development, but continual revelation, clarification, or purification of the true law, which is always struggling against wrong, obscurity, misunderstanding, and forgetfulness—neither evolution nor revolution, but reformation—that is the mediaeval principle.

If a law has become ambiguous or obscure, the doomsmen do not declare what ought to be established as law, but find in their wisdom or conscience what has always been right and consequently continues to be right. They may make a mistake, and actually declare a law that has never existed before. Indeed, they may even be aware that they have made an innovation. But they do not say so, and they cannot say so. They can no more say that they have created new law than a modern legislator can say that he has established a law out of self-seeking wilfulness, class-spirit, or the like. For even if the Middle Ages actually made new law every day, mediaeval ideas forced them to assert that the reasonable, equitable law is also the old law. The " first application of a law " is therefore never spoken of in those words in the Middle Ages. It is true that mediaeval law-givers, to quote *Saxo Grammaticus*, often deliberately " destroyed bad laws and granted new ones. " But they were not, in their view, replacing one positive law by another positive law; rather were they guiding the stream of genuine law back into channels which had been temporarily blocked by wrong. The typical expression for mediaeval legislative procedure is " *legem emendare*, " to free the law from its defects. Right and law are restored as they had been in the good old days of King Eric (in Sweden), of Edward the Confessor (in Anglo-Norman England), of Charles the Great (among the French and Germans), or of some mythical law-giver.

In public affairs, however, cases were more frequent than in what we should call private law, where older law could be neither brought forward nor pre-supposed. But even so, it scarcely ever happened, before the period of the " Reception " of Roman law, that doomsmen openly stated that owing to lack of legal rules, they had taken a decision in accordance with their own free-will. So unmediaeval a formula points to the existence of a learned jurisprudence. There were, indeed, certain instances of the creation of new rights that were tolerated even by mediaeval ideas; the monarch can freely bestow privileges, so long as no one thereby suffers wrong. He can, for example, make grants from his own possessions, so long as the community does not thereby suffer. The objective law is conceived of as a gigantic skein of interdependent subjective rights, none of which may be set aside, except by free agreement or by forfeiture. But when there are vacant spaces between existing rights, free-will may enter in and fasten new threads. But this obvious fact did not destroy the general principle that where a right is in dispute, the good old custom and not the arbitrary will of any living person must be authoritative. Through the idea of the restoration of good old law, mediaeval society won in general sufficient freedom for its need to expand existing law in harmony with the legal ideas current at any particular moment. They reformed, in theory, by returning to the past, and in this they had a free hand, in so far as recorded rights and privileges did not form a barrier and block the development of objective law.

§6. LEGAL CONCEPTS AND LEGAL PRACTICE

We have already had to consider the relations between legal concepts and legal practice, and cannot attempt to deal here fully with this large and difficult subject. Only two observations remain to be added.

Had mediaeval folk-right been recorded in any degree of

completeness, had it been preserved and referred to, and had the written version been accepted as authentic, we have seen enough to realize that the free development of customary law would then have been stopped and changed into a rigid and highly reactionary fixity.   For the decree of King Pipin for Italy, to the effect that a law once promulgated must never again be replaced by custom, was theoretically valid, although not so explicitly stated elsewhere, for all recorded folk-law and royal law.   It is true, of course, that customary law, if written down completely, and accepted literally, would have been reduced to absurdity by the extreme rigidity which would have ensued; or, in other words, customary law would then have necessarily been treated as statute law, and have been transformed into statute law.   The theory of codified law, and its defeat by more recent codified law, would have inevitably grown.   But the development of such a theory was unnecessary, even where folk-law was set down in writing, because recorded law in the Middle Ages was always deemed to be merely a part of the all-embracing customary law, a fragment and not a complete codification.   Statutes, capitularies, and so on, regularly point to the unwritten customary law as the criterion to be followed.

But here we must again distinguish, for practical reasons —though the Middle Ages made no such distinction in theory—between the development of objective law and the treatment of subjective rights.   The typical mediaeval instrument for the discovery or revelation of objective law is the abstract judgment of the doom.   Often it is created, without any real historical or documentary research, out of the memory and legal feeling of lawful and credible men. It often broadens the law unconsciously or tacitly, in so far as the lawmen in reality judge more according to their own reason than according to a perhaps obsolete or forgotten tradition.   On the other hand, where the doom or its equivalent was recorded and so remained unforgotten, it could bind the law more rigidly, and could hold it in ancient grooves longer than modern codified law.   For, unlike the latter, it could never be formally superseded.   Obsolete statute law can easily be set aside by new statute, if only the legislator is really convinced of its obsolescence. In the Middle Ages, there was no such method of getting rid of stale traditional law. It was not possible to declare :

> The trees are old: we must fell the wood,
> And plant new trees where old trees stood.

But, instead, the Middle Ages were marked by negligence in the preservation, handing down, and evaluation of recorded legal rules, and were consequently in practice often able to circumvent a law no longer suited to the times.

Legal innovation and legal fixity can both be useful and harmful ; we can observe in practice, even in the Middle Ages, the eternal struggle between the two tendencies. But there is also a second struggle bound up with the first, a struggle which we to-day, under the dominance of statute law, need not worry about any more—the struggle for legal permanence, for adherence to tradition, for the continuity of law. The more the legal circle expands beyond the neighbourhood and village community, the less can mere memory be relied upon. In Scandinavia (only there) the custom existed of declaring the law by word of mouth at set intervals, in order to fix it. Written records of custom compiled by expert lawmen performed a similar service, and although it could never have been made the duty of lawmen to memorize these writings, they commended themselves to the masses because of their reliability and comprehensiveness, and their comparatively systematic form. It is well-known that law-books of the thirteenth century and the later Middle Ages performed such a service. Even these private compilations of customary law could, for want of authoritative codified law, acquire the position of codes, and not only assist in the preservation of law, but also contribute unintentionally to the development of the law. Thanks to respect for the authors, such law-books came to be regarded as true store-houses of good old law, in the same sense as even the written laws of kings and people were in theory only confirmations, not creations of law.

But now the main point must be considered. For us such

trouble to preserve the law would in every case be laudable and profitable. It would not affect the problem of legal rigidity or legal change, because it would simply imply the handing down of the existing law, without touching the question what the law ought to be. In the Middle Ages, on the other hand, the law that is was regarded as identical with the law that ought to be. Any effort to secure the permanence of the law in the Middle Ages implied therefore at the same time a bias towards legal fixity, and as is now clear, unbroken continuity would portend a complete exclusion of legal change. Therefore, negligence in maintaining the law, which in the Middle Ages defeated the attempt to secure complete permanence, was a necessary evil, a necessary outlet for legal development. The negligence characteristic of the Middle Ages calmly ignored even the written law; passages in law-books were forgotten; legal rules, such as the example we have cited from the *Lex Salica*, were thrown over; charters were declared not genuine or were set aside by later charters, if development could not otherwise find an outlet.

So much for objective law. In the sphere of subjective law, on the other hand, the mediaeval combination of theory and practice at first resulted in conspicuous legal insecurity, which in spite of many advantages in individual cases, nevertheless made the transition to modern legal theory seem a decisive advance.

Not that private rights were of minor importance as compared with the public legal order. On the contrary, the lack of differentiation between objective and subjective, or public and private law, vested even the pettiest legal claim of an individual with the sanctity of the common inviolable legal order, in which no little stone can be loosened without the whole structure tottering. The moral tone of the Middle Ages scorned considerations of expediency, and always took right and wrong seriously, no matter how big or small the question at issue. So the mediaeval theory of law necessarily put subjective rights on a more secure footing than any other legal theories. But in this respect, as so often in the Middle Ages, the ideal was wrecked by inadequate technical equipment. Even legal security, so well-established in theory, inviolable for great and small, for the State and private person alike, was, for lack of legal fixity, in practice something quite different.

Here also, as in the case of objective law, what was decisive in practice was the scantiness and haphazardness of written record; the lack of systematic and full law-books, the varying knowledge and reluctant use of recorded law by succeeding generations; the want of registered charters and deeds, the non-existence of learned judges and legislators. Here again, subjective rights were strongest within the narrow limits of the immediate neighbourhood, and within the period of the events which gave them birth. The preservation of subjective rights became more difficult the more distant they were in space and time. Only the interested parties themselves, the possessors of subjective rights, concerned themselves, from their own narrow point of view, about the permanence of the law; only they took action about it, but their interests were naturally one-sided, and if, on the one hand, they maintained the law, on the other, they twisted it to their own ends. Only they created archives to to preserve the charters which contained their subjective rights, and impartial archives with public access, by means of which private archives might have been.controlled, did not exist in most places. The duty of the State to maintain equal justice for all was loudly proclaimed; the scholastics praised the *justitia distributiva* of the monarch; but in practice he had no means of determining impartially and exactly what every man's rights were. In practice he was forced to rely upon the *justitia commutativa* of private persons, always suspected of partiality. The most educated, the technically best equipped private parties were always the religious houses, churches and monasteries; these possessed archives, chartularies, and so on, and they made provision for the highest measure of legal security attainable in their time. At the same time, owing to the want of criteria of authenticity, and the technical helplessness of the public authorities, it was they who the most often and most easily obtained fabricated rights, by forging charters of earlier kings. The temptation to forgery, however, was very great not merely because control was almost precluded and success was as good as certain to skilful workers. On the contrary, we must concede the *pia fraus* some extenuation precisely because of the lack of established law. I am convinced that many a monk who fabricated charters for his house—to say nothing of great forgers like Pseudo-Isidore—thought he had won himself a place in Heaven. Was it not, so to speak, clear and evident from reason, justice, tacit or admitted tradition, and so on, that a particular field could not belong to the evil steward, because after all its very shape indicated that it " must " have originally belonged to the adjoining cloister garth? Was it not clear that Constantine, when he went to New Rome, " must " have appointed the Pope in Old Rome as his heir? Was not the constitution of the Church in the ninth century an intolerably misshapen thing as compared with the purer form that " must " have existed in the ancient Church? To be sure, written documents for all these things are lacking; centuries-old wrong has entrenched itself, and can be successfully challenged and defeated by the more ancient and unageing right, only if the old true law can bring evidence into the arena. But is it not pure chance whether or not such evidence still exists? Might it not have been destroyed by the burning brands of the Normans a hundred years ago? Might not some forbears, through negligence, have omitted to obtain or preserve it? Might not, finally, some earlier forger belonging to the opposite party have used his talents to supplant right, and make wrong triumph? And so the decision is taken to help truth and right to victory by a new forgery. The accidents of tradition are corrected, and the true legal situation is restored; by creating evidence, the forger re-creates the law itself. Thus two armies of skilful forgers are at work, secretly undermining each other's position, and yet with a good conscience on both sides; they repair the gaps in tradition in the only legally effective way. They do not talk about their activities, but their conscience is easy. If Pseudo-Isidore restored the law of the Church as in his view it " must " have been,

and if that field of which we spoke was won back for the
monastery, then the skilled exponent of the use of charters
could rejoice in a bloodless and truly lawful victory, and we
may believe that absolution was not made too hard for him.
The legal instability of the Middle Ages was an all too
obvious and attractive instigation to forgery.

So much for the motives of the mediaeval forger, which
we cannot understand without an intimate knowledge of
mediaeval legal ideas. The whole preceding discussion
serves in some measure to explain the extreme frequency of
forgery; it shows why the water with which the Church
cooked was not always clean. At the same time, it is undeniable that even in the Middle Ages these means were felt
to be questionable and suspicious. Only where the aim was
good or holy, and not merely a personal interest; only where
the conditions restored by the forgery were commonly
recognized to have existed previously, could such proceedings be justified in the sense we have explained.

Apart from forgeries, the immense number of charters of
confirmation in the Middle Ages reveal a certain disturbance
of legal conditions.

It is usual to explain the custom of confirmation by the
fact that the Middle Ages had no idea of a government
independent of the person of the ruler, and consequently
placed great importance upon the personal binding of every
new monarch. But we shall see later, when we come to
discuss the Constitution, that the monarch, though he did
not grant charters in the name of an impersonal State,
nevertheless did grant them in the name of the community
and the impersonal, imperishable law. The custom of
confirmation is, therefore, not explicable on the basis of any
general constitutional ideas, and we must turn to practice,
or the technique of mediaeval legal procedure, in order to
explain it.

Every monarch was constitutionally bound by his own
earlier royal acts as well as by the lawful governmental acts
of all his predecessors. Had the mediaeval State possessed
a good official register in which superseded charters were
cancelled, and all valid charters were open to inspection,

then the Middle Ages would not have needed to have a single charter confirmed. Confirmations were simply technical aids to obtain legal security, precautions, alarm signals against legal insecurity. Anyone who possessed rights authenticated by charter always lived in the expectation that opposing interests might suddenly bring forward a royal charter granting the contrary. The older charter was, of course, the better, if the subsequent diploma did not expressly abrogate it. But how lightly was the matter often decided in mediaeval chanceries, because of favouritism or superficial knowledge! The means of declaring law were defective, and the granting of charters part of this defective declaration of law. Notwithstanding the loftiness of legal theory, technique was weak. There was thus always the possibility that the good old royal charter which testified to one's rights might be defeated by opponents with a new royal charter, perhaps obtained surreptitiously, perhaps free from any vice, and perhaps even containing the express revocation of one's own charter. What guarantee was there that at any moment opponents might not " discover " an old charter which the reigning monarch would then confirm in good faith? In short, there was only one comparatively safe recourse in the potentially dangerous jungle of mediaeval legal confusion: to procure without delay a confirmation of one's subjective rights from every new monarch. Then for the duration of his life-time one was comparatively secure against undesirable incidents. The king had bound himself personally, and this undertaking could not be easily evaded by him. Security had not been obtained against unconstitutional and arbitrary revocation by the monarch of his predecessors' acts; but one was secure against his inability in practice to perceive at all times what actually were the rights which it was his royal vocation and duty to protect. Security had been obtained against the eventuality that the king might accept and act upon evidence brought forward by opponents which he was in no position to test and examine. Moreover, it was useful to possess, besides ancient charters which guaranteed the venerable age and high quality of the rights concerned, new charters granting the same rights. The confirming authorities had in practice a justified suspicion of old charters, because proof of their genuineness was so much more difficult, and perhaps still more because the legal relations of some past period could undergo so many alterations during the intervening period—a fact which made it very doubtful, if the chancery took its work seriously, whether confirmation was just and reasonable. Interested parties thus had every motive to add a new link to the chain of confirmatory charters every successive reign. A monarch was often asked to confirm his own charters—in the case of the German king, for example, after he became Emperor; not because he took on a new legal personality and put off the old one at his imperial coronation, and was no longer bound by his earlier royal acts, but because the royal chancery was often quite unable to determine whether or not it had issued a particular charter, even in the case of a diploma of the living ruler; and so under certain circumstances it might be awkward if one had only a charter of King Henry in the muniment-chest, whilst opponents had one issued by Emperor Henry. Double stitch holds better.

Thus the custom of confirmation is explained, on the one hand, by the exceptional value of royal charters in litigation, as contrasted with the vagueness of customary law; they were, so to speak, the solitary firm pillar of legal tradition. On the one hand, it is explained also by the unsatisfactory nature of the administrative machinery, which meant that it was left to the interested parties to preserve their charters, which were the principal evidence in litigation. The chancery fees that were exacted for the constantly-repeated confirmations, were insurance premiums not against any constitutional danger to particular private rights (such a danger, as we have remarked, hardly arose from a change of ruler), but against technical legal dangers arising not from absolutism but from the chaos prevailing in royal chanceries.

How the monarch himself suffered in major constitutional questions from the fluctuating conditions arising from technical incapacity to ensure legal continuity, cannot be discussed here.[5] This legal instability is in some places and times so great that it has sometimes been denied that mediaeval public life was in any way legal in character, and it is asserted instead that it was no more than a chaos in which force predominated—this of the Middle Ages, when politics as well as law were more firmly anchored in the eternal basis of morality than at any other period before or since! Here also the decisive fact in practice is the technical incapacity to transform the ideal into reality; and for this very reason the modern period, although it no longer attributes the same theoretical sanctity to law, secures for it much greater practical respect because its law is more effective and better preserved. If Barbarossa was called upon by the pope to act as marshall—certainly an important issue in the relations of Empire and Papacy—what means had he of deciding whether this claim was justified? Chance verbal traditions, the memory of the Emperor's companions on previous expeditions to Rome, and in the second place, charters which the pope, his opponent, produced against him: these were his only means. Hence it is understandable that the prince resisted such demands, and was still disposed to contest the credibility of the pope's alleged " right, " even if he submitted to it on political grounds. And yet the destruction of subjective rights that a monarch suffered in such a case, because he had no charters to bring forward against those of his opponents, was still more easily suffered by his own subjects.

The more prudent, therefore, the mediaeval possessor of rights was, the more he was intent on obtaining not only confirmations, but also as full a collection of charters as possible. As a precaution all possible rights were put into writing, not only separate rights but general ones also, and those which we should describe as public in character.

I quote here the apt words of STEINACKER: " The power

---

[5] In this connexion, such questions would have to be considered as why important laws and treaties, like the Concordat of Worms or the Golden Bull, were so infrequently carried out; why only the interested parties drew attention to them and asked for their execution, and so on. But it is better to reserve this aspect of the matter for a study, not of mediaeval law, but of mediaeval politics.

to secure and to create for the individual the subjective rights to which the general legal order gives him a claim—a power inherent in Roman and modern law—was lacking in the law of the Middle Ages. For this reason those who wrote down the law were very seldom concerned with objective law, and never with a complete and systematic codification of objective law, but rather with determining the subjective rights of individual persons. In other words, the predominant form of recorded law was the privilege. The individual had his subjective rights directly guaranteed in a charter issued by the head of the State, and this practice was not confined solely to privileges not possessed by his peers, and which therefore formed exceptions from the general legal order and were " privileges " in the true sense of the word, but was extended also to rights to which he should have been entitled without express privilege or grant, because, as the charters often specifically state, they customarily belonged to all members of a certain class, lords of manors, for example, or burghers, and so on. And the individual obtained such charters, quite without regard to whether or how they recorded the general principle, in virtue of which he among many others claimed the right which the charter specified. In fact, the privilege, the grant by charter of the subjective rights of a specific person, offered such a person relatively the greatest security, since the compilations of objective law made in the Middle Ages were always being superseded and made obsolete by the growth of new customary law.[6]

§7. TRANSITION FROM MEDIAEVAL TO MODERN CONCEPTIONS OF LAW

It still remains to sketch the transition from the mediaeval to the modern conception of law, from custom to statute; but here we can venture only some preliminary remarks.

A particularly important factor in the origin of the modern conception of law was, I believe, the technical imperfection

---

[6] H. Steinacker, *Über die Entstehung der beiden Fassungen des österreichischen Landrechtes*, Jahrbuch des Vereins für Landeskunde von Niederösterreich (1917), 261.

of mediaeval practice which has been discussed above. Practice, for example, must have led to the realization that new law defeats the old. Already in the law of the Ripuarian Franks, a naïve compromise was sought between the principle of the " good old law " and the " law that is born with us. " In case of conflict between two royal charters, the object in dispute was to be partitioned in such a way that the possessor of the older charter was to receive two-thirds and the possessor of the later charter one-third. Even in the Middle Ages, recent law constantly overrode old law in practice, although such a phenomenon could neither be admitted nor conceived of. On principle, it is only in statute law that the most recent statute is valid, just as in customary law the oldest tradition was valid. But before the principle that new law is stronger than old law could prevail, statute law had first to advance the claim to comprise the whole law, in the sense that any particular statute or code could extinguish or supersede all older law within its scope.

One instrument of transition from customary law to statute law was learned law, and here Roman law played its part. Roman law was easily absorbed into customary law, and then like a swelling kernel burst the ever-weakening husk of custom. The *Corpus Juris* is a collection of fragments, not a code of statutes. But being dead law, not living tradition, it compelled systematic study and discovery of principles. These principles, or the learned activity that led to them, welded the system of Roman law into a unity, and gave jurisprudence its character as a science for the interpretation of comprehensive statutes. But, just as the law of the Pandects became a complete system of civil law, so legal scholarship and the codification to which it led, welded other fragmentary legislation into complete systems of criminal law, procedural law, public law, and so on. Even if this modern unity of enacted law is no less a fiction than the mediaeval conception of law, still it had a decisive technical superiority, and is quite indispensable in present-day circumstances, where the law extends over an immense community. Customary law is only suited to small local communities. But it is in technical progress alone, not in progress in ideals, that the modern concept of law is superior to the mediaeval. We can observe the historical process by which customary law, fragmentary, and limited to one district, was gradually transformed into all-embracing statute law. The result was that law became both more fluid and more definite as well as more certain. Its currency grew; customary law was too inflexible, and when, in spite of its very nature, it could in fact be changed, it was too ambiguous and vague ever to be used over wide areas or for long periods.

The new conception that the law exists as a complete body in a code grew out of the need, which gradually asserted itself, to discover some means of imparting permanence and authenticity to the private, fortuitous, and fragmentary legal writings which the Middle Ages produced. But once legal scholarship or the State undertook this task, then it had set forth on the path which ended in the fiction that the written law is comprehensive, and the positive law a complete system. For the authority of legal scholarship or of the statute-books, which is considered infallible, gives an answer even where it is silent. For this reason, the State, from the very first moment when it took upon itself to promulgate law, was compelled, in theory, to promulgate a complete law, and to change the law which merely existed in the people's sense of justice into enacted law. The natural unity which resides in the general sense of justice, is in this way transformed into the artificial unity of a legal system, in virtue of the principles introduced by legal science, principles which build a bridge between codified law and the general sense of justice.

In conclusion, a glance may be cast at the way in which the mediaeval conception of law still resists the pressure of modern ideas, and is only gradually yielding exclusive dominance to them. For a simple person, in whom something of the mediaeval spirit survives, it is a strange thing that all law should exist in books, and not where God has planted it—in conscience and public opinion, in custom, and sound human understanding. The positive written law brings with it learned lawyers and scholars, cut off from the people. Although in fact statute law is more accurate and certain, unlearned persons become less and less sure what the law is. They can no longer take stock of it, and have the same suspicion of lawyers and advocates, whom they call " perverters of justice, " as they have of physicians and chemists. But if illness is sent by God, and so cannot be helped, the unintelligible laws seem to be made arbitrarily by men, or even to be taken over from the heathen Romans, and resurrected at Bologna—in lecture-rooms and folio volumes. The old peasant believes he is doing right if he cuts off at least the glosses from around the *Corpus Juris* which his student son brings home with him on his holidays.

Positive, codified law, in fact, often proves to be clumsier and less helpful than customary law. The latter quietly passes over obsolete laws, which sink into oblivion, and die peacefully, but the law itself remains young, always in the belief that it is old. Yet it is not old; rather it is a perpetual grafting of new on to old law, a fresh stream of contemporary law springing out of the creative wells of the sub-conscious, for the most part not canalized by the fixed limits of recorded law and charter. Statute law, on the other hand, cannot be freed from the letter of legal texts, until a new text has replaced an old one, even though life itself has long since condemned the old text to death; in the meantime the dead text retains power over life.

Customary law resembles the primaeval forest which, though never cut down and scarcely changing its outline, is constantly rejuvenated, and in a hundred years will be another forest altogether, though outwardly it remains the same " old " wood, in which slow growth in one part is accompanied by an unobserved decay elsewhere. The rejuvenation of positive written law, on the other hand, resembles the shock of an earthquake. When reason has become nonsense, and originally beneficent statutes have become nuisances, then sudden and deliberate change is necessary, but before that point is reached, no death of the old law is permitted. Nevertheless, the simple feeling of the people, when a particular circumstance contradicts its sense of justice, still raises the truly mediaeval question: why is what is right not also law—now, forthwith, without delay, and without legal formalities? The mediaeval idea of law is something warm-blooded, vague, confused, and impractical, technically clumsy, but creative, sublime, and suited to human needs; to that idea people gladly return, especially when the unwritten primitive laws of human conscience revolt against the cold callousness, as it seems to them, of written statute; the immemorial right of resistance, for example, persists in this way. But all this will be seen more clearly, if we now turn to the second part of our investigation—to constitutional law in the narrower sense.

II

Constitution

IN modern usage we mean by the term " Constitution " that part of the general legal order of a State which controls the powers of the government and the mutual relations between the government and the subjects. Was there a constitution in this sense in the Middle Ages? No explanation is needed of the fact that the word " constitution " is modern. But what of the thing itself?

The theory of the sovereignty of the people was not dominant in the Middle Ages. The monarch was subject to no man, but he was subject to the law. This sovereign law was, as will be understood from what has been said above, not written law. The monarch was subject not to a specific constitutional check, but to the law in general, which is all-powerful and almost boundless in its lack of definition; he is limited by this law and bound to this law. From the point of view of constitutional machinery, the control exercised in this way by the law will presumably be very incomplete and insecure—the very breadth of the mediaeval idea of law allows us to guess this. But in theory there resulted a complete control of the monarch, a subjection to law so thorough that political considerations and reason of State were excluded and out of the question. We come then to:

§1. THE PRINCIPLE OF LEGAL LIMITATION. (THE KING IS BOUND TO THE LAW)

We can name three sources for this binding of the mediaeval monarch to the law: Germanic custom, testified to as early as Tacitus; the Stoic law of nature transmitted by the Church Fathers; and the Christian idea that every ruler is God's vicar and instrument of action. The law stands over all men, even over the monarch:

Nieman ist so here, so daz reht zware.[7]

The monarch is subordinate to the law, but the people and the Church, in interpreting this principle, had in mind two different laws. Nevertheless, people and Church were one in holding that there was no special law of the State, and that the monarch was subordinate to the Law as such. Objective law as such embraced all the subjective rights of every individual within the community, or rather it was simply the sum of individual rights. Even the right in virtue of which the monarch ruled is no exception to this general principle. The ruler has his subjective right to rule, just as the meanest bondsman has his right to cultivate his clods. This unity and indivisibility of all (subjective) rights in the objective law is the decisive element in mediaeval constitutional thought, as we shall see later in the discussion of fundamental law. Here let us keep primarily in view the fact that there is no special public law, no differentiation of public from private right. Unless we bear in mind the indivisibility of subjective and objective law, as well as of private and public law in the Middle Ages, we shall never be able to understand what the mediaeval constitution was, nor how it is related to the modern.

With us, law is partly dependent upon and conditioned by policy. The State establishes as law what it needs for its life, and this law of the State overrides private rights. We are reconciled to this, provided that this law of the State is governed by necessity, and is not dictated by arbitrary will; and as guarantee for that, we demand that it shall not be made by an individual at his caprice and pleasure, but by the representatives of the community. But the Middle Ages, with their purely conservative idea of law, with their rejection of politics, their fusion of law and morals, and of ideal and positive law, could not recognize at all any law of the State which modified or destroyed these private rights. The limitation imposed by law on the autocratic mediaeval prince or administrator is, in theory, very much greater than in the modern State, greater even than that to which the constitutionally limited monarch or president has to submit.

[7] No one is so much lord that he may coerce the law.

For the latter can establish new law in conjunction with the other supreme constitutional organs, but the mediaeval monarch existed for the purpose of applying and protecting the good old law in the strictest imaginable sense. It was to serve the good old law that he was set up; that was his *justitia*, and the maintenance of every individual's subjective rights, of the *suum cuique*, was the source of the *pax*, the peace at home, which was the primary and almost exclusive aim of domestic government. The preservation of the law in the broadest and most conservative sense, also guaranteed the ruler security in his dominion; for the sanctity of the rights of all members of the " folk " down to the clod of the meanest bondsman, also secured the ruler's own right to rule.

At his accession, the mediaeval monarch took a vow to the law, and personally bound himself to the law. The beginnings of the modern constitutional oath lie in this coronation oath. Anyone who wished to write the history of the origins of written constitutions, would have to take this self-binding of the mediaeval king as the starting-point,[8] for it is an explicit binding of the government to the law which is its superior.

Now it is true that, along with the remains of ancient culture, mediaeval culture took over certain dicta and maxims which derived from the completely contrary ideas of Roman imperial absolutism. But here mediaeval learning made use of the methods which it already possessed, to neutralize unpalatable fragments of ancient tradition. The art of interpretation rendered the text " *princeps legibus absolutus* " harmless. Legal maxims handed down from antiquity, in which government was treated as above and not below the law, were so frequently .interpreted as moral precepts that even here the law seemed to retain the upper hand over the government. The *rex* is called *animata lex*, but this does not mean that the law is the monarch's pleasure, but that the monarch has absorbed the law into his will. In canon law also, the statement that all law is in the pope's

[8] Cf. Schmidt, *Vorgeschichte der geschriebenen Verfassungen* (Leipzig, 1916).

bosom meant not that the pope was absolute but that there was a legal presumption that papal decrees were issued in knowledge of and in harmony with the older canon law. In general, the absolutist formulae of Roman law should not be taken too seriously, especially in view of the fact that, as we shall see later in the section on the monarch's duty of obtaining consent, the Middle Ages did not attribute the character of absolutism to proceedings which seem to us to be absolute, owing to defects in the technique of popular representation. Later on, a time came when absolutist forms were accompanied by an absolutist spirit; but that was the end of both mediaeval political and legal ideas.

The lack of differentiation between ideal and positive law, which we have already discussed, enabled the Middle Ages to avoid too rigid a bondage to traditional law. Might not tradition be an abuse? In this respect, the Church in particular loosened the bonds which bound the government to folk-law. Even in the eyes of the Church, government was subordinate to the law, but only by grace was it subordinate to the law enacted by the State itself. For the Church, the monarch was bound to equity rather than positive law; equity is the " law " to which he is bound without reserve. Consequently, when positive law contains something inequitable, it is not law, and the ruler is obliged not to maintain it, but to set it aside.

The notion that the decrees of mediaeval monarchs were valid only during their own reign is completely false. Royal acts known to be unlawful will be revoked, whether they are ancient or recent. Acts admittedly lawful, on the other hand, have the force of law quite independently of any change of ruler; indeed, the older they are, the more sacred.

It is here, as a rule, that the modern historian's difficulties with regard to the peculiarities of the mediaeval constitution arise, unless he starts from the mediaeval conception of law. We have said that the Middle Ages knew no genuine legislation by the State. The ordinances or laws of the State aim only at the restoration and execution of valid folk- or customary law. The law pursues its own sovereign life. The State does not encroach upon that. It merely protects its existence from outside when necessary. Whole centuries elapse without the smallest signs of legislative or ordaining activity in our sense. The mediaeval conception of law explains this phenomenon,.just as it also comprises the question of fundamental law or the rights of man. For this reason, let us recapitulate what we have already said.

There is no public or constitutional law. The objective law is nothing but the sum or combination of all the subjective rights of the people. The law is prior to and above the State. The whole conception of the State or of magistracy depends on this: the State is, so to speak, the loser by the mediaeval conception of law. For the monarch is not above but below the law, to which he is answerable like every other member of the community, but unlike them he alone is responsible for the rights of all and for all rights. This sounds fine in theory, and seems to secure the rights of individuals better than any other constitutional arrangement; but once again the technical execution is defective, and this meant that the merit of the system, the protection of private rights, is less conspicuous in reality than its demerit—the fatal muzzling of the power of the State. For, since the sole aim of the State according to Germanic ideas is to preserve existing law or existing rights, and, according to ecclesiastical ideas, to carry out the divine commands, the State is prohibited from adapting its actions to its own needs, and from adapting the law of the community and private rights to meet its necessities, as modern constitutional law allows it to do. The mediaeval State, as a mere institution for the preservation of the law, is not allowed to interfere for the benefit of the community with private rights. A unilateral decree imposed by the State is possible only in the case of rightless persons, those, for example, defeated in war, or outlaws. Otherwise, all private rights of individuals against the State are, as later adherents of natural law would say, fundamental rights, none of which can be set aside by new law enacted by the State. The government had to preserve every subjective right of every individual, for the sum total of these subjective rights constituted the objective law, of which even the rights of the magistracy or the State itself formed a part. The State itself had no rights *sui generis*. It can, for example, raise no taxes, for according to the mediaeval view, taxation is a sequestration of property. The State therefore can accomplish this attack on private rights only with the free consent of all concerned (or at least of their representatives). Hence mediaeval taxation is a " gracious aid, " and the State or the monarch has an unquestionable right to a tax only when it has become traditional. The rights to property possessed by every individual member of the community are an absolutely sacred part of the whole absolutely sacred legal order; the criterion of the rights in property of the individual as well as of the State is the good old law.

From this example, we can readily understand why the Middle Ages neither could nor needed to single out any specially fundamental rights. For all subjective rights were, as we should say, fundamental and protected by the constitution, and were untouchably hedged around by the law. Special, distinct fundamental rights become necessary only when a separate constitutional law has been created and stands sovereign over private rights. Only the activities of the absolutist States which succeeded the mediaeval and representative States, and which ruthlessly encroached upon private rights, explain the demand for constitutionally protected fundamental rights and the Rights of Man, i.e., the demand for the recognition of certain limitations upon the sovereignty of the State in its interference with private rights. In the Middle Ages, there was, as should be clear from what has been said, no need for any separation of fundamental rights into a distinct category. It is also now clear why only the State, not the private person, was the loser by the mediaeval omission to distinguish public from private rights, law from morals, positive from ideal law. No place was left for reason of State or policy, and so the government was not free to act in accordance with its own needs. In practice, of course, the individual also suffered; but the first consequence was that the competence of the State was in theory restricted, and this in turn reacted profoundly upon practical life.

The technical deficiencies of the mediaeval constitution, notwithstanding its lofty ideals, can only be discussed in the following sections, where we come to the questions of popular representation and the sanctions of the constitution. Here where we are primarily concerned with the principles of the mediaeval constitution, only one practical expedient for putting the constitutional ideas of the period into effect has come to our notice: the monarch's oath at his accession. How little guarantee this oath provided in reality for the fulfilment of mediaeval constitutional theory, is obvious.

But how, then, was it determined whether the monarch's actions were in harmony with the law, or, as we should say, whether or not he was acting constitutionally? This was infinitely more difficult to ascertain with regard to the unwritten, fluid, good old law, than it is with regard to modern written constitutional law. In the last resort, there was only one single source of decision: the community's sense of justice. With that we arrive at:

§2. THE PRINCIPLE OF POPULAR REPRESENTATION. (THE KING'S DUTY OF OBTAINING CONSENT)

The monarchical order of the mediaeval State can for our present purpose be taken for granted, though it also had its ideal roots and foundations.[9] Even in the case of republican organizations, the fundamental constitutional ideas of the mediaeval State were no different from those applied in monarchies; for the head of the republican community and the people, the monarch and the people, stood in an entirely analogous constitutional relation to each other. Again, we may take for granted the representation of the people by the *meliores et maiores*, although here also it would be possible to discuss theories behind the facts. After this preliminary simplification of our task, we shall enquire neither about the difference between the monarch and the head of a communal State, nor about the rules as to how a people may be represented—instead, we shall proceed directly to the crucial question: Is the monarch bound to obtain the assent of the people? Wherein is he bound? Wherein is he free?

[9] Cf. *supra*, pp. 5–12.

We have seen that the mediaeval monarch is not absolute in theory. He is bound by the law. But in respect of form and practice, he seems to us to be absolute; for he is not obliged to attain that harmony with the law which is required of him, by any definite, formally prescribed method. The harmony between the ruler and the law is usually achieved without the observation of any fixed forms, though, in cases of doubt, the harmony of his actions with the law is demonstrated by the consent of the community or its representatives. But there is no binding rule as to what cases require this consent. In ordinary circumstances, it is presumed that all the monarch's acts are explicitly or implicitly in accord with the law and the community's sense of justice.

In order to make this point comprehensible, we must remember the peculiarly undefined and vague nature of the association through which, in the Middle Ages, monarch and people together formed the State or the " folk. " There was no distinction or antithesis possible between monarch and people, such as we later find in the doctrines of popular sovereignty or governmental contract. What the monarch does, he does in the name of and in accordance with the will of the people; he speaks as the mouthpiece of the folk. Monarch and people were both equally dependent upon the law; they declared it together and preserved it in common. Unless proof is brought forward to the contrary, all that is declared by the king is law, in the same sense as if it issued from the people, the community. Until proof were brought to the contrary, the monarch would be described as the standing representative of the people and its law. For this reason, the rules as to how the king attains agreement with the community, and at the same time his own harmony with the law, are exceedingly vague and undeveloped.

There are three degrees of popular participation in the government, i.e., participation of the representatives of the community, the *meliores et maiores*, and so on. The first is tacit consent; here the king acts formally alone, and so " absolutely " in form but not in substance. The second degree is advice and consent; the third is judicial verdict.

It is typical of the Middle Ages that there are no hard and fast rules regulating the application of any of these three forms of participation, and that all three without any distinction, could result in equally valid acts of State.

Under the present-day dominance of an independent constitutional law and a written legal code, we distinguish carefully between these three forms of popular co-operation, and have established a definite sphere for each. It is exactly determined which legal transactions shall be settled in the law-courts, and in the constitutional State this judicial process is removed from the personal intervention of the monarch or government. It is exactly determined which affairs of State may not be settled without the advice of popular representatives, and this duty of obtaining consent is, in the constitutional State, exalted into an irremovable right of veto for those representatives. Finally, it is exactly determined within what limits the government is free to use its power of issuing ordinances—a power for which the tacit consent of the community has been obtained once and for all by means of the written constitution enacted as statute law. None of all this is defined or determined in the mediaeval State.

Provided that he remained in accord with the law, it rested entirely at the monarch's discretion which of the three methods he adopted for the dispatch of business. Whether he settled the matter by personal decree, or after giving audience to, or even perhaps with the collaboration of counsellors, i.e., representatives of the community; or finally, by procuring the judgment of the high court or a court of the princes, was decided entirely at his option. If he ordains alone and purely personally, but in harmony with the law, then his decree stands for law, and the tacit consent of the community conferred by the absence of opposition is completely adequate. On the other hand, it can happen that the council or the popular representatives, or even the most solemn court of the realm makes a false judgment; then the wrongful decision, in spite of its promulgation with the express assent both of the monarch and the people, must be revoked. The form in which an act of government is executed is all one to the Middle Ages, provided that its substance is in agreement with the law.

All the same, certain customary ways of obtaining consent evolved out of this. Before we discuss them further, however, we must consider the contrast between folk-right and royal law. This debatable question is easily solved from the standpoint we have now gained.

Certainly, in point of law we have to distinguish between rules of folk-right and of royal law, between popular courts and royal courts, in, for example, the Frankish period. But the period itself, in theory, did not and could not know this difference. For even if the folk-courts and the royal courts made decisions in accordance with different principles, what they decided was still in both cases one and the same law, the Law. What the king establishes with the express or tacit approval of the community, is law; in so far as it accords with the community's sense of justice, it is part of the good old usage, even if it is quite new. Royal law passed as folk-law, and the king expressly recognized that folk-law was legally binding upon him and that it limited his power of ordaining.

Therefore, even if modern historians distinguish between royal (or official) law and folk-law, it is necessary to avoid implying that this modern contrast was observed in the Middle Ages. Folk-law in the mediaeval sense is the law, recorded or unrecorded, recognized by prince and people alike, and includes even the personal decrees of the king, in so far as the people recognize their legal force. The right of the king to issue charters, to command in war, his power to " ban, " and the like, are all part of folk-law, and are limited, like other rights, by the pre-existent objective law which is the sum of every freeman's subjective rights. In promulgating laws and granting charters, the mediaeval monarch and the people, though in theory completely bound to the traditional law, could in practice arbitrarily and almost autocratically pass over the laws and charters of an earlier period; but this glaring contradiction is explained by the technical deficiencies in the methods of handing down and fixing the law, which have been fully explained above.[10] In theory every lawful act of the king, like every well-established right, bound his successors and the whole community in perpetuity. But in practice very little was done for the preservation of the law; and the exigencies of politics, for which no place was reserved within the framework of mediaeval legal and constitutional theory, played a large and almost uncontrolled part. This could occur without the violation of finely-spun theory, because legal practice was sufficiently elastic. But this contradiction between theory and practice had nothing directly to do with the question whether monarch or government was bound to obtain consent or was free to act by personal decree. Arbitrariness in practice, in spite of theoretical limitation, was indulged in by the community no less than by the king. For the community, in theory, is as much bound to the law as he is. Actually no one cared a rap for outworn law, although in the theory of customary law, it was not and never could be annulled, unless the re-discovery of ancient charters compelled people to re-consider it.

At this point, however, a difference even in mediaeval thought between the legal obligation of the people and that of the monarch must be noted.

If the community set itself in opposition to the law, that signified nothing, so long as the community, or the predominant part of it, remained united in its interpretation of the law. It was a different matter if the monarch as an individual came into conflict with a considerable section of public opinion. In that case he was in a very dangerous position; on account, in the first place, of the deficiencies in the power of the mediaeval State, concerning which more could be said in a study of mediaeval politics; and, in the second place, on account of the theoretically heavy responsibility of the monarch for his acts, of which we shall speak in a later section.

The monarch, therefore, often secured himself against anticipated opposition by obtaining the consent of the community or its representatives, and putting it into

[10] Cf. *supra*, p. 173.

writing. There is no reason here to go into the detailed history of the practice of mediaeval representation and consent.[11] The decisive facts always remained, that the monarch had a free choice whether or not he would secure his position in this way, and that without any previous consent—mere " advice " was deemed to imply consent—the monarch might issue legally valid decrees.

But the community, or those who represented it, and naturally the monarch also, could never dispose of the well-established rights of their fellow-members of the community. In this respect, the limitation of the mediaeval State by the law is especially clear—a limitation which was infinitely more far-reaching than any restrictions imposed on the organs of government in modern constitutional States. With us, the State is sovereign. Even to-day only a certain small category of private rights or liberties ought, according to the theory of Natural Law, to be withdrawn from the grasp of the absolute sovereign State; this is precisely the significance of the so-called " Rights of Man, " the origin of which falls in the period after the idea of the sovereign State had become predominant.[12] In the Middle Ages, every well-established right, even a right to an annual tribute of one hen, had scarcely less sanctity than the Rights of Man have in certain modern constitutions. Only free renunciation by their possessors could lawfully set these rights aside; a royal decree could not do so even though it rested upon the broad basis of a vote by a representative assembly. No valid act of State could be promulgated without the assent of those whose rights were affected.

Strict interpretation of mediaeval legal theory implied, therefore, that it was possible for an individual to prevent entirely the formation of a corporate will, for according to mediaeval conceptions, the maintenance of existing political conditions, even down to the smallest details, was, in the

[11] Cf. M. V. Clarke, *Mediaeval Representation and Consent* (1936).

[12] Even then, it may be noted, their validity remains very dubious. For if the majority in a modern State resolved to suppress the Rights of Man, who on the basis of modern constitutional law would be able to assert their continued validity? On the other hand, the significance of the Rights of Man is precisely that normally a majority would never be found to allow their suppression.

ultimate analysis, a part of the subjective rights of every individual member of the community. The State which held on the longest to this true mediaeval principle, so far as the nobility were concerned, was Poland; and for this very reason, Poland was brought to ruin by an absurd extension of the right to veto. But even among the Germanic peoples, there were similar tendencies, which may be illustrated by this example:

King Clovis, it is related, wished to retain a costly vase over and above the share of booty lawfully falling to his lot, in order to give it to a church; all agreed to this, except one envious person who opposed the king in an insulting manner, and who smote the vase with an axe. He remained unpunished, for his opposition to the general will merely confirmed his indestructible subjective right to enforce that partition of booty which had been established as a part of the objective law and which must not be changed over the head of a single individual by a majority decision. As a matter of fact, the king revenged himself a year later by a similar exaggerated insistence on another part of the objective legal order, namely, his powers as a military commander, which he used to penalize his opponent. But the fact that the king had to make use of a favourable opportunity to wreak his vengeance and was not empowered to inflict punishment, shows that the Frank who opposed the king stood on good ground when he denied that a right shared by all could be changed otherwise than by a unanimous decision of all. It is true that his pedantic exaggeration of his right exposed him to revenge; but formally he was in the right even though opposed by the majority; for his right to enforce a strict observance of the rules for the division of booty could not be taken from him by any majority decision, because there was no State law that could override private rights.

Here, therefore, we have a case of the right of resistance, which we shall discuss in the next section, used in opposition not merely to the king himself, but against the whole people save only one member. Though only one single individual declined to renounce freely a well-established right, that was sufficient to prevent the State from changing the objective law, in which every subjective right was rooted. We see here the theoretical limits which the law imposed not only on the monarch, but also on the folk itself. No individual could be deprived of his law; there was no rule of the majority. *Fiat justitia, pereat mundus.* Any idea of political compromise and overriding governmental powers was completely obliterated by the unswerving logic of mediaeval thought.

We have here learnt two things: (1) that the monarch could, for example, exact taxation only after he reached an understanding with the community, and (2) that this understanding, at least in theory, took the form of negotiation with every individual, as to whether he was willing to pay. The mediaeval prince could not yet write, as Frederick William I wrote to his successor with reference to the Estates: " if they agree *de bonne grace,* so much the better. If they make difficulties, God has made you sovereign." Such a suggestion would have appeared almost blasphemous in the Middle Ages. Not only the law of the realm or the community, but also rights of property were considered laws which the king could not curtail on his own initiative alone. Hence there is a series of cases in which the king may not act unilaterally, but, at least in theory, must secure an understanding with the community. In practice, however, it was not always easy to define these cases beyond doubt, and still less easy to convince a powerful prince in what respect he might have violated his duty of obtaining consent. Here again, power was decisive. But such a heresy was never openly expressed during the Middle Ages; it was too discreditable a fact ever to be avowed. These remarks bring us to:

§3. THE PRINCIPLE OF RESPONSIBILITY. (THE RIGHT OF RESISTANCE)

It is the individual's task to protect the law against all, even against the State. This is a duty incumbent upon all; all are authorized and indeed obliged to undertake it. This is the true meaning of the right of resistance, upon which I have written at length elsewhere.[13] The right of resistance was, however, merely the mediaeval method, clumsy in idea and technique, for the realization of a far more general principle, for which a technically more suitable procedure of enforcement was afterwards found. This principle was that of the responsibility of the government which in the Middle Ages meant the responsibility of the king and his council.[14] Since the government is established for the protection of the law, it forfeits its own proper authority if it breaks the law. *Il n'est mie seignor de faire tort.* The monarch who violates the objective law at the same time destroys his own subjective right to dominion, which is part and parcel of the objective legal order. *Rex eris si recte regis*, or *recte faciendo regis nomen tenetur, peccando amittur.* The lack of differentiation between ideal and positive law meant that the king's forfeiture of his right to govern was a semi-legal, semi-moral process. By a breach of the law, the monarch *ipso facto* forfeited his right to rule. He deposed himself. The verdict of the community, the defection of individuals without any process of law, the election of a new (anti-) king, all this and the other incidents in the countless cases where the mediaeval right of resistance was put into force, had really only a declaratory significance, whereas the forfeiture of the right to govern was actually completed at the very moment the prince overstepped the bounds of the law, and so deposed himself.

This theory does not require any idea of contract. He who violates the subjective rights of others, places himself outside the legal order, and forfeits all claim to protection for his own subjective rights. Because as yet there is, as we have seen, no special law to safeguard the rights of government, this applies to the wielder of State authority no less than to the least member of the community. The senator whom the Emperor arbitrarily dismissed retorted: " I no longer regard you as Emperor."[15] The lawfully

[13] Cf. *supra*, pp. 81–134.

[14] The councillor of a prince in the Middle Ages had the dual character of a representative of the people against the king, and of a co-administrator against the people, a duality which the successors of the undefined mediaeval *consilium*—the later mediaeval Estates—carried further.

[15] Cf. *supra*, p. 88

established monarch had a claim to dominion, like the peasant's to his inherited farm; both claims are equally sacred, but both are equally exposed to the risks of forfeiture. The king's right is no different from any other person's right; it is, as we should say, a " private right." A monarch must be obeyed, but not a tyrant. The instant a ruler interferes with the rights of others without their consent, he ceases to be a king, becomes a tyrant, and simultaneously loses his claim to obedience, without any necessity for formal legal proceedings on the part of the community.

It is thus clear that there is no need to introduce the idea of contract in order to explain the right of resistance.[16] A full understanding of the mediaeval conception of law teaches us to avoid an exaggeration of the theoretical importance of the contractual idea. In the later Middle Ages, on the other hand, the idea of the governmental contract was applied to the relations we have just described, after it had been re-discovered in classical literature. The idea of contract is not Germanic in origin, but for learned thought it provided the most suitable explanation of the mutual duty of monarch and people to the law which was superior to both. The Germanic substitute for the idea of contract is the concept of mutual fealty, in which the obligations of both parties are anchored in the objective law. Through fealty the government is bound to the people, just as the people is bound to the government. But, in fact, the Germanic idea that a ruler who broke faith lost any claim to the fealty of the people came to the same thing as the ecclesiastical doctrine of the *tyrannus*, who deposed himself, and also was little different from the natural-law theory of the dissolution of the governmental contract by the ruler's breach of the law.

In order to understand fully the mediaeval right of resistance, we must see where it differs from revolutionary self-help as it is understood to-day. Even we in certain circumstances would still approve a rebellion to enforce a " Right of Nature " against the State, even if the government had

[16] Cf. *supra*, pp. 117–23.

kept within the letter of the law. For the law (by which in this connexion we mean only positive law) is for us neither final nor unique; it is limited, watched over, and in some circumstances, abrogated on the one side by reason of State or political considerations, and on the other by moral convictions. Thus the law is subordinate to politics and morals; and we recognize this subordination when we recognize that in some circumstances, revolution, though never lawful, may be necessary. But the mediaeval right of resistance is no revolutionary right, but one of the most prominent elements in constitutional law; a constitutional sanction for the protection of the rights of the subject. The explanation of this is not simply the lack of differentiation between public and private law, but rather the identification of ideal and positive law. The force of morality, which to us is extra-legal—politics or reason of State is not recognized at all in the Middle Ages—is embodied in the mediaeval idea of law.

Since the law was simply law, not positive law, it made no difference to its intrinsic merits or to its validity whether the government knew it or recognized it. So much the worse for the government, if it failed to recognize the law! Thus it might happen, and often did happen, that a single person recognized the law, or thought he did, whilst the government did not, or pretended not to. But since the government exists only by and for the law, and only possesses authority in so far as it dispenses or administers the law, a power which commits itself to an injustice ceases to have any authority for the man who knows himself to be bound to the law. The law is sovereign, and such power is a tyranny, and consequently void. The individual has therefore every right to resist the usurper of governmental authority, not merely because of any particular injustice against the individual, but still more because he has illegally represented himself to be the constituted authority, whereas in reality he who does not respect the law ceases to be *rex*.

§4. TRANSITIONS

Post-mediaeval constitutional development has gradually

effaced the picture we have here drawn. Above all, the modern conception of law, developing separate categories of positive, codified, and public law, has brought about the downfall of the very pillars on which the edifice of mediaeval thought rested. Even before this happened, the later Middle Ages saw certain technical innovations within the framework of the old idea of law, due to the improved and regularized practice of consent which appeared when political society was organized upon a basis of representative Estates.

Such societies (as compared with princely absolutisms) preserved and even accentuated the main principles of mediaeval constitutional thought; namely, the protection of individual rights, and the weakening, control, and limitation of the government. The personnel of those entitled to give consent, still flexible in the early Middle Ages, was defined; the limits within which the monarch was bound to obtain consent, still elastic in the early Middle Ages, were marked out. The populace as a whole receded in importance, the more the representatives—the Estates—were defined, and as a result, the Estates became a kind of community in or above the community, a subsidiary government or a class of co-regents. Even the right of resistance, still indispensable owing to the persistence of mediaeval principles, is restricted to the Estates, and consequently ceases to be a casual repressive device, becoming instead a permanent constitutional method of preventative action, and thus leading on to the modern forms of governmental responsibility, and of parliamentary responsibility. By this definition both of the personnel and of the authority of the representatives, the late mediaeval State achieved a highly important clarification of the constitutional situation, and the introduction of the majority principle into popular representation was a further technical improvement. The clear delimitation of the organs of government and of their competence, which the Middle Ages did not accomplish, and on which the healthy working of the government depends in practice, was also attained to a certain extent in the later period. The useful fiction arises that the will of individuals is merged, and expressed in such a way as to bind legally the whole community, in the will of the majority of the people's representatives. At the same time, the monarch knows definitely for what affairs he must obtain the consent of definite persons.

This progress of the representative Estates, the Middle Ages could, so to speak, evolve out of its own spirit. The Estates shared the true mediaeval spirit, and this they proved by imposing ever more rigid control on government, and by pressing forward private rights and interests. In consequence of this, the modern State could not grow directly out of the State based upon a system of Estates. A place had first to be found for *raison d'État*, and for State necessity, and this was the work of the period of princely despotism, which was based upon fundamentally unmediaeval and even anti-mediaeval ideas of the State and of Law. Because the mediaeval conception was saturated through and thro gh with moral principles, mediaeval constitutional ideas were too hostile to the State and to authority. The crude reaction of princely absolutism brought constitutional ideas completely into the powerful clutches of politics and reason of State. And only then, when private rights and morals, under the aegis of Natural Law, again sought a place within the power-satiated Leviathan, did the modern constitutional State emerge after long constitutional struggles, as a result of a fair settlement between Power and Rights, Public Law and Natural Law.

One may speak of an " eternal Middle Ages " that continue to survive even in the modern period, and I would accept this expression in a double sense; in the sense that the modern period has preserved fundamental mediaeval ideas, with better technical execution and far better results than the Middle Ages themselves could achieve; and in the further sense that the developed technique of modern civilized life has created a schism between learned, educated culture and popular thought, which has never got beyond mediaeval or semi-mediaeval notions—notions which in their own period were still accepted equally by educated and uneducated alike.

Let us consider first the realization of mediaeval aims by modern constitutions. No lengthy demonstration is necessary to show that the fundamental ideas of the modern constitutional State: the obligation to respect the law; the co-operation of popular representatives; the responsibility of the government, are definitely also the fundamentals of the mediaeval constitution. But the technical changes by which in the modern period these aims were attained, apparently less directly but actually more surely and with less friction than in the Middle Ages, are extraordinarily great.

Modern governments are no longer circumscribed by the " Law " as such, but by positive law, and wholly or partly written constitutions. Many modern constitutions contain two totally different parts; on the one hand, fundamental rights or the Rights of Man, formulated under the influence of Natural Law; on the other hand, purely technical rules. In the first category, for example, the division of powers would have to be reckoned; in the second, particular rules regarding the calling together of the representative assembly, electoral law, and so on. Yet both sorts of enactment are classified as positive law. Every single organ of the State, even the government, stands under this positive law, but the State as a whole stands above it. The State, not the positive law, is sovereign. Whilst, therefore, the government is bound to the law, even if a different law, in the same way as the mediaeval monarch, the modern State as a whole is bound to no law, but is superior to all law. Limits are set to the arbitrariness of the monarch or the government, but not, as in the Middle Ages, at the expense of the State's needs.

Whether or not the government was in fact respecting or violating the law remained debatable in almost every case in the Middle Ages, owing, on the one hand, to the ambiguity of the idea of law, and on the other, to the elasticity of the law. To-day, it is very easily established whether or not an organ of State is acting in accord with the law. Even if the individual to-day still possessed a right of resistance, it would be much easier now to determine when it might be legitimately exercised than was possible in the Middle Ages, and so the maintenance of governmental authority and the stability of the law would be much more firmly secured. But a right of resistance is no longer necessary. For the modern written constitution so interlocks the respective functions of the various organs of State, that any one organ which oversteps its competence is automatically checked and brought under control by constitutional safeguards. This does not, of course, always occur; here also actual power is decisive in the last resort. Breaches of the constitution, *coups d'État*, and rebellions are possible. But such events are extra-legal. Within the legal and constitutional spheres, the repressive right of resistance has been replaced by preventative supervision on the part of the subjects. The anarchy of the Middle Ages shows how beneficial was the re-discovery of the idea of " positive law ", and the differentiation between public and private law; it was worth many battalions of soldiers. In the Middle Ages, everyone, in order to know what was the law, could and must consult his own sense of justice. If, to-day, a minority wishes to enforce conceptions of justice other than those in actual existence, it has to strive to become a majority, and to dominate the will of the organ of State which determines what is to be law. In the Middle Ages, such a method was not recognized; for the law was not made by organs of State, still less by the majority, but was prior to all the organs of State, and heedless of majority decisions. The prince might, if he wished, consult selected persons in order to ascertain what was the law, and these persons were then in some measure held to be representatives of the people. But whether or not he would consult them, whom he would consult, and whether he would pay heed to their views, all this rested entirely with him. As regards the will of the popular representatives, moreover, the modern constitutional fiction did not exist (or rather it first arose in canon law)—the fiction that the will of the representatives supersedes the will of those represented, and that the will of the majority overrides the minority, so that a common will binding all comes into existence. Since in the Middle Ages, it was, in the absence of any positive law, impossible to nullify by positive enactment the minority's or the individual's conception of what was law, and since even the method of cutting down your opponent by the sword, characteristic of the Polish Diet, could not be relied upon to secure unanimity in all the innumerable cases which arose in practice, it was never possible to prevent minorities and individuals from believing and declaring that their knowledge and convictions really represented the true law, whilst those of the dominant party were perversions. And since at that time law existed of itself, and was not the result of State enactment, every person had the right, if not the duty, of protecting the law against wrong, and of becoming a Michael Kohlhaas; he protected the law, to which everyone is bound, against the unlawful practices to which the government was committed, because the fact that the government had entered into a pact with the Devil did not mean that individual citizens also were compelled to enter into such a pact.

The essence of the mediaeval attitude is the lack of any differentiation between ideal and positive law; it was this that made the attitude of the individual towards the law, the legislator, and the State, so different from that in modern life. If to-day an individual protests against a positive law, it can, constitutionally speaking, only be replaced by the individual's idea of law if he can change the opinion of the legislative body which then converts the desired ideal law into positive law. But if, in the Middle Ages, anyone detected an injustice in the conduct of the government (and "injustice" was then identified with "unlawfulness" and even with "force"), he could declare that the law was being forcibly stifled. In that case, however, there was no need to promulgate new law; it was merely necessary to get rid of the government's illegalities, and to restore the suppressed law, which alone existed. This was what Michael Kohlhaas demanded, and if necessary, he would have coerced the State, setting force against force.

Fortunately, when we see justice aggrieved, we need no longer resort to force in this way. Conceptual refinement and technical improvement have brought the aim of the mediaeval constitution to more peaceful and more certain attainment in the modern constitutional State, without in any way dissipating it. But these last remarks have already brought us to the " eternal Middle Ages " in the second sense which we indicated above—in the sense of the retention by the popular mind of mediaeval ways of thought even in the modern world, which, precisely because of its more com‑ plicated forms, has necessarily created a gulf between educated and uneducated thought. We have already emphasized this in general at the end of our section on Law, and we must now recapitulate it with reference to the Constitution.

It was and always will be difficult for naïve popular feeling to realize that something which it holds to be right is nevertheless not the law. For at all times the State ob‑ tains its right to exist from the fact that its government corresponds to the general sense of justice; but the necessi‑ ties of State are not always understandable without explanation. The path of statutory reform is long, and hopelessly closed to minorities. The common man does not readily comprehend how beneficial and necessary the technical restraints and the lengthy, complicated routine of modern public and legal life are. He may dimly surmise it, but the attitude of Michael Kohlhaas is dearer to his law-defying instincts. Nevertheless, the strong State of modern times has educated the people by means of its positive, written law, and of its public law, and so the murmurs of the people to-day are rarely expressed in actual rebellion. Except among oppressed peoples under alien government, to whom even to-day the right of resistance seems to be an eternal law, the right of resistance is extinct. The eternal demand for an ideal law is informed to-day by a knowledge not possessed in the Middle Ages; the knowledge that legal reform is more certainly attained, in spite of opposition and delay, by an absolutely binding positive law, by majority decision, and by codification, than by belief in a law existing by itself, with appeal to the sovereignty of the individual conscience, which is authorized to restore that law if it has been injured, and to turn against the State which has injured it.

Peoples such as the French and the English, who are politically well-trained, and have infused the spirit of *raison d'État* into the will of individuals, are less prone to revolutions than mediaevally-minded, unpolitical peoples like the Germans and the Russians.

In one respect, however, private citizens will in theory never be so well-off as they were in the Middle Ages. Never again will the pettiest of their subjective rights be as sacred and inviolable as the fundamental laws which safeguard the existence of the State and of society. But this boundless theoretical protection for private rights was in practice a very dubious advantage, not only from the standpoint of the State, which, entangled in the tentacles of overgrown private rights, could take no steps necessary for the maintenance of government without overstepping the law, but also from the standpoint of the private person. For where, owing to lack of refined conceptual distinctions, small things are venerated as highly as great things, there is always the danger that even the greatest things will be treated like petty ones. Many dangers lay in the lack of differentiation between ideal and positive law, for the private man as well as for the government. If—as for example in the case of John Hus— a prince promised a subject a safe-conduct to a Council, which then by the voice of the Holy Ghost declared that subject to be a heretic, the safe-conduct automatically lost its validity, because every right and every act of State is void if it be injurious to the Faith. It is true that the subject to-day is never quite sure that the sovereign State, in its dire need and in its insatiable lust for power, will not curtail his private rights. To-day, the subject knows only two securities, and these must suffice him. The one is the certainty that some rules of morality stand so firm that in the long run they can be abrogated by no State, whatever its situation. The other is participation in the government by popular representatives, who may be expected in the long run to guarantee the security of these moral requirements against the whims of individuals, no matter what may otherwise be the defects of popular representation. But it is quite indifferent, and of almost no importance for the essentials of modern constitutional government, whether such moral rules are wholly or partly incorporated into the written constitution as fundamental laws and the like. For the inviolability of these rules in no way depends upon their inclusion in the positive law, which is in theory easily changed. On the contrary, it depends on the fact that such rules represent an ideal law, which is ever sacred to all citizens, or at least to an overwhelming majority of them, and on the fact that in the modern constitutional State, the organs of government are so balanced that none of them can violate any one of these moral convictions with impunity. The fact that, in the eighteenth and nineteenth centuries, fundamental laws, i.e., a small section of these fundamental moral demands, were in certain countries incorporated into written constitutions, is not to be explained by the spirit of modern constitutionalism, but as a fragment of the " eternal Middle Ages " cast into the struggles against absolutism, under a misapprehension as to the nature of written law. The theories of natural law are characteristic of this transitional period, with its admixture of the mediaeval and the modern.

It is, however, not our purpose to go closer into these matters. It is enough for us to have noted not only the bonds of affinity between mediaeval and modern constitutional ideas, but also the contrasts between them. The strong executive power of the modern State impresses upon the people that even an " unjust " government does not cease to be a government, and that even bad positive law does not cease to be law. The mediaeval idea of law succumbed to learned written law and to the strengthening of the power of the State. The ambiguous mediaeval conception of law, mysterious and fertile as it was in its obscure depths, sufficed in the narrow limits of mediaeval society, when everyone knew everyone else, and each individual could survey the whole range of the legal order that mattered to him; but this simple idea of law was one of the vital obstacles to the construction of a stronger State; it was good enough for small communities, but it was anachronous and inadequate after the rise of great kingdoms.

INDEX

hostile to kin-right, 30; its
sanction necessary, 23–4; growth
of its constitutional influence,
45; revolution in its attitude
towards the State, 50–2; its
dominance over accession, 51;
royal control of, 53; unable to
eliminate Emperor-cult, 62; frees
executive power from custom,
71–2; provides judicial process
over the king, 102, 124
Church Fathers', the : definition of
government, 7; view of magistracy, 28; simile of bishops and
kings, 53; adoration of the
emperor, 62; legal philosophy,
152, 181
Cicero, 70 n. 37
Civitas Dei, xxiv, 53, 100, 102, 103
Clarke, M. V.: Mediaeval Representation and Consent, 126 n. 69,
192 n. 11; Fourteenth Century
Studies, 126, n. 69
Clovis, 35, 193
Cluniac reformers, 107
Code, legal, 167
Coggeshall, Ralph, 91 n. 47
Coke, Sir Edward, xxii
Cologne, the archbishop of, 109
Columban, St., 29 n. 18
Communa terre, 129
Community, the (v. also Folk):
elects the king, xix; confers a
mandate, 7; its acknowledgment
necessary for valid law, 74;
representation of, 73, 187; bound
to the law, 191
Conscience, 152, 156
Consecration, of the emperor, differentiated from that of a bishop,
55–6; of the monarch, xviii, 11,
26, 27–60; declaratory, not constitutive, 33; in the East, 34; as
a sacral rite, 34–50; introduction
of, 34–6; its ecclesiastical significance, 36–40; its political and
constitutional significance, 37–8,
40–50, 57–8; as a sacrament,
36–7, 54, 58–9; assimilated to
priestly ordination, 37–40; indelible character of, not accepted
by law, 44; question of its indispensability, 45–6, 50; combined
with election, 49; as the symbol
of office, 50–61; confers rights,
50; exalts the State, 51, 54;
exalts the bishops, 55–6; its
importance reduced, 56–7

Consensus fidelium, xxv, xxvii,
xxviii, 73–4, 132–3; absence of
rules for, 74–5
Consent, three degrees of, xx, 188–
190; fiction of majority, xxv,
198–9; practice of, 192, 198–9
Constantine, emperor, 27; Donation of, 49, 162, 163
Constitution, the nature of a, xiii,
181; aims of the mediaeval
same as the modern, xxvi, 200;
effect of mediaeval conception of
law on, 151
Constitutional History, presentation
of, ix; comparative study of, x;
subject-matter of, x; nature of,
xii, xiii; in perspective, xxvi
Constitutional Law, xv–xvi
Contract, Theory of, xvii–xviii,
not Germanic in origin, 196;
later than right of resistance,
xviii, xxi, 195; vows and homage
as elements in, 77–8; asserted in
XIth century, 78; governmental,
117–121, 188–196
Corpus Iuris Civilis, 62, 177, 179
Coronation, earliest mediaeval, 34;
of the emperor in Xth century,
38; in XIIth century, 56; of
the English kings, 55; of the
German kings in Xth century,
76
Councillors, the position of, 195
Coventry, Walter of, 86 n. 43, 91 n.
47
Cromwell, Oliver, 91
Crown, the, differentiated from the
king's person, 88
Crusading States, the law of, 74 n.
40, 122

Damiani, Peter, 40
Dassel, Rainald of, 66
Dei Gratia, 42–3, 52, 61, 64
Deification, of the ruler, 8 n. 2, 61–8
Democracy, principle of, 10; as
taught by Christianity, 114
Denmark, 84
D'Entrèves, A. P.: The Mediaeval
Contribution to Political Thought,
xvii n. 5
Derecho, 155 n. 1
Diffidatio, right of, xviii
Diritto, 155 n. 1
Divi, the, 62
Divine right of kings, 5–67; in
XVIIth century, xviii, 5, 11, 69;
origin of elements in, xviii–xx, 5;